# POSITIVE

---

# PARENTING

---

# FROM

---

# A TO Z

# POSITIVE

—

# PARENTING

—

# FROM

—

# A TO Z

*Karen Renshaw Joslin*

**another idea from becker&mayer!**

FAWCETT COLUMBINE

NEW YORK

A Fawcett Columbine Book
Published by Ballantine Books

Copyright © 1994 by Karen Renshaw Joslin

LIBRARY OF CONGRESS CATALOG CARD NUMBER: 93-90975

ISBN: 0-449-90780-5

*Cover design by Kathleen Lynch*
*Cover art by Karen Bell*

Manufactured in the United States of America

First Edition: June 1994

20 19 18 17 16 15 14 13 12 11

**SPECIAL RECOGNITION:**

To the memory of Blackburn Smith Joslin, M.D., one of the first pediatricians in Bellevue, Washington, a founder of Pediatric Associates, one of the founders of Overlake Hospital, and the first chief of staff there. When a parent called, he was there. He worked to help parents understand their children, he fought for the rights of children, every one, and he truly was my number-one supporter for the Positive Parenting program.

# CONTENTS

# ACKNOWLEDGMENTS

This book has been a year-and-a-half-long project. My sincerest appreciation to:

My husband, Richard, for his listening, calming, and caring, and for keeping our home and family intact. Also, for his professional expertise and his natural understanding about what children need.

Our children, Brett, Malia, and Elizabeth, for their reflections and ideas, for their computer help, and for the biking, the plays, the ball games, the skiing, the walking, and the time for special talks.

Anne Joslin Webster and Kathleen Renshaw Woodson and our extended family, parents and children combined.

I owe many thanks to the following experts and friends for their enormous interest and contributions. In random order:

For reading and offering their helpful and often witty insights, thanks to Maureen and Page Jenner; Jan Jackson, M.L.S.; Jim Becker; and my Ballantine editors.

For their time in consultation, thanks to Robin Gilleland, M.D.; Leslie Russell; Missy McIver, M.S.W.; Lark Young, R.N.; Bob Bradbury, M. Div.; Toby Gonzales, Ph.D., and the Puget Sound Adlerian Society; Elaine O. Percival, R.D.; John A. Leaf; Jo Anne Holt, M.S., CCC-SLP; Kathryn Koelemay, M.D.; Terry

Whitman, Ph.D.; Russell Trevena, M.D.; Glenn Lux, M.D.;
David W. Montgomery, Psy. D.; Jerri L. Wolfe, Ph.D.; Rebecca
Perbix, M.S.W.; and H. E. Runion III, D.M.D.

For their support, I am grateful to the staff at Pediatric
Associates, Bellevue, Washington.

For the many hours at Main Street Kids Book Co., thanks to
Andy Pickard and Kari Peterson.

I am indebted also to the many parents who have come
to my Positive Parenting course, and to others who have shared
hours discussing their parenting with me. To name just a few:
Pete, Kathy, Chooch, Russ, Suzanne, Diane, Cathy, Babette,
Maureen, Cheri, Carol, JoAnne, Joan, Heidi, Bob, Sue, Judy,
Nicki, Robin, Willy, and Jan.

Thanks to the experts, Jean Illsley Clarke, Lee Schnebly, Stephen
Glenn, Rudolf Dreikurs, Jane Nelsen, Mary Sheedy
Kurcinka, Barbara Coloroso, and Adele Faber, for their
research, writing and personal training.

Finally, I am grateful for the Family Education Center, Kailua,
Hawaii (which I attended from 1971 to 1974), the
counselors there at that time, Ray Corsini and Geneviève
Painter, and the first text I learned to share with other parents,
*Children: The Challenge* by Rudolf Dreikurs.

# POSITIVE

---

# PARENTING

---

# FROM

---

# A TO Z

# INTRODUCTION

Even with a master's degree in education, I never in a hundred years would have thought I could write a book, and it is without a doubt one of the hardest tasks I've ever tackled. This book is proof that you can do what you set out to do if you believe in yourself. I am a wife, a mother of three children, a classroom teacher, a parent educator, and a staff trainer, and I do believe that only my own mother, a true encourager, would have initially said, "Dear, you can be an author, too, if you want to."

I'd just finished a day of substitute teaching a second-grade class. At home I listened to a string of messages on my answering machine. The last message caught my attention. "Karen? Jim Becker. You may not remember me, but I took your Positive Parenting class two years ago. I need some parenting tips. Please call when you have time. I wish you would write a book that I could just pick up." Beep. I reversed the machine and replayed Jim's message three times, trying to remember him from his enthusiastic voice and reflecting on his crazy idea about writing a book.

I called Jim, and we talked about his five-year-old daughter who would not stay in her own bed. Then he said, "Karen, I'm serious about your writing a book. When Barbara and I took your Positive Parenting class, parents raised countless problems and you always had something helpful to say. How about thinking of all the misbehaviors parents have to deal with and putting them into an A-to-Z format similar to a medical handbook?"

I'm not one to avoid a challenge, and the idea of reaching thousands of parents with such positive help was exciting. I set out to write a book that would be simple to use, like a first-aid guide. This is the parents' emergency guide for difficult behavior, set up for ease of access in a handy A-to-Z format.

I have been a parent for twenty-three years, and I fall into the category of those who teach what they want to do better. Over many years I studied and trained with experts in the field of human development and Positive Parenting. I have taught this program to hundreds of parents on a one-to-one basis and also in group settings through hospitals, pediatric practices, community services, schools, and workplaces. The Positive Parenting material is the best I know for anyone wanting to help good people (whether parents or not) reach their highest potential. I also took this program into the restaurant world to help management work more positively with staff. Every year I continue my training, learning new ways to explain important Positive Parenting principles and techniques.

This book is the result of hours of reflecting on my many experiences working with wonderful parents and others involved with kids. I interviewed skilled professionals, all experts in their fields, whom I have admired and to whom I have referred parents. I reread books, listened to training tapes, and reviewed educational videos. I wrote at all hours of the day and night, then captured my family, friends, and colleagues to read my text and discuss it with me.

The challenges of parenting are both demanding and rewarding. Being a parent combines the demands of the most complex professions with continual opportunities "to make a difference." We are on duty twenty-four hours a day, seven days a week. When we add this to other adult daily stresses and responsibilities, it is easy to feel overwhelmed. I recently had a call from a woman who sounded both tearful and angry. The elementary school counselor had called. "Your son is being a very disruptive kid. He doesn't seem to have any self-control. He is interruptive in the classroom and hurting children on the playground." I clearly felt the fear in this mother's voice. My heart went out to her. Her son's self-esteem—how he felt about himself and what he perceived others felt about him—meant so much to her. She did what all concerned parents do, she focused on what she was doing wrong. How could she improve his behavior? Feeling guilty, she blamed herself and her circumstances for his disruptiveness. She wanted to know what to do.

I met with this mother, and we covered the Positive Parenting approach just as it is presented in this A-to-Z guide. The concept is clear, and the principles and techniques are positive. This mother learned that making positive change is not a simple process; it takes effort, time, and consistency. The encouraging principles and techniques gave her courage and something tangible to work with and believe in. She traded in her nonproductive guilt for new things to say and do. In time, good things began to happen.

This guide is written to help you help your children (and every other person you come in contact with) to be happy, contributing members of society who feel capable of tackling any situation this world presents.

What we all want for our children is for them to grow into responsible, caring, happy, creative, self-confident, and respectful beings. Basically this means having healthy self-esteem. However, parents don't always say and do the right thing. We may know what we should not do and say, yet when faced with a problem, our words and actions seem to slip right out without our thinking. The punishing words that roll off our tongues and the hostile actions we use are often those that were directed at us as children. I have learned that punishment is not conducive to raising children with healthy self-esteem. Punishment is anything you say or do that lowers your child's self-esteem, anything you say or do that makes him feel worse, even if you are trying to make him be a better person.

This book includes 145 disconcerting behaviors that parents have brought to me. You can see the whole list in the table of contents. I've approached each behavior with the same format that I use in my Positive Parenting classes when I help a parent with a concern, using strategies developed from training I have had and from my experience working with parents to help them cope. This book, in effect, is parent tested.

•    •    •

Note: These behaviors occur with both boys and girls. I have used "he" or "she" singly throughout this book to simplify the text. Boys and girls are equally significant, and each entry applies equally to both.

## USING *POSITIVE PARENTING FROM A TO Z*

### Understanding the Format

"When my eight-year-old son talked back to me, I got so angry I washed his mouth out with soap. Then I scolded him: *'Don't you ever talk to me that way, young man. You show me respect! You stay in your room and think about what you have done. When I tell you you can come out I'll expect an apology. And by the way, young man, you can forget the help I was going to give you with your airplane model.'* Then I sent him to his room for the afternoon."

I listened to this father describe the most recent parenting experience that had brought him to my Positive Parenting class. He was not describing this easily. He was troubled. I asked, "What did you do after you sent Freddy to his room?" He looked down and spoke. "I felt really bad. I couldn't stop thinking about the incident. I guess I regretted blowing up at him, but I didn't know what to do when he was so rude to me. I want to be his friend, but I feel like I'm on him all the time. I want to teach Freddy to be good, to respect others, yet I only created an opportunity for him to feel angry, to want to do worse, and to lower his self-esteem."

All children throw unexpected curves to their parents just as Freddy did to his father. I hear, "What do you do about biting?" "My son's language is vulgar." "My older child beats on my younger son, and I am afraid to leave them alone." "She will not let me comb her hair." "We leave the house every morning with me yelling and screaming."

To help you deal with your particular challenges, I've formatted each entry as follows:

1. The experience is stated.

When I'm speaking to a parent directly, I listen to and restate the parent's experience. I try to establish what the parent typically says and does. For example, in this father's experience with Freddy, Freddy talked back and then his dad angrily responded by scolding, punishing, and restricting him.

While we're talking about the incident, we try to understand what the child may have believed—in essence, why Freddy talked back to his dad. I want to help the parent understand that every behavior does have a social purpose. Just because he misbehaves does not mean he is "bad" or "abnormal." Too often we respond only to the child's action, not to his real need. In this case, Freddy was angry with his father. Freddy wanted to feel he had some control over what was happening to him.

2. I suggest what to say and do.

This section gives several suggestions for what to say and do when you are in the heat of a problem. In Freddy's case, his dad should not have responded angrily. Both he and Freddy needed to take time out to cool off.

3. Preventive tips are provided.

These guidelines are to help you keep the negative situation from happening again. Use these preventive tips! These are great suggestions to help your child feel a strong sense of belonging, to build his healthy self-esteem, and to prevent discouragement and misbehavior.

With joint problem solving, a technique you will learn shortly (see page 26), you work with your child to find a solution to the problem instead of resorting to rage and punishment.

4. Books are suggested.

I have selected a few children's and adult books to help you. You may feel the children's books are too young for your child. Try them. My children, even now much older than ten, enjoy the lightness of younger children's picture books. Sometimes I just leave them around the house. Sometimes I share with my children what I have enjoyed about them, the illustrations, the wonderful way they show such understanding. When a person is upset and confused about feelings such as anger, fear, or jealousy or is otherwise discouraged, the basic ideas found in books for younger readers can be very helpful. Each of the authors suggested is keenly sensitive. Some of these children's books are written by professional counselors or physicians and give a helpful prologue.

## When You Face a Problem

First, when you have a concern about a behavior, before jumping to your problem in the A-to-Z guide, review the principles of Positive Parenting on page 10. These principles have been proven to work worldwide. They are taught throughout the country at leading universities and are used nationwide in schools, community services, and businesses.

Then read "Tools of the Trade" on page 15. These are useful techniques for you to use as you learn what to say and do in difficult situations. These techniques are parent tested and can be very helpful. When you see italicized words used with an entry (for example, you may be reading about "Biting" and see the words *use actions with few words*), refer back to "Tools of the Trade" to review the important details about the suggested course of action. These are great tools. If you use them creatively, they will work in many situations. They even work with adults.

Next, look up the behavior that concerns you. The behaviors are arranged alphabetically, and there may be several entries that apply. I've included cross-references at the end of many entries to guide you, but you should also check the list of entries in the table of contents to see what looks helpful. You also can refer to the index. Freddy's dad could read "Anger, parent's," "Talking back," and "Arguing," just to begin with.

Many entries are divided by age ranges, usually 2½–5 and 6–10 years. The age spans are large. Whole books are written on each age and stage of development. You have to keep your expectations reasonable for your situation. Freddy's dad needs to keep his expectations reasonable for a boy Freddy's age.

## SUCCESS TIPS

- Read the entire entry designed for your child's age and follow the suggestions. You will profit from the techniques suggested only if they are comfortable for you. Have fun being creative with your child at each age and stage of development.
- Tackle one problem at a time. It will be overwhelming for your child if you try to change many behaviors at once, and often several other behaviors improve when one is corrected. For example, when our daughter Elizabeth at age three learned to sleep in her own bed all night without going into our bed, her other babyish behaviors such as whining and not wanting to dress herself also stopped.
- The problem may get worse before it gets better. I once had a mom tell me her eight-year-old son started wetting his pants when their new baby came. When this happened she yelled at him and changed his clothes. With new information, Mom decided to turn the problem over to her son. He was to change his clothes and put the wet ones in the laundry. Because she had previously yelled at him when he wet his pants, he mistakenly felt she did not care about him at all when she *stopped* yelling. It did get worse; he began soiling his pants too. She remained patient and consistent, gave him lots of encouragement, and spent more special time alone with him. Though it took three weeks, the problem disappeared.
- Be consistent with what you decide to say and do, do not give up on your child, show your faith, and allow time. Some behaviors do take a lot of time to change—some months, some years.
- No parent is perfect. You will make mistakes, many of them. You will say and do things you regret. You are human. Don't beat yourself up when this happens. Maintain a good sense of humor, use positive talk when you make a mistake *("That's not like me!"),* and realize that you can be honest and make amends with your child. Each entry will help you know how you can

handle a challenge differently next time. Mistakes are okay. If we are not falling down, we aren't learning!

# SOME IMPORTANT PRINCIPLES OF POSITIVE PARENTING

These principles are based on the works of Alfred Adler, one of the fathers of psychiatry. My first exposure to these principles came more than twenty years ago at the Family Education Center of Hawaii. Here families came together with a professional counselor, either for family counseling or parent education based on these principles. Adlerian ideas are found in the works of Rudolf Dreikurs, Eric Fromm, Fritz Perls, Carl Rogers, Abraham Maslow, Erik Erickson, William Glasser, Eric Berne, Virginia Satir, and many other prominent psychiatrists.

Following are five essential principles of Positive Parenting:

## 1. UNDERSTAND YOUR CHILD'S NEED TO BELONG.

When my child misbehaves, she is usually discouraged. She is no different from you or me. Her basic human need is to belong, to feel loved and needed. Haven't we all experienced times when we felt a lack of attention? Occasionally we've all felt a lack of control, or powerlessness over what happens to us, and have pushed back with anger or frustration. Most of us have been terribly hurt from a disappointment or someone's actions and have wanted to lash out in anger because of the hurt. Remember the anxious feeling when all seems to go wrong—*"I can't seem to do anything right"*—and the resulting impulse to give up? Bad feelings create mistaken beliefs, *even if subconscious*, and misbehavior happens. All positive parents work to understand the discouraged feeling behind their child's action. When we put less emphasis on the misbehavior and begin to pay more attention to what is right with her, spend time with her, and encourage her appropriate behavior, she feels better about herself and begins believing, *"I belong when I cooperate for attention, contribute to feel powerful, communicate how I feel to keep from being hurt, and have the courage to make mistakes and try again so that I do not feel like giving up."*

## 2. FOSTER MUTUAL RESPECT.

*"I respect you. I respect myself."* This is very different from *"You need to respect me,"* which becomes a control issue, a power struggle. Positive parenting is not a permissive approach, and it is not excessively strict. Like most parents, I have grown tired and stressed at times and have fallen into dictating what I expect from my children. At times I even spanked and punished, trying force and control. It never helped. I felt worse, and they acted worse. It was not respectful, and it did not help them develop an inner sense of responsibility. I took ownership of their actions when I punished. Mutual respect means establishing a sense of order, setting limits appropriate for a child's age, teaching and modeling expected behavior, being consistent, and working with him with firmness, kindness, and understanding.

When I wanted Brett at age three to allow me time on the phone, I could not order him to cooperate or just expect him to leave me alone. Both of those approaches would end in my yelling and screaming. I needed to establish a sense of respectful order with him. I told him that I would be on the phone and for how long. I needed to respect his age and attention span. I tried to keep the calls short. I also worked with him to plan what he could do while I made the calls. I might set him up to watch "Sesame Street" while I made two calls.

I also let him know what to expect after good behavior. *"We will have more time at the park together because I will finish my calls faster."* The opposite was also true: *"If I do not have time for my calls, we will not have time for the park."* Then he accepted the responsibility. He had a choice, and he usually chose to go to the park.

Mutual respect means "I will never treat you any differently from the way I would want someone to treat me" and "I will never talk to you any differently from the way I would talk to a best friend." You show your children respect when you use joint problem solving, make decisions together, allow choices, and use mistakes as opportunities to learn. In this atmosphere a child learns to understand and express feelings, and he grows confident, cooperative, and responsible to himself and others.

### 3. LOVE AND ACCEPT UNCONDITIONALLY.

In order for your child to become a responsible person with healthy self-esteem, she must know that no matter what she does, no matter what she feels, no matter what the mistake, you will love her. If your love is based on what she does, when she does well she will feel good about herself, yet when she makes a mistake such as wetting pants, getting poor grades, or breaking a window in a ball game, the fear or threat of not living up to your expectations or of losing your love and respect may make her feel diminished and cause her to hide. She must also know that you will love her even if she gets angry. She must be able to show fear and vulnerability and know that you will not mock her, belittle her, or love her less. It is important to accept your child's feelings, understand and show empathy, and help her develop emotional control. Most kids will share their good with their parents. You want yours to have the courage to share their bad as well. The principle of unconditional love resounds in the best parenting books today. Remember to separate the deed from the doer. You will find this mentioned again in the next section, "Tools of the Trade."

### 4. TAKE CARE OF YOURSELF.

I asked a psychologist for the one important message he would want in this book. Without hesitation he spoke about the tremendous need he sees for parents to take care of themselves. When parents come to him they are often stressed and are dealing with difficult concerns about their child. He sees fear, guilt, and anxiety pulling them down. He begins by encouraging the parent to self-nurture. He suggests setting small goals each day. List three things you know you will do and pat yourself on the back for doing them well. Many parents are guilty of having unreasonably high expectations, of starting the day with too many things to accomplish so it feels as if nothing is completed well at the end of a day. Just like children, adults are guilty of carrying around mistaken beliefs. This is baggage that pulls down our energy level, such as believing *"I cannot make mistakes, I must be perfect, my children must be perfect, I need to work and be productive to be important, I need to please people."* Out of Apples by Lee Schnebly (Tucson: Manzanas Press, 1984) is a wonderful book of light-hearted psychology. She suggests that to build self-confidence, you should start watching what you do well. Look for the good you do. Just getting up, dressing, and getting a family fed and out the door in the morning is a real accomplishment. Do something nice for yourself occasionally. Make a wish list of things that would make you feel good, small as they may be: a fifteen-minute walk, a hot bath by candlelight, a long-distance call to an old friend, a date with your spouse or partner.

A parent needs to have strong feelings of self-worth to impart confidence to a child. It takes a terrific amount of energy to be the best cheerleader your child will ever know. In those years of rebellion—age two, age five, ages nine through the teens—when he may test you, you must feel confident that you are a capable parent who sets reasonable limits, who can say no and be consistent, and who has the courage to make mistakes. Take care of yourself.

## 5. MODEL IMPORTANT SKILLS.

It has been said that children are mimics—they learn best what they observe, not what they are lectured about. Stephen Glenn, in his training program "Developing Capable People," refers to four major skills necessary to maintain healthy self-esteem. High-risk children, or children who find themselves in trouble, usually lack one or more of these skills. Each entry in this book suggests ways for you to model these necessary skills.

## A. THE SKILL OF COMMUNICATION

Communication is both listening to others and expressing yourself clearly, working with others to negotiate and solve problems. Your child will learn to listen to you when you show your interest and listen to him. When you establish eye contact, get down to his eye level, he will learn to do the same with others. When you nag, lecture, judge, and criticize, he will become "parent deaf"; he will learn not to come to you and will shut you out. He will learn to negotiate with others to solve problems if you do the same with him.

## B. THE SKILL OF EMOTIONAL SELF-CONTROL

When you share your feelings and show emotional control, you help your child begin the process of learning his own self-control. This, combined with your helping him assess and manage his own feelings, will help him mature into a capable person.

## C. THE SKILL OF SELF-DISCIPLINE

When your child watches you follow the limits imposed by society, act responsibly, or experience consequences, she will learn to be more responsible for her own actions. If she observes even something seemingly trivial to you (such as your fudging her age to get her into a movie at half price, or avoiding paying a parking ticket), she will likely learn that limits don't matter.

## D. THE SKILL OF USING GOOD JUDGMENT AND MAKING GOOD CHOICES

We are often too quick to impose a consequence for a child's behavior because we feel we need to teach him a lesson. Instead, by having an open dialogue when a mistake occurs *("What hap-*

*pened? Why did that happen? What could you do differently next time to prevent the same mistake?")*, you encourage good thinking skills. Discussing results of mistakes without blaming, and finding solutions to problems, will enhance mature thinking and reasoning. Open discussions in which you explore values and judgments and share your experiences are necessary to mature development.

If you pay attention to the above four principles to the best of your ability, you will face normal parenting dilemmas more confidently and consistently. Many parents today know enough not to want to parent like a rigid brick wall, yet what to do instead is sometimes baffling, and in place of rigidity we use a permissive, waffling approach. These Positive Parenting principles will help you stay on track. In the long run, you will help your child grow to be more resourceful, responsible, and respectful of others.

# TOOLS OF THE TRADE

There are ten suggested tools for Positive Parenting. These tools can be used in handling the behaviors discussed in the A-to-Z section of the book. Do not hesitate to refer to this section when reading the entries. It is important that you understand that these tools work only when used with a loving, respectful attitude. Your child will do better when she feels you talk *with* her, not at her, and treat her as you would your best friend. This is possible. Be kind, firm, and very consistent.

## Tool #1: Setting Limits

Believe it or not, your child craves limits. She truly needs a flexible sense of order and will grow anxious without it. Think of limits as an expanding corral. Limits provide a physical environment in which your child can feel safe and can learn. As she grows more capable, the boundaries will expand. She begins in the womb, expands to a bassinet, then to a crib, and then to her bed. You may feel your three-year-old is too young for an overnight visit to a playmate's home. By the time she is five or six you may occasionally consider it, and by the time she's ten you may be ready to say yes to a slumber party. Your child's readiness determines how the boundaries expand. Your child does not want control or dominance but a structure that encourages her to think, to make choices, and to take chances.

Post your important guidelines. Do not have too many (have no more than five or six), but post them where you can refer to them with your child. (The refrigerator is a good location.) Even a two-and-a-half-year-old can see *Bedtime, 8:00* and review it with you occasionally.

### FOUR TERRIFIC FAMILY GUIDELINES
### FOR HOW WE SHOULD TREAT EACH OTHER:

1. We use appropriate words to tell each other how we feel. We do not name-call or use bad language.
2. We do not hurt others physically or emotionally.
3. We do not hurt property, others' or our own.
4. We work to get out of a problem, not to stay in it.

When a problem arises, review these guidelines. *"Hilary, tell me your understanding of the family guidelines."* The rules that are posted may change with the needs of the situation.

Your child will test the limits and "buck the boundaries" at times, and you will need to be consistent in enforcing them. Follow through no matter how she protests. *Some* limits can be negotiated, such as bedtime. *"Holly, yes, you may stay up past your bedtime for Bill Cosby on Thursday nights provided you can get up on time in the morning and show that you can handle our morning routine."* Other limits cannot be negotiated, usually for reasons of safety or values. *"Brian, I need you to fasten your seat belt before I start the car engine. That is the law; there is no choice."* For some parents, setting limits is often the most difficult part of parenting. Do you say no too quickly and then give in after much pleading? Don't be afraid to say, *"I'll need some time to think about that."* How do you say no to someone you love so very much and for whom you would do anything? Remember that limits will make her feel more secure and be a more confident person. Finally, it is important that parents work together to agree on the rules— don't allow your child to play one of you against the other.

## Tool #2: Time Out and Cooling Off

This combination is for both the parent and the child. When your child misbehaves, he is discouraged and often can get out of control. Time out provides a place to go and some time to feel better and cool off. It is not to be enforced with anger, as isolation in the "dunce chair" used to be. A child under three years needs you to remain calm, to stay near, and to judge the time needed for him to gain control. Children three years and up will learn how long they need their space for time out and will learn to judge for themselves when they are ready to come back. Your positive attitude and the way time out is executed determines whether it is punishment or a positive tool for teaching self-control. Saying, *"Morgan, please take time out to feel better. Come back when you feel like playing nicely"* is very different from yelling, *"Morgan, you take time out right now until you can behave yourself!"* You need to recognize when you need time out as well. All parents can use a cooling-off time to release anger and frustration away from their children. When you take time out to cool off, you may keep from saying or doing hurtful things you may later regret, and you will model emotional self-control to your child. You may do this by taking a deep breath and counting to ten, by leaving your child with another responsible person and taking a long walk, or by calmly ducking into the bathroom and locking the door to give yourself some private space for a few minutes.

Be sure not to storm off in anger. Let your child know that you will return (or come out) when you cool off or when he calms down. (Many younger children worry or become frightened when a parent disappears. If so, use another technique that will not leave a feeling of fear or rejection.)

## Tool #3: Poker Face

Many experts use this term to define a calm, relaxed body language. When you keep a straight face, you appear unimpressed with hassle and show no emotional involvement. Keep your eyebrows up and you will not frown. If you speak, keep your voice calm and quiet. This is a very effective tool when you do not want to give undue attention to a negative behavior but you must remain involved. For example, I was counseled to put our two-year-old Brett back to bed each time he popped up, kindly and calmly, with a poker face and action with few words. The first night I stayed calm and kind and marched him back to his bed thirty-five times. (It helped me to count.) He fell asleep in the hall on the floor. The next night it took fifteen times, and he again fell asleep in the hall. The third night he cried for five minutes and fell asleep next to his bed on the floor. The fourth night he cried five minutes and stayed in his bed. After that he went to bed happily and willingly. This was *very* hard to do, requiring a great deal of patience. When Brett received no social benefit, no sweet-talking, no reminding or scolding, the behavior stopped.

## Tool #4: Time for Teaching

Much misbehavior can be prevented if you avoid the mistake of expecting your child to know everything that you know. By taking time to teach her and reasoning with her, she will do better. Here are some examples. When you have a problem, stop to think, have I taught her all I can about this situation?

• If you are having a problem with your young child running into the street, have an adult stand with her while you drive your car over a toy truck or a grapefruit. *"Morgan, see how heavy the car is? Tell me why we stay out of the street."* You still will have to watch her closely near the street, but she will have a better idea of why you are concerned. Your reasoning with her is not to instill fear but to show her you feel she is capable of understanding.

- If your child is terrible in the toy store, take time to teach by making a trip to the store for practice. She will not know it is practice. Tell her before you go into the store what you will do if she begs or cries. *"Samantha, we are going into the store for Billy's birthday present. We will choose it and pay for it and leave. If you beg and cry we will come back to the car without the present."* Follow through as you discussed. This training will save you time in the long run because she will believe you will do what you say you will do.

- If dressing is a problem, remember to never do for a child what he can do for himself. Most two-and-a-half-year-olds can dress themselves with training. Take the time to shop for easy clothing, teach him how to put each item on, and then let him do it.

- Try a training chart. It helps children to learn good, responsible habits. It is not a system of rewards. You are merely helping your child with a visual, hands-on method of monitoring his own behavior. If you give big, pricey rewards you defeat the purpose, which is to create a good feeling of accomplishment and an inner sense of responsibility. Furthermore, as he grows he will begin saying, *"Well, what do I get if I do make my bed?"* When he is five a toy tractor may work, at age ten he may expect a skateboard, and at age sixteen it may be a car he is bargaining for. Work on only one problem behavior at a time. The following training chart helped three-year-old Malia learn to stay in her bed. She used it for two weeks, and then she did not need it anymore. Each time she succeeded, she put a sticker on the chart the following morning.

## STAYING-IN-MY-BED CHART

| MON. | TUES. | WED. | THURS. | FRI. | SAT. | SUN. |
|------|-------|------|--------|------|------|------|
|      |       |      |        |      |      |      |

At the end of the week, celebrate with a special time together, such as a trip to the zoo or an outing of her choice. Celebrate when you take the chart down: *"What an accomplishment. What a terrific effort!"*

Nine-year-old Anne was often not ready to leave for school on time. She used the following chart to help her learn organization and stay on task in the morning. Anne put a sticker on the chart when she completed each task. This eliminated morning hassles and her mom's nagging, and it taught organization at the same time. A difficult chart can be overwhelming. A chart such as this need only be used for two weeks for teaching, although a child may need to use it again in the future.

### MORNING TASKS

7:00 **Wake up**
**Dress**
7:45 **Eat breakfast**
8:00 **Practice piano**
8:15 **Organize books and lunch**
8:30 **Leave for school**

## Tool #5: Action with Few Words

Your child will tire of your lectures and constant reminders. She will become "parent deaf" when you nag, nag, nag, and she often will wait to cooperate until she knows you mean what you say, or until she sees you lose control and get extremely angry. Say what you need to say once with a positive message. For example, instead of *"No running!"* say, *"Please use your walking feet,"* and then act. Stop reminding and coaxing! If she does not stop running, stop her kindly and firmly. Five-year-old Samantha was great at conning her parents into a little more: *"Please, oh please."*

Sometimes Mom would give in. Dad always did. When it did not work with Mom, Sam pouted and sulked until Mom either gave in or got angry and began yelling and screaming. When both parents learned to say only *one* time what they meant and began to follow through kindly and calmly with action with few words, the conning stopped.

## Tool #6: Choices

When encouraging responsibility, offer reasonable choices instead of demands. Choices empower, giving your child a feeling she has control over what happens to her, which is crucial to self-esteem. Instead of telling your three-year-old to brush her teeth, try giving a choice: *"Mindy, it's time to brush teeth. Do you want the pump toothpaste or the striped?"* She has no choice in negotiating whether she brushes or not, just in the toothpaste she uses. Be sure either choice is acceptable. Choices, like limits, broaden as your child grows and becomes more responsible. For eight-year-old Molly: *"Molly, you know what you need to do before bed. You choose when you do it and be in bed by 9:00."* There is no negotiating what needs to be done before bed, just choosing how she may do it. Choices encourage cooperation and responsible behavior. Four-year-old Heather chose to play quietly without interrupting while her mom talked with a woman about a business deal. Her mother had wisely prepared her: *"Heather, if I am not interrupted I will be finished in time to take you swimming. It is your choice if you want to swim or not."*

## Tool #7: Special Time

Your child needs one-on-one time with you and/or any other significant person caring for him daily. You don't have to indulge in expensive, busy activities; you can do something free, something you both enjoy. You might take a walk, go to the park, or stay home and play a game. It is uninterrupted time: no peeling carrots, no answering the phone, no sibling disruption. A very important part of special time is to let your child know when it will happen. *"Ryan, I have a half hour set aside after school to have some fun with you."* Another important part is to do what your child chooses and enjoys. *"What would you like to do with our time together?"* Once in a while, make a special date to go out to dinner. *"Just the two of us."* Your child will remember these times, feel loved, and seek less attention in negative ways.

## Tool #8: Encouragement

Hang on, this is a biggie! Encouragement is what you use to create positive change, to help your child grow self-confident. Punishing never builds courage or healthy self-esteem. Find many opportunities each day to offer encouraging remarks.

Learn to separate what your child is doing from her self-worth. Do not use *good* or *bad*, as in *"You are a good girl because you peed in the toilet."* Instead, concentrate on the deed or how she feels about herself. *"Alright Abba! Dry pants. How do you feel?"* If she then has an accident, she will not feel like a bad girl.

Mistakes are okay; they are for learning. *"Abba, what will you do differently next time?"*

Love is unconditional. *"You are very important to me. I sometimes feel frustrated with what you do. You know I will always love you."* It is encouraging when you separate what she does from how you feel about her.

Give positive messages with enthusiasm when she is not expecting it. *"I just love you so much!"* is very effective when she is surprised with it.

Watch for what she does right rather than what she does wrong. Find many ways during the day to say *"Atta girl!"* with great enthusiasm, and work hard on limiting the nagging and criticism.

Catch him being good! *"James, you poured your glass of milk and one for your sister. That's great!"*

Focus on the process, not the finished product. *"Elizabeth, you look so happy coloring!"* Rather than praising her (*"I'm so proud of you for coloring the picture"*), it's better to encourage her enjoyment and effort and to inquire how she feels about it. Be specific. *"The colors! You have worked so hard on this! How do you feel about this picture?"* You want to separate her self-worth from what she does. That way, when she is not happy with her picture her self-worth is not diminished.

Maintain the positive attitude that the glass is half full, not half empty. *"The grape juice did spill and stain the new rug. We're lucky it is a small stain, and right in a spot where we can put an area rug over it."* (True, this is a tough one.)

Use a sense of humor. Lighten up, life's not that serious! *"Jenny, you seem to like different-colored socks and the laces are tied on the toes instead of at the top of your shoes. I guess I can live with it. Maybe I should try it."*

Rather than blame, help look for the solution to a problem. *"Let's not worry about who left the gate open. The puppy got out. We all need to walk the block and look for her."*

Set expectations appropriate to age level. If you have unreasonable expectations, loosen up. *"Andrew, the cover is pulled all the way up on your bed! Great job!"* (He'll learn to smooth the lumps out in time.) No one flourishes with a perfectionist parent.

Overprotection and rescuing are discouraging. Unless the result of not interfering would be hurtful to others or would have immediate or long-range dangerous results, try to let the natural or logical consequence run the situation. *"Tommy, if you leave your lunch home again you will have to go without. I cannot bring it to you."* You are encouraging your child by showing faith and confidence that he is capable and will learn from the situation.

Rather than pushing hard and creating a power struggle, empower your child by letting go. *"Meg, I am leaving the room. As soon as you brush your teeth I will take you to play."*

Be patient and interested in the process of her childhood rather than longing for or concentrating on her as a finished product. *"I love watching you grow and learn!"*

Use "yes" rather than "no." Say *"Keep your feet on the floor"* rather than *"Do not put your feet on the couch."* You can find positive ways to say almost anything.

Use questions beginning with "what," "why," or "how" to check that her perception is the same as yours. Instead of assuming she knows what you mean, tell her what you expect. *"Holly, we are going into the store. I need you to stay with me in the cart or at my side holding the string on my belt. We will go faster and you will not lose me.* " Then say, *"Holly, how will you go through the store? Why do I want you to stay near me?"* Questions will help her think. Do not say *"Do you understand?"* If she nods or says "yes," you still will not know whether or not her understanding is the same as yours. Checking out her perceptions saves a lot of misunderstandings at any age.

Do use "please" and "thank you."

## Tool #9: Family Meetings

The family meeting is a direct, team approach for parents and children to connect and practice all the skills presented in this book. Your family is a team. Decide together what you want to call your meetings. I've heard some children do not like the term *meeting.* Some families use *pow-wow* or *team time.* Family meetings will help your child feel his contributions are needed. In this setting his ideas and feelings are heard and taken seriously, and he has opportunities to feel some control over what happens to him. Family meetings, class meetings, and meetings in the workplace are important motivators. People do better when they belong to a group and know they make a difference.

### A model agenda for young children three and older:

Time: Fifteen minutes. Keep the meetings short and your expectations reasonable. Plan for success, be organized, and clip along. Let go of perfection. It's okay if you don't make it through your agenda.

1. Appreciations, compliments, and thank-yous.
2. Minutes from the previous week. Lightly touch on what was discussed.
3. Family jobs. Select daily and weekly chores from a list. Use pictures or illustrations with words for nonreaders.
4. Weekly plans. Mark a calendar to show daily individual schedules for the week. (Children do better when they know what to expect.)

5. One family issue. Discuss ideas and solutions. For instance: We need to keep the sand in the sand box. Or: Toys are not being picked up.
6. Plan the week's family fun activity.

## A model agenda for school-age children:

Time: Twenty to thirty minutes. Again, plan for success. Be organized. Model and teach skills: You are the parent. Stop hurtful or insulting language or actions. This is the arena in which to model and teach emotional control, good communication, responsibilities, good judgment, and choices based on family values.

1. Post an agenda to which family members can add items during the week.
2. Rotate leader, refreshment person, and secretary to take minutes.
3. Celebrations, affirmations, and thank-yous.
4. Agenda issues:

Name      Issue, concern      Suggestions      Solution chosen

5. Weekly schedule. Each person gets calendars out and marks individual schedule. Arrange rides, appointments, etc.
6. Select family jobs.

Name      Daily jobs      Weekly jobs

7. Family fun. Play charades.
8. Refreshments.

*Raising Kids Who Can* by Betty Lou Bettner, Ph.D. and Amy Lew, Ph.D. (New York: HarperCollins, 1992) is a short, helpful book on successful family meetings.

## Tool #10: Problem Solving

Many parenting experts use the following approach to problem solving. The idea is to talk and listen to help your child develop good decision-making skills and to encourage her cooperation. Sometimes one or two of these steps work well, and sometimes you will decide to use them all. Before your child will listen to you, she most likely will want you to listen to her. This will not work when you are angry or engaged in a power struggle. You will need a cooling-off time first. Before jumping right on her with *"Gretchen, I have a problem with all the TV you are watching,"* try this approach:

1. State her feelings. Show genuine concern. *"Gretchen, it seems that you are really very sad that your friend Zoe moved away."* Pause and listen and reflect very sincerely what she says and feels. *"It sounds as though you feel . . . because . . ."* or *"You really do feel . . . because . . ."* This may seem awkward at first, but stick with it. When you do not jump in with criticism, judgment, or an immediate solution, she will grow into a fine decision maker and will want to listen and talk to you more often. You will be amazed at the results, and it will become easier and easier for you. Do this as long as she seems to want to share her feelings or until you feel she may be sucking you into an attention-getting situation. *("This is great. I have really got Mom's attention.")*

2. Empathize. You may say kindly, *"Gretch, I'm sorry you miss her so."* You may show that you understand how she feels by telling her of an experience you had when you were her age. *"I remember when I was eight and my best friend moved away."*

3. Express your feelings. Now she may be ready to listen to how you feel about the problem. Use the word *I* this time instead of *you*, which can sound blaming. *"I'm sorry you miss Zoe. I'm concerned that you won't accept any invitations to play with other children, and all you want to do is watch TV."*

4. Brainstorm solutions. Invite her to think of ideas to help resolve the problem. Give your ideas only after she gives hers. *"Gretch, what do you think you might do to feel better besides watching*

*TV?"* If she has no ideas, suggest one or two to get her started. *"Would you like a couple of ideas that I have thought of?"*

5. Follow up. In a day or two, evaluate. *"Gretch, you agreed to write Zoe a letter and have two friends make a video of you all dancing. Did that make you feel better? I haven't had to bug you about the TV. You sure are a good problem solver!"*

The ten Tools of the Trade—setting limits, time out and cooling off, poker face, time for teaching, action with few words, choices, special time, encouragement, family meetings, and problem solving—equip you to be a Positive Parent. When you experience too much chaos and you want your child to show more responsibility, try *setting limits*, using *time out* and *cooling off* instead of lecturing, use a *poker face* and/or *action with few words*, or perhaps more *time for teaching*. If your child ignores you, try to build cooperation with *family meetings* and *problem solving*, and when you want to build your child's courage use *special time* and lots of *encouragement*. These tools, combined with your patience, consistency, and loving firmness, will help you be the Positive Parent you want to be.

# ADOPTION, QUESTIONS ABOUT

*"My child is asking questions about adoption."*

## UNDERSTANDING THE SITUATION

Historically, adoption was an embarrassing topic, considered shameful and hidden from common public discussion. Today, however, many people know someone who joined their family through adoption, and the topic is openly discussed at school and at home. Questions about adoption may make you feel uncomfortable. The more you learn and open your mind to current adoption situations the better you will be able to communicate proper attitudes to your child. For instance, today it is common with infant adoptions that the birth parents choose the adoptive parents they want to raise their child. It is also recommended that if a child is adopted, the words *birth mother* and *adopted mother* are common terms he hears long before he can understand the issues involved. In other words, adoption is not hushed as in the past. Be open to new ideas and if you do not know much about the subject be honest and admit to your child, *"I don't know much about that. Let's find out together."*

## WHAT TO SAY AND DO

As soon as a young adopted child begins asking questions he may hear, *"Nick, I am your adopted mom and I love you so much!"* *"We picked you because you are very special."* *"We are very lucky."* This loving attitude will build the confidence he will need to handle questions children may ask him as he grows.

As your adopted child grows, provide good talk times and be aware of issues he may need to discuss. He needs to hear that his adopted parents loved him very much but had many grown-up problems. Help him understand your empathy for them.

The most common question asked by a young child is, *"Did I grow in your tummy? Suzy says she grew in her birth mommy's tummy."* Explain, *"Yes, you grew inside me. I am your birth mommy. The mommy who gave birth to Suzy could not raise her, and she found another mommy and daddy to raise Suzy. They adopted Suzy so that they could help her grow up. Now they are a family together just like us."* A young child might understand better if you draw the people as you explain.

The loss of parents is a primal fear of every child. Your child may be concerned that she will lose you through adoption. You can reassure her by saying, *"Kate, Daddy and I were so happy that I got pregnant and that we could give birth to you! We wanted you very much! We will always raise you. Erin's mommy could not get pregnant. That happens sometimes. They were so lucky to have Erin join their family by adopting her. Now they will help her grow up."*

Your birth child may say, *"Billy says he's adopted. I guess his real parents didn't want him."* Explain, *"Billy joined his family through adoption because his birth parents could not raise a baby. They had too many grown-up problems at the time. I'm sure they were very sad, but they found Billy's adoptive parents to raise Billy. Billy's parents are his adoptive parents, but they are his real parents now and always will be."*

Sometimes school-age children will tease the adopted child out of curiosity to see how he'll react. Encourage your child to ask questions and not tease. Kindly say, *"Mary, teasing hurts. What would you feel like if you were teased like that? Joe is an expert; he was adopted. Ask him if he minds your questions. Joe can help you learn a lot about adoption."* Teasing is very hurtful no matter what the situation, but being teased about having been adopted is traumatic.

If you hear that your adopted child is being teased or is upset by other children's questions, spend time exploring the feelings. *"Mindy, you are very upset about the teasing."* Listen, do not try to fix. *"Why do you think she is asking you that?"* *"What do you plan to do?"* *"What do you need from me?"* Questions will help her understand her feelings and think out her own solutions.

**PREVENTIVE TIPS**

- Keep photo albums available and look through them together, often, just as you would read a book together. Your child, adopted or not, will love to hear the story of her birth or how she came to be. Share it with fun and humor.
- Read aloud together children's stories such as *How It Feels to Be Adopted* by Jill Krementz (New York: Knopf, 1988).
- Arrange for a field trip to an adoption agency with a scout troop or other group.
- Keep well informed on current adoption practices. Whole books are written on this important issue. Read *Making Sense of Adoption* by Lois Melina (New York: HarperCollins, 1989), *Raising Adopted Children* by Lois Melina (New York: HarperCollins, 1986), *Shared Fate* by David Kirk (Port Angeles, Wash.: Ben-Simon Publications, 1964).

# ANGER, CHILD'S

*"My child seems so hostile and angry all the time."*

**UNDERSTANDING THE SITUATION**

A common, major concern of many parents today is how to deal with their child's anger. Many parents share the shock and frustration of a constant angry mood: kicking or hitting, saying very bad, threatening words, and sometimes going into a sullen sulk for long periods of time. It is very hard not to react with your own anger. Typically a parent scolds, *"Don't you talk to me that way, young lady,"* strikes back, or threatens to remove privileges. This doesn't help. Your anger pushes against hers and creates more anger and hurt. She may think, *"I'll get even"* or, *"She hates me and I'll show her, she'll be sorry."* Likely your child is feeling hurt or powerless. *"I never get to do what I want."* The stresses of our fast-paced lives and the personal daily pressures make it difficult to give this important issue the time it deserves. *Take the time.* Your long-term goal is to help your child have emotional self-control, a skill very important to healthy self-esteem. We all experience angry feelings, and we all need to know that we have choices about how we act on those feelings. *Gaining emotional self-control is learned over time, many years, with a great deal of patience, consistency, and modeling of your own emotional control.* Keep the faith and do not give up on your child. Over time you will lovingly teach her:

1. to identify and begin to understand the feeling of her anger.
2. to understand what makes her angry and how she might communicate her needs to prevent a bad situation.
3. to soothe herself before she gets out of control.
4. to accept her anger and decide what she will do to vent the anger without hurting herself or others.

**WHAT TO SAY AND DO**

Do not overreact to your child's anger. Anger creates more anger. Calmly, with a *poker face*, identify his anger. *"Casey, you are very angry and you may not hurt your sister. Please take a* time out.*"* You may need to sit with your young child through his anger. Some very intense young children respond to a tight, loving hold. He may struggle but hang in there. This will help him feel safe and trust himself to calm himself and gain self-control. Stay close with your older child as well. You may be in the next room or hallway if not with him. Staying near sends a clear message that you won't desert him when he loses control.

Instead of ranting and raving, stay calm and say, *"Shelby, do you need a hug?"* She will learn from this that what she may be feeling is hurt, not anger, and a cuddle or a hug is very soothing. In time, if you do this consistently, she will learn to ask for this instead of manipulating with her emotion.

You may need time to *cool off.* Take three deep breaths if you can't leave the room. Timing is important. No listening or good thinking happens during the adrenaline rush of anger.

Pouting and passive aggression, such as not cooperating, coloring a wall, constantly needling a sister are signs of anger. Say what you need once, do not nag, nag, nag. Set a timer to direct him rather than your voice.

## PREVENTIVE TIPS

- At good talk times, *problem solve.* *"Pat, you seem to feel very angry. I remember a time when I was eight and I felt so frustrated that my father would not let me do what I wanted. Do you feel that you can't do what you want or that you can't be your own boss? Let's talk about some things that will help you feel better."*
  - At a good listening and talk time discuss with your child what signals her body gives her before she hits the peak of anger. She may describe a tightness in her stomach, clenched fists, or that her heart beats faster. Talk about getting in touch with the feeling before she loses control. Talk about what she may do to calm herself before she gets carried away with anger. Here are parent–child tested ideas:

  1. Ask for a hug or to be held. *"Caitlin, tell me when you need a hug."* (Many parents and teachers have remarked how well this works.)
  2. Take a warm bubble bath.
  3. Blow bubbles. (This teaches taking deep breaths for soothing.)

- At a good listening and calm talk time brainstorm what she might do to release her anger.

  1. Jump on an old mattress.
  2. Punch a punching bag.
  3. Shred paper in a designated area.
  4. Ask to be held.
  5. Run around the house outside.
  6. Throw hoops.
  7. Write a letter or draw the angry feeling.

- Be aware of the media. Your child will see violence live on every news station. He'll hear about live drive-by shootings in his city on the radio. His favorite TV shows likely display an angry, out-of-control character; cartoons are often the worst. Children often act out what they see. Screen what your child sees when possible, and discuss what he sees and hears when you can't avoid it. Ask questions to promote thinking. *"Andrew, shooting is not a good way to settle a problem. What do you think he could have done instead?" "What happened? Why did that happen? Do you think that was a good choice?"* Your discussions about your values are very important.

- Have *family meetings.* Your child is growing quickly and at each stage of development he will need to know that you are valuing his opinions, including him in problem solving, and giving him increasing responsibilities. Involve your child in family decision making and in finding the solutions to problems.
- *Encourage!* Your child needs to hear what he is doing right. Give affirmation. *"Patrick, I will always love you, no matter what. I may not like what you do some of the time. You need to know that I will always love you. Nothing can change that."* You don't want him to feel ashamed or guilty for his anger.
- Your child needs to feel in control of what happens to him, to feel needed by those close to him, and to feel capable. His anger is a red flag that he is not perceiving this to be true. Read the Principles of Positive Parenting and Tools of the Trade at the beginning of this book. Read other individual entries that may discuss issues you are experiencing at home. You will diffuse your child's anger by the positive way you respond to sibling fighting, getting your child to bed, morning hassles, temper tantrums, etc.

See also: Anger, parent's; Feelings; Temper tantrums

# ANGER, PARENT'S

*"My child makes me so angry I lose control. It scares me!"*

## UNDERSTANDING THE SITUATION

Anger of a parent is an emotion that deserves careful attention. You are not alone if you have felt the urge to call your child terrible names, yank him, or strike him. These are scary feelings that can leave you feeling terribly guilty and incapable of being a good parent. You will be very angry with your child now and then; that is a fact. *Do not take your anger out on your child. Cool off*, then deal with your child's actions. Learn to feel the emotion build before you lose control. Express your feelings, be specific about what you are angry about, and remove yourself to relieve your anger. Punishing with anger takes the responsibility away from your child. Fighting back creates power struggles. Hitting or yelling only teaches him to react with violence when he is angry and creates feelings of more anger, blame, shame, guilt, or lowered self-esteem. If you do lose it, do not beat yourself up over it. You are human, and you will make mistakes. Apologize to your child and act differently next time. This takes courage. Be sure your child knows that you feel *"I will always love you, and yet I do sometimes get very frustrated with what you do."*

## WHAT TO SAY AND DO

Do not try to impose consequences when you are angry. It will only result in punishment. Use *time out*. Don't be afraid to say, *"I am angry! I need some time to think about this. We both need time out to think and cool off, and then we will talk about it."* When you calm down you may see the situation differently. It may take several hours to be able to discuss what happened without anger. Sometimes it may take a whole day.

Before you jump to enforce consequences, check your child's perceptions of what happened. Children are often punished for something they did but did not intend to do. The surprise of a ball accidently hitting and breaking a vase is powerful. Your child does not necessarily have to be punished to learn a lesson.

Separate your child from what she did to make you angry. Tell her how you feel by stating emotions, not by calling names. Do not use "you" messages, like *"You are such a loser, a real klutz! You can't be trusted!"* Use an "I" message: *"I am angry that the ring was lost!"*

Take a walk to *cool off* if someone is there to stay with your child. If not, leave the room (but not with rage), leave with a *poker face*, and go into the bathroom for *time out*. Take ten deep breaths slowly, gain control, and return to discuss the situation.

If you are in public with no other adult help, take deep breaths and as calmly as possible with a *poker face*, remove yourself and your child. Stand outside or go to the car. *"Jeana, I am really angry. We are going to the car until I can cool down."* Firmly and kindly fasten her in and stand outside. *Cool off.* Often just taking a brisk walk to the car will cool you down.

If you do blow it and get very angry, apologize at a cooled-off time. *"Mike, I felt very angry when I saw you eating the cake. I really screamed at you. I am sorry. I don't like to speak to you like that."* Then ask for his help in sharing some of the responsibility. *"What might you do differently next time that could help us both?"* Your apology is important. It is also important he think about the role he played, and this method does not blame or criticize him.

Leave a note. *"Ian, the record is broken. Plan to talk about this after dinner."*

## PREVENTIVE TIPS

- Take time away from your child regularly. Trade childcare with friends, ask help from a family member, or hire a sitter.

- Stress management and regular exercise are crucial to good mental health. Take time for yourself, and keep your energy level up!
- Read together children's books to stimulate discussions about feelings. *Grandpa's Face* by Eloise Greenfield (New York: Putnam, 1988), *I Was So Mad!* by Norma Simon (Morton Grove, Ill.: Whitman, 1974), and *Sometimes I Get Angry* by Jane Watson, Robert Switzer, M.D., and J. C. Hirschberg, M.D. (New York: Crown, 1986) are picture books that are fun and helpful.
- A small bear pin on your collar means *"Bear with me!"* It's a great way to let family members know you may have a shorter fuse than usual.
- If your anger feels out of control, see a professional counselor. This is very important to both you and your child.

# ARGUING

*"My child argues with almost everything I say."*

### UNDERSTANDING THE SITUATION

A two-to-three-year-old's job is to say no, an irritating but essential part of developing assertion and independence. An older child challenges in much the same manner, and again it may be irritating, but it's important in developing good thinking and reasoning skills. It may seem she rudely challenges your every word, what you do and even what you wear. If you say it is black, she says it is white. This can be very frustrating, but do not scold or punish her. When you feel she is disrespectful, tell her and stop her firmly and kindly. Do this consistently, and remember a basic of Positive Parenting: *"I respect you, and I respect myself."* *Encourage* her assertive skills, compliment her good choices, and notice when she thinks for herself. This will help strengthen your relationship and build her cooperation. Later, in teen years, she will be able to say no to her peers when good judgment dictates that response. Be patient with her, and accept that her maturing is a process that will take years. This is her practice arena in learning about life!

## WHAT TO SAY AND DO

The predictable response—*"Don't you ever talk to me that way"* or *". . . because I said so. Now do as I say!"*—isn't constructive. These are fighting words that create a win/lose situation. Your child may be critical, challenging, and testing. She needs to know you love her and that you won't reject her when she pushes against you. Let go of the need to be right all the time.

1. Use questions, not a lecture, to make her think. *"Mindy, how could you say that more respectfully to me? How would you feel if I spoke to you that way?"*
2. Avoid giving her orders and telling her what you won't do. *"I certainly won't let you go when you talk to me that way, young lady."* Instead tell her what you will do. *"Mindy, I will listen to you when you use a softer tone."*
3. Set your limits with *choices* instead of orders. *"Mindy, I will listen to what you want if you talk nicely to me, or we can discuss this another time. You choose."*

Walk away if she is disrespectful and you grow angry. Take *time out.* *"Heidi, we aren't getting anywhere. We need time out. You can bring it up later if you want to negotiate with a nicer attitude."* If you are in public, lead her away from people, stand outside (if it is rainy and uncomfortable, so much the better), and wait with her. *"When you are ready to be more respectful we can go back into the mall."*

Show you care about her opinions. Teach her to think about what she feels, to negotiate her needs or ideas with *problem solving* discussion, and not to flair into an argument.

1. Listen and reflect her feelings. *"Julie, you feel you should be able to go to Mary's after school and miss choir."*

2. Show understanding. *"I think I understand. You haven't had much play time with Mary, and you do go to choir every week."*

3. State how you feel. *I'm concerned about you missing choir this week because you only have one practice before Sunday night's perform-ance and it is very important to the choir that you go."*

4. Work together to come up with options. *"You are committed to choir Wednesday. How about having Mary over Thursday, and I'll be home from work early."*

Use *"I need to think about it,"* or defer to the *family meeting* to avoid her insistent pleas. *"Jen, it sounds as though you have some important thoughts and concerns about our rule. Put this on the agenda for the family meeting, and we will discuss it then."* Do not feel rushed or pressured to answer right away. Inevitably you will an-swer no; if you back down later and change your mind, that teaches your child that you don't mean what you say . . . and in-vites a hassle.

Some rules should be negotiable. *No guests overnight on a school night* is a rule that is okay to waive if you feel persuaded to do so. For example, *"Katherine, the rule is no guests on school nights. You need to convince me that I should be flexible on this one."* Watch terrific creative problem solving happen. *"Jenny has never slept at my house"* won't work, but *"Jenny and I have a report to do together, and we will work all evening and go right to sleep"* may be a consid-eration.

Notice and comment on her good thinking and reasoning. Be specific about what you noticed that was right! *"Amy, I noticed you stayed very calm talking with Dad last night. You really had your ideas well thought out, and you were convincing. Bravo!"*

**PREVENTIVE TIPS**

• Read books together at good talk times, possibly evenings be-fore bed. Books are good door-openers to humor and friendly conversation. Two suggestions: *Mrs. Piggle Wiggle* by Betty MacDonald (New York: HarperCollins Children's Books, 1985) and *Seven Kisses in a Row* by Patricia MacLaughlin (New York: Harper Trophy, 1988).

- Spend *special time* together. Do something you both enjoy once a week. A long car ride to get to the ski hill is a great time to share music and stories.
- Make time to be around your child and his friends, and spend time watching his sports and activities when possible. The better you know him, the better you will understand and be able to talk to him.
- Find time for yourself, take needed breaks, and keep your own self-esteem up!
- Develop a support group with parents of children your child's age.

# BABYISH TALK

*"My child talks like a baby to get my attention."*

## UNDERSTANDING THE SITUATION

"Babyish talk" is different from the baby talk you hear when a child has late-developing speech. It is usually spoken in a tone of whining or cutesiness. Your child may revert to substituting words, as in *"Me don't want dat!"* and simpler language forms. This behavior, though irritating, is normal and temporary. Your child may be responding to some uncomfortable situation causing her to feel a need for extra attention. Babyish talk may be triggered by any new circumstance, such as a new baby in the family, a leap from preschool to kindergarten, a parent taking a trip, Mom going back to work, or a stressful situation at school with a teacher or a friend. Your child may revert occasionally to less mature behavior when she is tired, hungry, or feeling ignored. Coaxing her to stop is giving her too much attention. Keep faith in her; it will end more quickly if you give little attention to the behavior and lots of specific acknowledgment when she shows effort in maintaining self-control, making good choices, and being helpful and responsible.

## WHAT TO SAY AND DO

Babyish talk will usually stop as quickly as it began if you ignore it. Do not ridicule or make fun. Talk with your child just as you would a good friend, straight. Firmly and kindly, say, *"Jill, I cannot understand that voice, and I cannot help you get what you need."* Comment with pleasure when she uses her grown-up voice. Say, *"Thank you! I can understand you so much better."* Even if she does not want to act grown-up, she does want to be understood.

Do the unexpected. Rather than show annoyance, which is what your child expects from you, find a chair, pull him close, and cuddle him. You must be sincere. Rock him and give him a few minutes of your time nurturing him like a baby. You may be surprised how good it feels for you both. Try to wait until he is the one to signal he is ready to stop.

Be honest. If you grow tired and irritated, let him know, but separate what he is doing from him. *"Alex, I am tired of listening to that talk."* Let him know ahead of time what you will do when you feel irritated with the talk. *"Alex, when you use babyish talk I will leave."* Follow through with consistency. Exit with a *poker face*. Go to the bathroom and close the door.

If you will be in public and you won't be able to ignore her behavior, tell her ahead of time. *"Lori, as long as you use your grown-up voice we can stay at the Center. If you don't, I will leave with you and sit in the car."* Give a second opportunity should she test you—a knowing glance that says, *"One more chance."* Then take her away.

## PREVENTIVE TIPS

- Take time to listen to your child and reflect her feelings. Read books together and talk about the characters' feelings.
- Begin *family meetings*. Put family responsibilities on the agenda, and make her a chore chart. Two chores a day is possible and will encourage your child to feel capable and needed. Babyish behavior may then stop.
- Do not do for her what she can do for herself. Show her that you know she is growing: Give her an alarm clock to wake herself up, let her choose her own clothes, ask for her help with grown-up tasks such as cutting vegetables or watching the baby.
- Help her internalize the feeling that she is growing up and is a capable person. Find an area where she can experience success: sports, art, music, dance, or other encouraging activities.
- Examine the current outside demands on her time, and adjust her schedule if possible to help reduce stress.

- Talk with her teacher to make sure he or she has no concerns about your child's socializing or work at school.
- Plan *special time. Encourage.* "You are as much fun for me to be with as my good friend. We can do things we both enjoy now that you are so grown-up."

# BABY-SITTERS

*"My child does not like being left with a baby-sitter."*

## Ages 2½–5

### UNDERSTANDING THE SITUATION

It is definitely unnerving when your youngster cries, begging you to stay home and not leave him with a sitter. His cry triggers mixed feelings—concern, guilt, and often anger—whether you are leaving him out of necessity or only for a much-needed break. Your child may subconsciously or consciously be testing his limits and acting out for attention, he may be trying to manipulate you with tears, or he may truly be scared and unable to cope easily with change and separation. Show your confidence and faith in him. With each success, he will become more independent and confident. Guilt and worry are not productive. This stage sometimes takes months, but it will pass. Do not give up.

### WHAT TO SAY AND DO

Build his confidence and courage with small steps of training, such as leaving him for short periods of time with familiar family members or friends.

Choose a sitter with experience, and use that person consistently. Have a familiar backup sitter for an emergency.

Invite the sitter to visit with you and your child. Watch the interaction and the rapport with your child. You may need to meet several people before you find the right one. Explain these visits by saying, *"Justin, a girl named Julie is coming to have juice with us today."* Later, when he is having fun playing with her, say, *"Julie will come stay with you sometimes when Daddy and I go out."*

Put together a "sitter box," a box pulled out only when the sitter is coming. Keep it full of fun activities, and occasionally add a new surprise to be unwrapped after Mom leaves. You might include modeling clay, a box of crayons, paper, watercolor paints, magazines, scissors, and a box of instant pudding or Jell-O to mix. Your sitter may interact more with your child if you have suggestions for a planned activity.

Let your child know earlier in the day that a sitter will be coming. Be positive, upbeat, and not afraid of his reaction. Limit the discussion. *"Martin, Daddy and I are going out on a date! Rebecca is coming to play with you and put you to bed."* If he cries when you tell him, take time and get down to his level, hold him, and reassure him with firm and kind words. This is the time to try to work through feelings, not when you are walking out the door. Help identify his feelings. *"Yes, you are unhappy to have us leave."* Listen without offering advice. Hold him until he offers to get down.

When it is time to leave, say good-bye and leave. Hesitation will create more anxiety for your child and make it more difficult for the sitter. Never sneak out; that only fosters worry and mistrust.

### PREVENTIVE TIPS

- Read *The Good-bye Book* by Judith Viorst (New York: Macmillan, 1986).
- Take pictures of sitters when they come to stay, and make an album to look at often with your young child.
- Leave your sitter well prepared and organized. Supply the phone number of the place where you'll be, the physician's number and a signed release for the physician, and remind her to dial 911 in an emergency. Tell her about snacks and meals she can serve, games and activities, and your child's schedule. She needs to know all about his routine. The better you prepare her, the more comfortable she will be with your child—and he with her.

• If leaving your child is difficult for you, speak to your pediatrician or daycare provider about your feelings. Your feelings are very important. What you reflect is what your child will feel.

## Ages 6–10

### UNDERSTANDING THE SITUATION

Your older child may complain about being left with a sitter. He doesn't want to be bossed or told what to do. If he is an only child he may feel you are leaving him behind. He may embarrass you by being rude or hostile and give sitters a bad time. Bribing and rewarding, or scolding and threatening, will not help him develop responsibility for his actions. Gain his cooperation. Indicate that you expect grown-up actions and that you trust him to be responsible so that you can take time away. By giving him responsibilities, working with him to *set limits*, letting him know the behavior you expect, and following through with kind and firm consistency, you will help him become a more confident and cooperative person.

### WHAT TO SAY AND DO

As with a younger child, choose a mature and experienced sitter. Many teens attend sitter training programs through schools or hospitals. Invite the sitter for a visit with your child and have the two become acquainted. Have the sitter come early and have fun with all of you before you have to leave. A few extra dollars is worth the peace of mind.

You will be lucky to have a choice of sitters. When possible, offer *choices*. Do not use the term *baby-sit*. *"Toby, Dad and I are going out Friday night. You have been invited to Grandma's, or either Dana or Scott are available to spend the evening with you. You choose and let me know by dinnertime."*

State your expectations and give an incentive for cooperative behavior. *"Rachael, if you have a good evening and get to bed on time, you may go to the overnight tomorrow. If it is a bad evening, you will have to stay home."* Follow through.

Have your child plan the evening. He can plan a simple meal and snack and be in charge of preparing them. He can choose the entertainment, a video to watch or games to play. *"Scott, tonight Randy is coming to be with you while I go out with Uncle Page. He really enjoys staying with you because you plan fun things to do. You are a great host!"*

## PREVENTIVE TIPS

- Comment on your child's efforts the next morning. *"Brian, thank you for being so cooperative last night. I had a nice evening and I needed it. Let's go to a movie together tonight."* Or *"Tonight I'll be home and you can have a friend over."* He will see how he helped you to raise your energy level.
- See Preventive Tips for ages 2½–5.

---

# BATH TIME

*"Catching my child to give him his bath is a hassle."*

## Ages 2½–5

### UNDERSTANDING THE SITUATION

Common, but very frustrating, is the battle to get your child into the tub. Your child may be frightened of the bath. He may have always liked it and all of a sudden is afraid of the drain swallowing him up, hot water, or stinging soap in his eyes. Some children hate baths because they are an interruption. Ironically, they are the ones that hit their preteen years, begin to shower, and never want to get out. Baths are not necessary every day; a casual two to three times a week may be enough during the temporary

period when your child is resisting them. Decide together on the
bath-time schedule, then let him know what to expect and consistently follow through.

## WHAT TO SAY AND DO

Be patient and take small steps. A fearful child may learn to
bathe with you in the tub at first, then alone. Climb in with her.
Hold her initially and gradually let her gain confidence to sit independently. Have a nonslip pad in the tub for safety. Make sure
the water temperature is comfortable, that your hands are not icy
cold, and that your touch is gentle and respectful.

Agree together on a bath-time schedule. Some families find
that bath time before dinner is calming and helps with the five
o'clock "arsenic hour." Others like bath time right before bed as
part of the bedtime routine. Some like morning baths when they
are not overtired.

If your child is overtired it is best not to push too hard. A
break with a story or a special toy is sometimes needed. Then try
again.

Avoid a battle getting your child into the tub by giving a
warning and offering incentive. *"Jeremy, bath time is in five minutes, after this cartoon. As soon as you have your bath you can come
back and watch 'Sesame Street.' "* Try also, *"When the timer rings it
will be bath time. After your bath, we can have story time."*

Be involved at bath time. Make time to stay with your child
when she's in the tub, for safety of course, but also *"just 'cause I
want to be with you."* Say, *"Amanda, let's sing 'Row, Row, Row Your
Boat.' "* or *"I'd be happy to tell you the new Troll adventure that just
happened"* or *"I have a story to tell you about the three bears in the
woods."*

Lighten up over removing dirt. Begin her bath with games
and songs. Sing "The Itsy Bitsy Spider" or "I'm a Little Teapot."
Supervise play with kitchen spoons, plastic bowls, funnels, and
utensils. As you have fun, begin introducing to her the idea of
washing herself.

Take *time for teaching* and then *encourage*! Teach her to put the
shampoo in her own hair and wash all her body parts. *"Mary, you*

*are growing so big. You are learning to wash all by yourself! I'll read you a story while you wash."*

PREVENTIVE TIPS

- Be very consistent. With your follow-through, the bath can be as routine as eating a meal.
- Try alternating bathing with an occasional shower with you or your spouse. Give her the *choice*. This is a good way to get your child used to water on her face and head. She may prefer the shower to the tub.
- Do not leave bathing to a baby-sitter if your child has been difficult. It may be a situation for you to handle until she outgrows the battle.

## Ages 6–10

UNDERSTANDING THE SITUATION

When your older child refuses a bath or shower, he's probably unwilling to interrupt his activity or to be told what to do. *"I want to be my own boss."* If you coax continually, he's likely to become "parent deaf" and ignore your requests. Together you can turn this into a full-blown power struggle. You will be smart to win his cooperation, set agreements together, and follow through with consistency and kind firmness. One of the best remedies for the temporary I-don't-wanna-take-a-bath syndrome is humor and try to appear unimpressed with his obstinacy.

WHAT TO SAY AND DO

Work on building a cooperative relationship. Plan together a weekly bathing chart. *"Hilary, let's mark the days on this calendar when you will bathe and wash your hair. Remember, on soccer days you will need a bath."* If the schedule is to be altered, she needs to make the change with you in advance. *"Maria, you agreed to take your shower before 'The Simpsons.' You did not make other arrange-*

*ments with me."* Missing "The Simpsons" then becomes her choice, not your punishment.

You cannot physically get a child this age into the tub. Use a respectful, logical consequence: *"Lauren, as soon as you have your bath you may watch TV or use the computer."*

Stay flexible. Your child will feel a sense of control when making a deal with you. *"Mark, I'd say no, but it is Friday night. Just this once. Promise to take your bath tomorrow morning, and if you do, I can be flexible more often."*

Don't nag him about not washing well. Take *time for teaching.* *"Eric, tell me what you consider to be a good washing. Right! You need to wash your hair at least once a week. And the soap and washrag?"*

Use a kitchen timer to signal when it's time to bathe or time to get out of the tub.

## PREVENTIVE TIPS

- *Problem solve* at a neutral time. *"Bryce, when I remind you to take your bath you seem annoyed and then get angry."* Pause, listen, and reflect his feelings. *"It seems you feel . . ."* State briefly how you feel. *"I don't like having to coax you. You are old enough to be responsible without my being involved."* Gather ideas together. *"Tell me your ideas to resolve this problem, and let's agree to try one this week."* Follow through during the week to evaluate how it went.
- Getting your child involved in sports is a great way to introduce the need for a bath. Children love being part of a team sport with good friends and positive coaching. Say, *"Elizabeth, you may continue playing soccer as long as you shower after practice and the game."*

*"My child refuses to get out of the tub."*

## UNDERSTANDING THE SITUATION

When it is time to get out of the tub, your youngster may balk. Do not get sucked into a battle. Remain calm, firm, kind, and consistent.

## WHAT TO SAY AND DO

Use a timer, and give your child notice when the time is almost up. Be clear with your *limits* with an agreement before he gets into the tub. *"Joey, you are a good bath-taker and love your bath. It's been hard for me to get you out of the tub. Tonight the timer is set. I'll give you a warning, and when the bell rings, I will drain the tub and you'll need to hop out. Agreed? Good!"*

When it is time to get out, give him *choices*. *"Randy, do you want to pull the plug yourself, or would you like me to? Would you like me to help dry you off, or do you want to do it yourself? Green towel or yellow?"*

Use *action with few words*. Let him watch the water drain out and then help him out kindly and firmly. Remain *poker faced* even if he is obstinate. Muster up the energy not to get emotionally involved. Be clear about consequences if he has dawdled: *"You have chosen to miss your story and go straight to bed."*

## PREVENTIVE TIPS

- Before she climbs into the tub, seek her agreement about how she will get out. Instead of directing her, use, *"Shelby, when it is time to get out of the tub, what will you do?"* When children agree to do something, they usually follow through.
- Before she needs to get out, tell her what she will do next. *"Katherine, as soon as you get out of the tub, I will tell you a story with the puppets."*
- Notice and comment the times she cooperates in the tub.

*"Holly, you are really growing up. You rinsed your own hair!"*
*"You handle the job of getting into the tub and washing really well."*

## BED MAKING

*"Getting my child to make his bed is a hassle."*

### UNDERSTANDING THE SITUATION

Most children do not see bed making as a necessity, and it is clearly not a priority to them. You may feel very strongly that your child should make her bed each day. You may have made her bed when she was younger for efficiency, and now when you expect her to be responsible she balks. If you find yourself feeling angry and nagging regularly, you may be caught in a win/lose situation. You'll need to lighten up about the bed, work on building a cooperative relationship, and turn this into a win/win situation. You may want to evaluate whether you over-value the importance of a made bed over a good relationship with your child. Remember to *encourage* and to use your sense of humor. Be sure your own bed is made just as you expect hers to be.

### Ages 2½–5

### WHAT TO SAY AND DO

Begin bed making when your child has his first bed. Age two and a half is not too early; a child is easily motivated at this age. Have fun, and make a game out of piling the stuffed animals on. *"Randy, put the animals in their places so they feel happy."* Keep your expectations reasonable for his age.

*Encourage*, make the bedding easy to handle (one comforter to pull up is enough), leave the lumps unnoticed, and comment on his effort.

Make bed making part of the morning routine. Post a training chart and take *time for teaching*. Do this routine together initially. Have him put stickers on his chart when tasks are completed.

### Eric's Wake-up Schedule

| Wake Up | Bathroom | Hug Mom and Dad | Make Bed | Dress |
|---------|----------|-----------------|----------|-------|

Create an incentive. *"Eric, as soon as you finish your chart you may pop the waffles into the toaster."*

## Ages 6–10

WHAT TO SAY AND DO

Put bed making on the agenda for a *family meeting*. With joint *problem solving*, agree on a plan for a routine. Establish consequences with your child ahead of time.

Take *time for teaching* what you expect; demonstrate how you want the bed made. Do it together several times. Make it easy by using sheets and a comforter and eliminating blankets.

Put bed making on your child's morning training chart as one item to check off before coming to breakfast.

When she doesn't make her bed, say only once, *"Mary, you agreed to make your bed before school, understanding you may miss the bus if you don't. If you miss the bus today I cannot drive you until 9:30. It is your choice."* If she slips away without making her bed, catch her before her next activity. *"Megan, make your bed. Then you may go to Girl Scouts."* Your follow-through is imperative.

PREVENTIVE TIPS

- Encourage her to be excited about her room and involve her in arranging and decorating it. *"Heidi, you are growing up so fast. Choose new sheets and a new comforter, and we can make some pillows if you'd like."*
- Notice her efforts and comment often on what she is doing well.
- Be flexible once in a while. *"This has been a busy week for us. Next week we will get back on schedule."*
- Take the time to listen to feelings and work on *problem solving.* Your child may have issues other than the bed. She will more likely cooperate after being listened to and when involved in the decision making.

# BEDROOM, CLEANING UP

*"My child refuses to keep his room clean."*

UNDERSTANDING THE SITUATION

When your child ignores your first request to pick up his room, you probably feel annoyed. You might say, *"Come on, Joey, cooperate"* or *"Your room looks like a pigsty!"* Ignored, you wind up angry, at your wits' end, and you scold or punish with unreasonable threats: *"Joey, you'll stay home forever until you clean your room"* or, *"Jessica, that's it! I'm not buying you any more clothes or toys."* You have in essence just punished yourself. You have threatened with a grounding you will not enforce. This is the training ground for manipulation. Your child may think, *"She knows I have a birthday party tomorrow"* or *"How can I get Mom to feel sorry for me and buy me a new toy?"* Your child has gone from trying to get your attention to waging a full-blown power struggle in a short time. You have escalated from annoyance to anger.

Anger only creates more anger; it does not win cooperation. Bedroom cleanup is an ongoing process you will deal with all the years he is in your home, so be patient, hang on to your hat, and know that these years pass quickly. Before you know it, you will be sitting in your son's empty room wishing you had a couple of wet bathroom towels on the floor to complain about.

## Ages 2½–5

### WHAT TO SAY AND DO

Structure a daily routine, especially if the toy room is the bedroom. Choose a time of day that consistently will be room-cleaning time, preferably when your child is not tired and you have time. If you are home at 4:00 P.M., try it then. This is usually a high-energy hour. Young children do better when the mess does not get out of hand. A week's worth is overwhelming.

Take *time for teaching* hands-on with your younger child. Walk through a room cleaning together. Play games, such as *"Johnny, you pick up the red Legos, and I'll pick up the blue"* or *"See if you can toss the dirty clothes into the laundry basket."* He may try to coerce you into doing the whole job. Do not do it all for him but encourage a good time while doing some to show him what you expect.

Your young child will do better when you stay reasonably near his work area. When he has learned how to pick up and understands what you expect him to do, you should be able to go to another room nearby.

Motivate with consequences: *"Lucy, when you have picked up your room you may watch cartoons."*

## Ages 6–10

### WHAT TO SAY AND DO

Establish expectations at a *family meeting*. Decide what is meant in your family by "clean room." *"Meredith, when your room gets too messy it is too hard for you or me to clean up. We both get very frustrated. Let's agree on what 'clean' means."* Make a list together of what is expected. Have a chart listing what needs to be done to have a clean room.

1. Allow no food or drinks in room.
2. Put dirty clothes in laundry room.
3. Hang towels in bathroom.
4. Put clothes in closet or drawers.
5. Keep toys in proper places.

Do not nag all week. Appoint a specific day of the week for all housecleaning. Let your child know what to expect ahead of time. *"Jamie, we decided to do all housecleaning on Saturdays before baseball."* Between cleaning agreements, don't nag.

### PREVENTIVE TIPS

- Have a structure that meets your child's current needs. Go through her room with her at each new stage of development. She will be happy to know that you feel she is growing up. She'll grow from cubbies for toys to shelves and a desk for schoolwork. Arrange her room with proper storage units that are easily accessible. Put storage baskets under her bed and in closets for her to store unused or seasonal clothes.
- Keep expectations reasonable. Perfectionism sets impossible goals, and seldom leads to improvement; more often it leads to giving up. Watch for what she does right and comment on her efforts.
- Your child should earn the right to more privacy as he gets older by treating his room with respect. Respect his privacy. A child over eight years old does not want a parent to wander into his room and pick things up, read his notes, etc. when he is away.
- Keep your own room clean. You need to model the behavior you expect from him.

# BEDTIME, GETTING TO BED

*"Bedtime is a major hassle!"*

## Ages 2½–5

### UNDERSTANDING THE SITUATION

Dawdling over getting ready for bed, asking for one more drink of water or one last hug, indicates loud and clear either that your child does not want you to leave him for the night or that he is not done with you for the day. You may tell him that he is tired and needs his sleep, when in reality *you* are the one needing time to yourself. As the hassle unfolds, each time he reappears or calls you, you grow irritated and begin nagging, then yelling, which leads to threatening and spanking. Bedtime often ends in his crying and your feeling terribly guilty. This is the wrong way to end the day! Bedtime is an important time for children and parents to listen and share feelings and experiences. As hard as it is, especially when you are tired at the end of a long day, you or another important caregiver needs to muster up the energy to show interest and caring right up to the last good-night kiss. Follow-through in putting an unhappy child back to bed is hard, but *follow through you must, with loving directions and consistency.* You will teach him important skills: to be responsible for his own bedtime routine and to get his own needed sleep. This is a long process. It takes years.

### WHAT TO SAY AND DO

Plan together with your child a bedtime routine. You will need to discuss:

1. What are routine responsibilities?
2. What is enjoyable and calming?

3. *Limit setting* together.
4. Understanding consequences and consistent follow-through.

*"Margie, bedtime will be more fun if we plan to do what you like best and do it each night. Let's list what needs to be done and what you want to do."* These are suggestions. Establish a time frame for the routine to begin and end.

### Bedtime responsibilities

1. Take bath.
2. Brush teeth together.
3. Have short drink of water and use toilet.
4. Lay out clothes for morning.

### Bedtime fun

1. Enjoy stories and songs: tell a story to a favorite stuffed toy about your child when she was little, read three favorite books, sing and recite favorite rhymes. Lie on the bed and cuddle. Share a secret.
2. Explore feelings. Ask, *"Cory, what one thing happened today that made you feel happy? Was there something that made you feel sad?"* A variation that takes more time is to have her draw her feelings with a pad and pencil. Share an experience of yours with her. *"Do you want to hear about mine?"*
3. Hug and give one last good-night kiss and recite a familiar poem like *"Nighty night, sleep tight, don't let the bedbugs bite. If they do, chew 'em in two, just like the monkeys do."* Or say good night to all the wonderful things and people you know. *"Good night moon, good night sun, good night Rufus . . ."* Or have your child name all those who love her. *"Nanny loves me, Daddy loves me, Woody loves me, Auntie Cheri too!"*

### Bedtime limits

1. Look at a book quietly or listen to a tape for five minutes.
2. Turn lights out, settle into sleep.

3. Understand that Mom and Dad are having their adult time. Make no further requests and have no social interaction. Lead back to bed poker faced, use action with few words, consistently.

Note: if he needs to use the toilet, work toward him doing it himself. If you need to help him, use *a poker face* and *action with few words*.

## Understanding consequences

Start bedtime routine earlier the following night. (Perhaps missing a favorite TV show.)

Take the time to stop what you are doing and begin the bedtime ritual. Your task is to give her your time for fifteen to thirty minutes, then her task is to be in bed. Be firm if she hassles you about staying longer. *"Good night."* Exit without hesitation, use *action and few words*.

Let your child know what to expect with one reminder. *"Marti, ten more minutes to bedtime"* or, *"Jenny, please remember bedtime after this TV program."*

Giving *choices* will help her feel in control of going to bed. *"Amy, it is bedtime. Do you want your red pajamas or your yellow ones?" "Do you want me to read a story or make one up?"* Try setting a timer for fifteen minutes when you start story time and when the bell goes off, exit. Use *action and few words*.

### PREVENTIVE TIPS

- Use *family meetings* to review the routine, to renew or make changes.
- Be consistent with the bedtime ritual before allowing flexibility or changing the schedule. A late night here and there because of company, etc. can be very disruptive to establishing a regular schedule with cooperation.
- Anticipate bedtime demands. Take care of drinks, toilet, hugs, and kisses before bed.
- Make time for telling or reading stories together at bedtime.

Your child's listening level is higher than her reading level. When you are enthusiastic about the stories you read at bedtime you will motivate her to hop into bed and want to read as she grows older. *For Reading Out Loud!* by Margaret Kimmel (New York: Delacorte, 1988; Dell paperback), *The New Read-Aloud Handbook* by Jim Trelease (New York: Viking, 1989), and *Hey! Listen to This: Stories to Read Aloud* edited by Jim Trelease (New York: Viking, 1992) provide stories and are wonderful guides to teach parents about reading aloud to children. Read together *A Bedtime for Frances* by Russell Hoban (New York: HarperCollins, 1960) and *Mrs. Piggle Wiggle* by Betty MacDonald (New York: HarperCollins, 1985).

• Notice and comment often on her efforts to follow routine and hop into bed.

## Ages 6-10

### UNDERSTANDING THE SITUATION

Your school-age child needs to be gradually taking more responsibility for himself. Bedtime is an opportunity for teaching him to organize his personal time, schoolwork, bathing, plans for the morning, and getting to bed on time. Remember the concept of the expanding corral. As your child grows, so will his boundaries. You'll need to walk your four-year-old through using the toilet, bathing, laying out clothes for morning, and getting to bed on time. With gradual broadening of boundaries, your eight-year-old may do all of that himself. Stay involved with the bedtime ritual of reading or playing a game with him, listening to him tell you about his day, rubbing his back, etc. Be patient with him as he learns how to be organized and stay on a schedule. It takes time to learn this process, so your patience and consistent follow-through are musts. Your child will be ahead of the many college freshmen who have not mastered the skill of personal organization so integral to maturity and independence.

*See also: Bedtime, ages 2½–5*

## WHAT TO SAY AND DO

Use the *we* approach. Develop a training chart. *"Ben, bedtime has been a hassle. I nag, nag, nag and you take longer, longer, and longer! Let's develop a chart."* Make a plan for school nights on the chart.

|  | M | T | W | T | F | S | S |
|---|---|---|---|---|---|---|---|
| 1. Homework |  |  |  |  |  |  |  |
| 2. Bathroom |  |  |  |  |  |  |  |
| 3. Laying out morning clothes |  |  |  |  |  |  |  |
| 4. Reading a story, talking |  |  |  |  |  |  |  |
| 5. Good night |  |  |  |  |  |  |  |

Let him know what to expect if he doesn't follow through. *"As soon as you are in bed, either Papa or I will come up to read stories. If you are fast we will have time for a story and time to talk. If you are not in bed by 9:00, we'll have to cut out the special time."*

Do not coax, nag, or remind. Ignore his excuses with a *poker face*. Rather than hassling him, use the timer when you feel he needs more direction sticking to the decided time. Use your energy to notice what he is doing well, and invite him to spend some fun or interesting time with you. Be creative and *encourage*. *"Alex, as soon as you've brushed your teeth I want to show you these photos of you as a baby."* Or *"We bought a new indoor/outdoor thermometer today. Come help me understand the directions. I need your advice about where to hang it."*

Gradually give him more control. A responsible ten-year-old can handle the privilege of judging his own bedtime, reading and turning his own light off when he is ready to go to sleep. Follow this with the further responsibility of morning wake-up. Give him his own alarm clock. The natural consequence of being tired the next morning is more effective than a lecture by you. If he is late or tired, refrain from saying *"I told you so."* Instead, say, *"Ricky, you are looking pretty tired. What do you think you could do to avoid feeling so tired in the morning?"* Show faith in him to work through this, and be patient. This is lifelong training and will take time.

### PREVENTIVE TIPS

• Use the *family meeting* to establish agreements about the bed-time ritual. Your older child will do better when you involve him in making the agreements and setting the limits.

• Journal writing is a wonderful bedtime activity and a tool for building healthy self-esteem. Teach him journal writing by helping him think of important events and feelings about his day. He will want to do this alone in time. Honor his privacy and do not read his journal unless he offers to share it.

• Be available! In today's hurried, fast-paced life it is easy to overcommit and become frenzied and unavailable to children in the evening. Your child needs to end his day with your loving hugs and your listening to his feelings.

• Do not stop reading with your child just because he is older. Bedtime is one of the nicest times to read together. Picture books are fun, though more involved narrative books are on-going and provide suspense and something to jump in bed to hear. Refer to book suggestions, Bedtime, ages 2½–5.

*See also: Bedtime, ages 2½–5, Preventive tips; Bedtime, staying in bed; Sleeping with parent; Dark, fear of*

# BEDTIME, STAYING IN BED

*"My child will not stay in bed."*

### UNDERSTANDING THE SITUATION

Getting your child to bed is only half the battle. Next comes his test: *"How can I keep Dad involved with me a little longer?"* This may really anger you, especially if you are tired and have given a lot of energy to the bedtime ritual. Do not yell or lecture. It will only invite more of the same behavior. Your child knows how many times he can bug, bug, bug you before you'll really do what you say you'll do. Your job is to remain patient, calm, and consistent, telling him once what he needs to do and then following through with a *poker face* and *action with few words*. Remember that no matter how old your child is, there will be times when he has trouble settling down for the night, just as you sometimes do. That should be the exception, not the rule. Parenting is not easy. Twenty-four hours a day and seven days a week is quite demanding. Take some breaks, alternate responsibilities with significant others, and if you are a single parent, plan to have family or hired sitters help relieve you at bedtime occasionally.

## WHAT TO SAY AND DO

Check with your child at bedtime. *"Michael, what will you do after I hug and kiss you good night?"* Tell him what you will do if he gets up. *"You may get up to use the toilet and then go straight back to bed. This is my quiet time."*

Use a *poker face* and *action with few words*, and kindly lead him back to bed. It may take days to teach him, but keep the faith.

Allow your child to use the toilet if he needs to. If old enough he should do it on his own. You are working toward giving more freedom as he shows more responsibility.

## PREVENTIVE TIPS

- Be sure his bedtime is appropriate. You may need to wake him early from naps. When he's adjusting to giving up naps, bedtime may need to be flexible.
- Before he climbs into bed, make one last check to see if he has any last-minute needs.
- Comment often when he goes to bed well. *"Jason, bedtime was a breeze last night. Thank you for your effort. I sure feel good today. How do you feel?"*
- Be very consistent.

*See also: Bedtime, getting to bed; Sleeping with parent; Dark, fear of; Night wandering*

# BED-WETTING

*"My child wets the bed at night."*

### UNDERSTANDING THE SITUATION

You may be quite concerned if your child still wets the bed at night, especially if you compare him to other children his age who are dry. Bed-wetting does not stop magically at age four or six, and some counts indicate 25 percent of seven to ten-year-olds still wet at night. It is common, yet embarrassing and not often openly discussed. It happens with both boys and girls, and gender does not alter the recommended approach. *Discuss this concern with your family pediatrician at your child's annual physical.* He will reassure you and your child that bed-wetting is common.

Physicians feel the most common reason for bed-wetting is lack of maturation. The doctor may check for organic problems, allergies, and stress in the family and may want to discuss family history. (Incidence is higher when one and especially when both parents were bedwetters.) He will likely set up a program to help you and your child, based on your individual needs. Whether your doctor recommends a special diet, decides to use a device that delivers an electrical signal when wetting occurs, or, more commonly, determines to give your child time to grow out of it, studies show that the most successful program includes conscientious parents who share their unconditional love and *encourage* their child to take responsibility for his actions. After age five a child likely feels upset with his lack of "self-control," embarrassed, sometimes afraid of going to sleep, and fearful of sleepovers, camp experiences, etc. He needs your *encouragement!* Do not listen to negative advice or comments from friends or family. Muster up the energy to be patient and keep your faith in your child. Some take years, but they do stop. Your message should be, *"I know you will stay dry when your body is ready. I know you want to, and you will! I have faith and confidence in you!"*

## WHAT TO SAY AND DO

Arrange for your child to have a physical with your family physician to explore the problem and offer good counsel or make a referral. Your child needs to hear that he is healthy and normal. You do not have to tell your child your concern is bed-wetting, just that he is going to have a physical. Let the nurse know to tell the doctor why you are there.

Design a program with your child to show your support and invite her responsibility. Help her feel she has some control. Use *problem solving.*

1. Identify her feeling. *"Kelly, when you wet the bed you feel upset."*
2. Show understanding. *"Wow, I think I'd feel the same way. It is frustrating, I'm sure."*
3. Briefly, share your feelings. *"I love you and I want to do what is best for you. I am never mad at you for wetting your bed. Sometimes I am tired of doing laundry and I seem grumpy. You will be dry when your body is ready."*
4. Discuss solutions *"You are a very capable person. I will help see that you have what you need. I will be happy to help you when I feel you need it."*
5. Follow through. *"Kelly, we will talk at the end of the week about how it's going."*

Before going to bed, some parents wake young children up and put them on the toilet. The idea is to help the child's body wake up to the need to void. A seven or eight-year-old may learn to wake up with an alarm and be responsible to go by himself. Some children sleep through the alarm and need parental help. When escorting your child, do not socialize. Be kind and use *action with few words.* Then quickly back to bed.

After problem solving, do not nag or remind. Take *time to teach* your child to be in charge of the situation. This is a team effort. Show your support by using *we.*

a. Help your four or five-year-old strip the bed and put on fresh sheets, but give him the responsibility of dumping the wet sheets and clothes into the washer. *"We're a team, Tyler. We both strip and make the bed, you dump the wet sheets and clothes, and I'll wash."*

b. Your older child can assume more responsibility. *"James, I know you want to stop wetting the bed. I know you will. I'll work with you; we're a team. From now on, if your bed is wet in the morning you take the sheets off and put them in the washer. I'll wash them. The dry ones are in the closet. I'll help you put those on until we feel you can do it yourself."* If his bed is wet, appear unimpressed. Be consistent with having him take on this responsibility. Do not do this for him. It is easier to do it yourself, but a true *encourager* takes the time. Do not pity him or do for him what he can do for himself.

If your child does not cooperate, do *problem solving*. Set consequences together. *"Heidi, if the wet sheets and clothes are not taken care of at the agreed-upon time, you will miss after-school play to take care of it."* Or *"I only wash what is in the laundry. It's not fun to sleep in wet sheets or wear wet clothes."*

Be supportive about how she feels. When she wets her bed, empathize. *"Megan, you seem upset that your bed is wet."* Pause and listen and reflect back what she says or feels. *"You are frustrated."* (You may be surprised to learn she has a reason for the wet bed. Perhaps she is afraid to get up in the dark.) Reassure her. *"You are not alone. Many other kids wet the bed."* When she is dry through the night, do not cheer with bells and whistles. She may get the idea that you are pleased with her only when she stays dry. Instead, say calmly, *"Megan, you were dry all night. How do you feel?"* (Pause. Reflect her feeling rather than judge.) *"You feel happy and you know you can do it. You will be dry again. I feel happy for you too."*

## PREVENTIVE TIPS

- Make his bedding as waterproof as possible to reduce the strain on you. Flannel-covered rubber mattress covers are helpful, and they don't cause your child to perspire.

- Have him put a sleeping pad and dry pajamas near his bed so that if he is wet in the night he can get comfortable without disturbing you.
- Take time to listen to feelings. At bedtime ask, *"What was the best part of your day? What was the hardest?"*
- Read children's books together regularly. The following suggestions are picture books with mature messages to help all ages understand emotions: *Dry All Night* by Alison Mack (New York: Little Brown, 1989), *Feelings* by Aliki Brandenberg (New York: Mulberry Books, 1986), *Double Dip Feelings* by Barbara S. Cain, M.S.W. (New York: Magination Press, 1990).
- Spend one-on-one time with your child often, and let her know when you will spend *special time* with her during the week.

*See also: Toilet training*

# BELCHING

*"My child belches loudly to irritate me."*

## UNDERSTANDING THE SITUATION

It is truly irritating and embarrassing when your child deliberately belches to annoy you or show off in front of friends. Coaxing him to stop, or becoming obsessed with designing a consequence to make him stop, will likely make him belch more. Belching is a great attention getter. Act, do not react; with no social gratification, this typical behavior will disappear. Give attention for positive, more mature behavior. And remember, the behavior you model will be the behavior you get!

## WHAT TO SAY AND DO

It is always best to try to remove yourself from attention-getting acts, if possible. Exit to the bathroom, close the door, and read a book or magazine. If with a friend, suggest you both move to another room. If you are eating at the table, pick up your place setting and meal and move with a *poker face* to another room.

Agree ahead of time about what you will do. Then, *"Scott, that is annoying behavior at the table."* Calmly, *"Please take* time out *to think about it. Come back when you are ready to act nice at the table."* Or *"The deck or the bathroom is the place to belch. You choose."*

Logical consequences are best designated ahead of time. If one comes easily to you and it fits, use it. *"Auntie Babs called and wanted to take you horseback riding next Saturday. If you agree to go the rest of the week without belching, you may go."*

If you are in public, calmly remove yourself and your child. Go outside or to the car. *"Mike, you have a choice. Either be polite and we will go back to the fun, or we will go home."* If he chooses to not cooperate, go home. This may ruin the day for you, but he'll believe you next time.

Use humor to defuse the behavior. Say, *"Randy, even the dog has better manners than that. Please, no more."* Be sure that you feel the humor and can say this without sarcasm or anger.

## PREVENTIVE TIPS

- Work on *encouragement* and building a positive relationship with your child at neutral times when he is not misbehaving.
- Ask for his cooperation at good times with *problem solving*.
- Identify his feelings. *"Scott, you seem to really enjoy belching."*
- Show understanding. *"I remember learning to burp real loud on cue. I was so excited, I felt so proud because I could be like my brother Eric. Boy, did we make Grandpa mad."*
- Tell him briefly how you feel. *"I'm annoyed at your belching for attention, just like Gramps was with me."*
- Ask for ideas. *"What do you think you could do to help me with this problem?"* A suggestion from you is appropriate if he has

nothing to offer. *"I'm going to ask that you not go to friends' homes while this continues in our home. The behavior is too rude."*

- Follow through. In two or three days, evaluate his progress together. *"Scott, I haven't heard any belching in the last three days. How do you feel?"* (pause) *"It sounds as though you feel . . . I appreciate your efforts! Jimmy wants you to come over Friday night. What do you think?"*
- Catch him being good and tell him that you appreciate his efforts.

# BIRTHDAYS

*"My child doesn't enjoy his own birthday party."*

## UNDERSTANDING THE SITUATION

Birthday parties are very important to children today. Most children count on one every year, when twenty years ago many families gave one party a year, alternating among siblings. Today younger and older children anticipate six months ahead, planning the friends, presents, food, entertainment, games, and prizes they will have at their annual event. At any age, expectations may build to the point that your child dissolves into tears the day of her party. Small situations may set her off: She loses it when the guests arrive with gifts and she's not able to open them NOW; she sees another child playing with one of her favorite toys; or the day is not going quite as she pictured it would. As you stand feeling helpless, weary, and a little embarrassed for her, your child is feeling overwhelmed or frustrated. Proper planning can help prevent this kind of trauma. Consider your child's temperament and the kind of event that is best suited to her (and to you as well). Keep the party manageable both in terms of the number of guests and in scope. Prepare her to know what to expect, and be sure your planning doesn't reflect a desire to relive your own birthday dreams. She will have many years to grow into bigger events that both you and she may be ready to handle better.

## WHAT TO SAY AND DO

Discuss possible trouble spots before the party.

1. Presents: *"Erin, you will be opening many presents. Last year you were upset when the other children played with them."* Role-play what might happen. Involve her in solving the problem. *"What do you think we should do this year to help prevent your being upset?"* You could have other toys available, or put the new gifts away after opening them. Emphasize giving as well as receiving. *"Morgan, let's choose a party favor for each guest to open after you open your presents. Giving is as fun as receiving."*

2. Manners: Do not nag her about manners during the party. Before the party ask questions to make her think. *"What do people like to hear when their present is opened? What do you say when you already have what they gave you? What do you say if you do not like what they gave you or you feel disappointed? What happens when you rip through the presents real fast?"* If she forgets her manners during the party, do not embarrass her. Say, *"Jennie?"* and give her a knowing glance.

Involve her. The day of the party she can help set the table and decide where she wants the balloons. *"Megan, you are a great party giver! Your friends will have a good time. Let's set your table, and then we'll blow up the balloons and you can decide where to hang them."*

Have your young child (ages 2½–5) open each guest's gift as the guest arrives. The guest will be delighted at having all the attention focused just on her gift, your child will be eager, and the rest of the children will not have to sit through a long gift-opening process.

Let all the children know the plan at the beginning of the party. Children do better when they know what to expect. *"We are glad you are here. First we will open gifts. Then we'll eat cake and ice cream and play some games."*

Help your child through a bad situation. A child can lose control at her own party at any age. Don't get angry, threaten to send everyone home, or lose your temper. You may feel embarrassed, but do not worry about what others think. Have another adult take charge of the party and calmly take your child into another room away from everyone. Wait with her while she calms down. Help her understand her feelings. *"You are upset that the children are playing with your toys. We will wait here until you are ready to go back to your friends."*

**PREVENTIVE TIPS**

- Keep the planning low key. Keep the group small (one friend for every year your child is old is suggested). Talking about her party weeks in advance can set her up for overanticipation and unrealistic expectations.
- Before guests arrive ask her to choose any favorite toys that she doesn't want anyone playing with. Put them away out of reach. Say, *"You understand that everything left out on the shelf in the toy room is for your birthday guests to play with."*
- An alternative to hiring entertainment: Plan to have adult help, and involve the children in an activity (paint or bead a shirt or hat, etc.) or assemble a food (pizza, ice cream sundaes, etc.).
- Read together *A Birthday for Frances* by Russell Hoban (New York: HarperCollins, 1968).

# BITING

*"My child bites other children or adults."*

## UNDERSTANDING THE SITUATION

If a social situation is too difficult for a child, she may resort to biting to express herself. Biting is often an expression of frustration: She cannot make herself understood, so she bites. It may be for attention or control. She may subconsciously feel *"I belong when I bite. Look at everyone scurry. I actually made her cry."* Biting is common, but it is not socially or medically acceptable. You may be embarrassed or be so angry that you want to strike her or even bite her back. This is a very difficult parenting issue. No one wants a biter; we all want our children to be liked. Your job is to act immediately, kindly, and with a firm *poker face*. It may take several incidents to allow this behavior, but it can be done! Do not let other people's negative opinions dictate what you do. She will stop the biting, so do not give up faith in her. Remember your unconditional love: *"I love you very much, though I do sometimes get frustrated with what you do."*

## WHAT TO SAY AND DO:

Never bite your child back. It is never okay for anybody to bite.

Have plenty of adult supervision to prevent biting before it happens. Help you child express herself before she bites: *"Tracey, you want the truck. Let's find a toy to trade with Trevor."*

Use *time out.* Cup your hand over her mouth and say, *"Tracey, no biting!"* Direct her to *time out.*

Give her a warning: *"Tracey, we are going over to play at Trevor's. If you bite anyone, we will have to come home."* If she bites, cover her mouth with your hand and say, *"I'm sorry that Tracey bit you,*

*Trevor."* Immediately leave with a *poker face* and go directly home. *"Tracey, I see that you have chosen to go home."*

If biting is a persistent problem, give the child a biting pillow, a small pillow to be used just for biting. When biting occurs, give her *time out* and say, *"Tracey, we do not bite people. If you are angry, here is a pillow to bite."*

Do not give undue attention to the victim. If another adult is available have that person attend to the bite. Comfort the bitten child with a hug and quickly and calmly wash the area. If the skin is broken, use a topical antibiotic cream, and tell the parent exactly what happened.

**PREVENTIVE TIPS:**

- Simplify the play situation. Your child may do better with fewer children, or there may be children with whom she plays particularly well.
- Keep play sessions short and successful. Leave before she gets frustrated and bites. Comment on how well she has done.
- Take *time for teaching* with an authority. On your next visit to the pediatrician, have the doctor talk with you and your child about biting.

---

# BOSSINESS

*"My child bosses other children and adults."*

## Ages 2½–5

### UNDERSTANDING THE SITUATION

When your two-year-old places his hands on his hips, stamps his foot, and throws orders like a little tyrant, the family may chuckle and encourage his humorous bossy behavior. Unfortunately, when he is older, others may find his bossy ways irritating and come down on him or avoid him. He may consciously or unconsciously feel, *"At least I get attention when I irritate,"* and his behavior may escalate. He may become a bully, believing, *"If I get meaner, it will make them notice me."*

A child is often bossy in early childhood. It may be part of his makeup, his strong-willed temperament. It grows irritating. Handle his bossiness as you would any attention-getting behavior. Ignore it when possible, and catch him sharing and getting along with others. *Encourage* him to use good communication and emotional control. When managed properly, a bossy character will develop into an assertive and strong leader. Have faith. He can and he will learn to be thoughtful. It may take some time, but he will.

## WHAT TO SAY AND DO

When your child becomes bossy with you or other adults, do not laugh, mock, or encourage the behavior. Do not embarrass him with scolding or lecturing. Stay calm and say, *"Justin, that is your bossy voice. Tell me what you need with your pleasant voice."* It is best not to give in to what he wants until he is pleasant.

Spend time with him socializing. Join a small play group of three or four children with other parents. Think of this as taking *time to teach.* Encourage positive leadership. *"Brett, show Brian your big toy and your slide. Ask him what he would like to play."* Comment on his successes. When he shares and plays well, celebrate!

If he bosses and disrupts others, do not embarrass him. Remind him with a whisper, *"Brian, you are bossing."* If he continues to disrupt, take him to *time out.* Do not overreact; address it calmly. *"Brian, we can go back when you talk nicely to the other children."* Check his understanding. *"When you want Susie to play with you, what is a good way to ask her?"*

## PREVENTIVE TIPS

• Do not use or accept negative labels. Think of positive adjectives such as *assertive, dramatic,* or *persistent.* When you begin thinking of your child in positive ways, and catch him as much as possible when he is good, he will begin feeling positive about himself and acting it.

- Use good communication skills with him. Listen to him. Reflect his feelings, and rather than direct him, use questions: *"How will you get the toy you want? What do I need before we go to the park?"*
- Begin *family meetings* and give him a job so that he feels important and a contributor at the meeting.
- Increase responsibilities to encourage independence and add new chores to show him how capable he is.
- Find positive ways for him to be in control. Family pets offer loving experiences. Learning to be assertive through feeding and training a dog with Mom or Dad is a good *special time* activity. *"Andy, you are a good dog trainer. Dogs like you to give directions. People don't always like that."*
- Play noncompetitive games at home with the family. Emphasize the fun of playing, not the winning.

## Ages 6-10

### UNDERSTANDING THE SITUATION

Bossy school-aged children will often run through a string of friends and find no one wants to play more than once. Your child may boss others with the misunderstanding that it is the way to feel needed and capable. She may have a serious temperament and show intolerance for others less serious. Only children and older siblings often don't learn until school starts that others don't want to be bossed. If you have been a very directive parent, your child will direct others. This is different from bullying, though if not discouraged it could become bullying. When you hear her boss a friend you may cringe and feel embarrassed or annoyed by her actions. Do not overreact. It is best left alone and addressed later. Do not feel sorry for her when friends turn her down. Empathize and check what she thinks may be happening. *Encourage* and take *time for teaching*: Socializing, teaming, and leading all require her positive assertion and will help her internalize *"I feel good about myself when I work with others."*

## WHAT TO SAY AND DO

When you observe her bossing friends, do not embarrass her with your comments. Later, at a happy time, tell her your observations. *"Sarah, today I heard you telling Jenny what to do on the playground. It sounded so bossy. How might you have done that differently?"* Be ready to discuss feelings. She may be ready to talk about why she was so bossy; anger or frustration could be the reason. This will lead to *problem solving*.

If she bosses at home, identify what she is doing. Take *time for teaching*. Sincerely and kindly say, *"Julie, that is a very bossy way to treat Joey. It sounds like you want to be his boss."* Identify feelings. *"How would you feel if he talked to you that way? How could you say that more nicely?"*

Name a stuffed animal to be bossed when she feels she needs to boss. Say, *"Hilary, Jamie doesn't want to listen to that. Go boss Bozo."*

## PREVENTIVE TIPS

• Talk with her at a happy time. Eventually you will win her trust and she will begin to share her feelings. Do not lecture her on how to make friends.
• Read together children's books on friendship. *I Want to Play* by Elizabeth Crarey (Seattle: Parenting Press, 1982) is a good problem-solving book. Other suggestions: *Chrysanthemum* by Kevin Hanks (New York: Greenwillow/Morrow, 1991), *Bailey the Big Bully* by Lizi Boyd (New York: Puffin Books, 1991), and *Lofcadio, the Lion Who Shot Back* by Shel Silverstein (New York: HarperCollins, 1963).
• Observe your child's interactions at home. An older sibling may be bossing him, or he may be bossing a younger brother or sister. Use a *family meeting* to discuss how we treat others and want to be treated ourselves.
• Team sports such as soccer or basketball provide wonderful op-

portunities to build skill and confidence. Seek out a coach who works well with children, one who stresses the fun and skills of teaming rather than the winning and competition.
• Seek out Brownies, Cub Scouts, or like groups with good, experienced leadership.

*See also: Bullying; Sharing*

# BRAGGING

*"My child brags to other children or adults."*

### UNDERSTANDING THE SITUATION

We all know adults too tiresome to listen to as they spout off exaggerated, self-centered experiences. Bragging is a symptom of needing attention in order to feel important and to belong. Your most important job is to help your child learn self-love and to be proud of himself. Loving oneself is critical to loving others. That is very different from bragging about being the best or the first in order to feel good about oneself. When your younger child brags, it is cute and you most likely feel good about it. When your school-age child brags, you may feel embarrassed and annoyed. Both age groups need the same approach. Refrain from laughing at the four-year-old and scolding the eight-year-old. Do not worry about what others think. With your modeling and patient guidance and your faith in him, your child will learn to stop bragging and still have his ego intact.

### WHAT TO SAY AND DO

When your child boasts about himself, celebrate! Be specific about what he did and identify his feelings. *"Wow! Ryan, you are a good kicker. How does it feel to kick that far?"* When he puts someone else down (*"I kicked way better than the other guys"*), do not overreact, do not put him down, but do respond. Say calmly, *"Ryan, the other boys put in a lot of effort. Someday they may kick that far."*

Teach your child to feel proud of her accomplishments and to tell you about them. When asked if she can ride a bike, she should answer honestly: "I can ride a bike well. On Saturday I rode all the way around Mercer Island." This is different from *"I can ride better than anyone else."*

Older siblings will put younger ones down. *"Mikey can't read as good as me."* Give an affirmation to both children. "Susan, you are a very good reader. And Mikey, you will read very well too when you are as old as Susan."

Do not overreact to your older child's exaggerated bragging. Do not embarrass him in front of others by correcting him. If you cannot remain *poker faced*, leave the room or give him a knowing glance, and *problem solve* later. *"Johnny, you are proud of your water-skiing and I love to hear you talk about it with your friends. But I'm not sure they like to hear bragging, like 'I'm the best skier my age.' How do you think they might feel when you say that? What could you say differently? Why don't you make a good, honest statement and then express interest in your friend? 'I worked hard to learn to ski and I really feel good because now I can ski on one ski. Have you ever skied before?' "*

Older children can understand the difference between put-downs and put-ups. Many elementary school teachers are presenting this concept in the classroom. *"Greg, I like it when you share your accomplishments, like telling others that you are a good swimmer. That is the truth and a good self put-up! When you say that you beat the pants off them, you put down the others to make yourself feel bigger. How do you think that makes the others feel?"*

## PREVENTIVE TIPS

• Play down the competition, which sets children up to believe that if you succeed, I fail.

- Teach and model positive talk. Say, *"Ryan, when you make a mistake, say, 'That's not like me.' When you spill the milk, say, 'Well, I did get most of the milk in the glass.' "*
- Model and teach affirmations. At bedtime say, *"Brian, we had a great bike ride today. Repeat after me, I am strong and well coordinated. I am a good biker! I like myself! Now you make up one for me!"*
- Read aloud *Loudmouth George and the Fishing Trip* by Nancy Carlson (New York: Puffin, 1985). A fun book to read aloud together about all kinds of values is *You Can't Sell Your Brother at the Garage Sale* by Beth Brainard (New York: Dell, 1992).

# BRUSHING HAIR

*"My child won't let me brush her hair, and she won't brush it either."*

### UNDERSTANDING THE SITUATION

Though no one likes starting the day with anger and tears, hairbrushing is a common hassle in the morning before work and school. It's a win/lose issue, and fighting about it is not worth it. Lighten up. Your child wants to feel in charge of herself: *"I want to be my own boss."* Work on building a cooperative relationship; offer your help but do not demand. When she is young get her a good haircut that requires little care. Though it is difficult, try to let go of what you believe others will think and ask yourself, *"Is my self-worth wrapped up in how my child looks?"* You are the loving parent, she is the child, and most likely, when you give up your end of the rope in the tug-of-war over hairbrushing, she will begin coming to you for help.

**WHAT TO SAY AND DO**

Do not nag. Suggest *limits* that make sense. Keep it light and humorous. *"Emily, I just ask that you keep your bangs out of your eyes so that we can see in and you can see out. Wash and brush your hair to keep it healthy, with no bugs or tangles."*

Long hair is often the issue. If she wants long hair and you want her to take care of it your way, the stage is set for a power struggle. Let go and give a *choice*. Sincerely and kindly say, *"Carolyn, you want long hair. Your hair tangles, and you tend to chew the ends when it is long. As long as you keep it brushed and pulled back from your beautiful face, you may keep it long. If you won't take care of it, we will have it cut."* Do not nag. If the problem continues, follow through and cut the hair.

If you are in a power struggle over hair, do not fight. Say with sincerity how you feel. *"I would like you to brush your hair before school so that you feel clean and good about yourself. Your friends and teacher will like it too."* Or *"I enjoy helping you with your hair because I like spending time with you in the morning. I don't like fighting before school."*

Put her in charge with her own equipment. *"Michelle, you are growing up! You can be in charge of your hair. Here is some hair conditioner just for kids with tangles. Spray it on, then brush."*

Make hairbrushing part of the morning routine, after morning hugs. *"Jamie, as soon as your hair is brushed and you are dressed, breakfast will be ready."* Let go of your perfectionism, and comment on his efforts.

Avoid a power struggle with a school-aged child with a sincere question. Ask, *"You didn't brush your hair. Would you like to tell me why?"*

Your younger child may like to play the "You brush and I'll brush game." Say, *"Caitlin, you brush my hair, and I'll brush yours"* or *"You brush your hair first and I'll brush it next."*

**PREVENTIVE TIPS**

• Schedule an appointment with a haircut shop specializing in cuts for kids. Tell the beautician that you are having a battle over hairbrushing when you make the appointment. A fun, young operator can encourage your child to get the kind of cut she needs, show her some hair products she can use herself, and emphasize the importance of hair care.

- Allow your child the opportunity to make her own decisions about how she wants to keep her hair. Give her opportunities to make personal choices. (Some boys have their initials carved in their hair.)
- Let the natural consequence of frustrating, matted, and tangled hair or unfavorable comments from peers motivate your child.

## BRUSHING TEETH

*"My child won't brush his teeth."*

### UNDERSTANDING THE SITUATION

It is normal to feel angry and impatient when your child refuses to take care of her teeth. Brushing teeth must be nonnegotiable. It is one thing to lighten up about brushing hair and another to permit tooth decay. The needs of the situation are critical and demand an organized, scheduled routine. You are the parent. Be clear about your rules, and allow her *choices* within those *limits* so that she will feel, *"I can be my own boss and be in charge"* and learn to use good judgment about caring for her teeth. Oral hygiene habits are established at a very young age. Extreme stubbornness often occurs if something else is going on. Spend time listening and exploring what might be bugging her. Be very consistent in following through with the routine. Parenting does take time. Each time you let her run out the door and avoid her routine tooth brushing, you weaken your stand.

## WHAT TO SAY AND DO

Establish together a scheduled time for tooth brushing, morning and night. This can be included in the bedtime and morning routines. Do not schedule it for a time when your child will be exhausted.

Most dentists recommend helping young children with brushing. Make it a game and have fun. Sing while brushing, "This is the way we brush our teeth. . . ." (Some families, as part of the bedtime routine, gather on the parents' bed and have Dad or an older child read a story while everyone flosses their teeth.)

Your young child will love her own toothbrush set, perhaps with a Little Mermaid or Ninja Turtle theme. Her own personal satchel with floss, toothpaste, and toothbrush is an incentive. Say, *"Kelly, you have beautiful teeth! Here is your very own equipment to keep them healthy and clean."*

Some rules are negotiable and some are not, and brushing teeth is not negotiable, though how it is done may be. Say, *"Bryce, you need to brush your teeth; that is not a choice. Dad can help brush your teeth, or I will. You choose."* Or say, *"We have two kinds of toothpaste. Which would you like tonight?"*

You should not struggle to brush your child's teeth against his will. Let him know what you will do, not what you will make him do.

1. Your very young child may button his lip. *"Johnny, you brush yourself or I will brush for you."* Remain calm, use a *poker face*, and let go of it. Try again later. Your persistence with unemotional involvement will win in the end. At age two and a half, a spell of nonbrushing is not a life-or-death matter. Letting go may win a lifetime of cooperation.

2. Your four or five-year-old may cooperate if you say *"As soon as you brush, you may go play."*

3. Your older child may respond to *"You will miss your soccer practices until I can get you to the dentist for an appointment to talk about brushing. He'll fit you in during your soccer time."*

4. A ten-year-old will understand *"I pay for dentist visits and preventive care. You pay to have your cavities filled when you eat candy and don't brush."* Say what you mean to do, and do it.

## PREVENTIVE TIPS

- See that your children visit the dentist regularly. The hygienist can teach proper care of teeth to children as young as two years. Tell your dentist about your wonderful brushing routine. This is also a time to ask about tooth-brushing problems. A commitment to the dentist, with your added encouragement, will make your child feel responsible and proud to cooperate. Plan home tooth care together at the dentist's office.
- Read children's books together about good, healthful foods and dental care.
- Use a training chart. Have your child put a sticker on the chart when he completes tooth care for the day. He will be pleased at the end of two weeks to see the accomplishment.

*See also: Dentist; Bedtime, getting to bed; Morning hassles*

# BULLIED CHILD

*"My child is picked on by other children."*

## UNDERSTANDING THE SITUATION

Children's temperaments vary greatly. Some are much less aggressive than others and stand back and observe a situation to become more confident before joining in. Some are very sensitive and never join in large or active situations. Others jump into play impulsively and with vigor. Some are quite aggressive and may tend to bully the timid child, who often becomes the victim. If your child is often bullied, help her gain confidence and teach her to be more assertive. Never label her a wimp. If this is your first child, it is very hard not to feel sorry for her and pity or overprotect her. Rather than rescue her, encourage her to handle the situation and to have her needs met. She needs to learn she will be bullied only if she allows it. She plays an active role; there is never a bully without a victim. It will take small steps to gain confidence, and for some children this takes a long time, perhaps months. It is very painful to watch your child feel hurt. Hang in there; offer support but do not coddle.

## Ages 2½–5

### WHAT TO SAY AND DO

Limit play time to well-supervised, small groups and alert caregivers to encourage assertion and avoid overprotection. Be sure you and other caregivers take *time for training* in skills, especially social skills, that will instill confidence.

When two young children are in a hurtful situation, deal with both the bully and the bullied in the same boat. *"Johnny, hitting and grabbing are not okay. Tell Matt what you would like with words, or trade with him. Matthew, rather than crying, tell Johnny what you need from him."* This is teaching a process of negotiation. It takes time to learn.

When a child bullies yours, do not rush to the rescue. When he comes to you for comfort, sit with him until he is calm. Then:

1. *Problem solve.* Talk about what he needs and feels. *"Ryan, you had the truck and Jason took it from you. You wanted the truck. Jason scared you and you didn't know what to do."* Show empathy. *"I would be confused too. We don't grab toys at home."* Give affirmation. *"You can get what you need."*

2. Take *time to teach.* *"Ryan, you can walk away. You can trade a toy."* (Show him by trading with another child.) *"You can find something else to play with until he tires of the toy you want. You can*

*tell a big person you need some help."* (Role-play.) Eventually he will feel good about his decision to leave the bad situation or to stand up to the bully and claim what is rightfully his.

Give your child words she can use. *"Kate, you need to tell her how you feel. Say, 'It is not all right to hit me. I do not want to play with you when you hurt me. I do not like to be pushed.' "*

**PREVENTIVE TIPS**

- Arrange for some of your child's playmates to be her age or younger. Ask her teacher or caregiver which children may have similar interests and less aggressive temperaments. She needs to practice her assertiveness and gain confidence.
- Never label your child a baby or a sissy. Give positive affirmations. *"You are very sensitive and tenderhearted. You are loving and a good thinker. Noise and commotion bother you."*

## Ages 6–10

**WHAT TO SAY AND DO**

Listen to your child, help her identify her feelings, and explore with her what she can do instead of remaining a victim. *"Jana, you are very sensitive and loving. It hurts when someone is mean to you."* When she learns to assess her own feelings she will be better at asking for what she needs.

Be a good observer of your child's interactions, but do not rescue. Do not try to reason in the heat of the problem. Later, when you are alone with him, empower him. Help give him control by taking *time to teach* him what he can do or say to an older sibling or bully. Say, *"Mark is learning not to try to get his way by pushing you. You are strong and can leave the room when he bullies. You need to continue to let him know that what he's doing is not okay."* Teach strategy, a little clever negotiation. *"When your brother wants you off the Nintendo, tell him he can have your time now if he will give you his time on Monday and Tuesday."*

*Set limits.* This is a good time to review your family guidelines on how we treat others and want others to treat us:

1. We use words to tell others how we feel. We do not name call or use bad language.
2. We do not hurt others physically or emotionally.
3. We do not hurt each other's property or our own.
4. We work to get out of a problem, not stay in it.

Watch for bullying at home. Older brothers and sisters may be bullying, and this establishes a pattern. Do not scold the bully or pamper the victim. Stop the behavior and treat them together. *"Roger, you and Michael are hurting each other. Take time out to cool off."*

*See also: Bullied child, ages 2½–5*

### PREVENTIVE TIPS

• Regularly give your child meaningful jobs at home. Comment on how much she is contributing. Help her find something special to her to take to school to share with the class. Let the teacher know that she needs jobs to feel important—all children do.
• Have her care for a pet. Feeding and training build confidence.
• Read together children's books based on friendships, self-esteem, and bullying. Try *Bailey Goes Camping* by Kevin Henkes (New York: Greenwillow/Morrow, 1985; Puffin paperback), *Fat Fat Rose Marie* by Lisa Passen (New York: Henry Holt, 1991), *I Am Not a Crybaby* by Norma Simon (Morton Grove, Ill.: Whitman, 1989; Puffin paperback), or *Making Friends* by Fred Rogers (New York: Putnam, 1987).
• Sign your child up for a physical activity such as gymnastics.

*See also: Crying; Sadness*

# BULLYING

*"My child bullies other children."*

## Ages 2½–5

### UNDERSTANDING THE SITUATION

When your young child asserts her territory, claiming toys and defending herself from aggressors, you may feel proud and cheer her on. A two-year-old can be "cute" yanking away an object from your hand or giving you a shove with a giggle. However, if this behavior becomes her mistaken way of feeling that she belongs, children won't want to play with her anymore. Your task is to encourage her strong, assertive spirit and defuse the bullying aggression. An early age is the best time to make changes. Remain patient. It may take many months to modify bullying behavior, but it will be worth the effort!

### WHAT TO SAY AND DO

Do not label your child a bully. Keep your perceptions of her positive. If an acquaintance criticizes or comments on her bullying, play it down. *"She is dramatic and demonstrative, and she is learning to play nicely."*

When she grabs for toys, suggest negotiation. *"Heidi, Jeremy had the truck. If you want it, try trading the tractor."* If that doesn't work, say, *"You are a good thinker. Think about what else you could do."* Then, *"Find another toy; leave Jeremy and the truck alone."* Then, take *time out. "Heidi, time out until you can come back and play nicely."*

Teach her to use strategy. Say, *"Margie, if you go play on the horse and stop bugging Danny for the truck, maybe he'll put the truck down and go play with something else. Then you can have the truck. If not, please find another toy."*

Before play time, make a plan together, establishing *limits* and consequences. Offer suggestions about what your child can do when she feels like bullying. *"Renèe, you often get very excited when you want the toy that Erin has. You are a good sharer. Today try offering some of your toys that you have brought in your bag."* Let her know what to expect. *"I know you want to play with Erin. If playing becomes difficult I will remind you once. You decide if we need to go home and try again another day."* If you need to go home, use a *poker face*, say once what you agreed to do, and go. Use *action with few words*.

Point out feelings. Get your child's attention by gently holding her shoulders, and get down on her level. *"Jessie, that hurt Kevin. How would you feel if he ripped the toy away from your hands? Would you like it if he tried to hurt you?"*

## PREVENTIVE TIPS

- Discuss your child's behavior with her teachers or day care providers so that discipline is consistent.
- At a *family meeting* make rules about respecting others. *(See: Preventive Tips, ages 6 –10)*
- Provide opportunities for her to be in charge and in control. Give her limited choices, and provide jobs she can handle and be successful with. Your young child can be in charge of a pet, make a dinner salad, toast bread for sandwiches, or make pizza.
- Read children's stories about friendship together. *The Hating Book* by Charlotte Zolotow (New York: HarperCollins, 1969) and *Bailey the Big Bully* by Lizi Boyd (New York: Puffin Books, 1991) are fun books that stimulate discussion.
- Give lots of love and recognition for specific times she does not bully!

# Ages 6-10

## UNDERSTANDING THE SITUATION

If your school-age child develops the mistaken belief that he must bully or control others to belong, his friends may abandon him. This is one of the hardest situations a parent faces. We all want our children to be liked by others and be happy. You worry and feel sorry for him, you try fixing his poor social situation by tantalizing would-be friends with treats or invitations, and you may even blame other children for not being nice. These are all natural reactions. However, they are discouraging to your child and will not help him internalize *"I feel strong and belong when I contribute and work with others."* He can handle this issue, and with your Positive Parenting techniques he will learn to understand his own feelings as well as others' and do better socially. Over time, keep the faith, be consistent with the program, and do not give up.

## WHAT TO SAY AND DO

Do not label your child or let others label him a bully.

Do not pity him when friends leave him. Empathize and use a little fantasy for humor. *"Mark, I am sorry Sam didn't want to stay. I bet you wished he'd stay for five nights."* Involve him in exploring. *"Why do you think he wanted to go home? Could it be that he wasn't having much fun? What do you think he was feeling? How would you feel if Sam would not share with you?"*

Appear calm when he bullies. When he is home and bullies a sister or brother, intervene with *action with few words*. *"Mark, that is not a good action. Time out."* When he *cools down, problem solve.* Do not judge or criticize. Listen and explore. *"Mark, you are feeling irritated with your brother. You seem to want him out of your way. How do you think you can get the space you need from him? Let's come up with some ideas."* Encourage him to come up with ideas and choose one to try. Follow up with him in a couple of days to see how it is working.

Refrain from pitying or overprotecting the bullied sibling. Empower him. *"Mark is learning not to try to get his way by pushing you. You are strong and can leave the room when he bullies. You need to continue to let him know that what he's doing is not okay."*

When your child's bullying is offensive and becomes disrespectful, warn him once and then take him home, using *action with few words.* Do not fear his angry response. Say, *"Roger, I see by your actions you have decided to go home."*

After he cools off and you are calm, encourage him to think, explore feelings, and ask questions. *"David, you were fighting with Nick for the bat and ball this morning. He was hurt. How would you feel if someone older and bigger, like Roger, did that to you? What can you do instead of fighting? I don't want to control you. You are a good thinker. Please think about it and let me know."*

## PREVENTIVE TIPS

- *Family meeting*: Discuss how we treat others and want to be treated. Post family guidelines, *set limits*:

  — We use words to tell others how we feel. We do not name call or use bad language.
  — We do not hurt others physically or emotionally.
  — We do not hurt each other's property or our own.
  — We work to get out of a problem, not stay in it.

- Read together *I Want to Play* by Elizabeth Crarey (Seattle: Parenting Press, 1982), a book on how to make friends. *Hello Mrs. Piggle Wiggle* by Betty MacDonald (New York: HarperCollins Children's Books, 1985) has a bully remedy.
- *Encourage* and take time to train socialization, teaming, and leadership, which all require power in a positive way.
- Teach negotiation and strategy at home at neutral times. *"Lanny, you bullied Mark today for the ball. Let's brainstorm. How about trading? Tell him, 'I'll let you use my soccer ball at your practice if I can use yours now,' or 'Let me use it today and you can have it tomorrow and Saturday too.'"*
- Downgrade competition at home and do not compare children. Treat each child as a unique individual.

- Encourage team sports such as soccer or basketball. Seek a coach who will emphasize having fun, building skills, and teaming before winning.
- Encourage your child to join a club with good leadership such as Indian Princesses or Boy Scouts. Find opportunities that allow your child to work in a group and involve Mom or Dad as well.
- Join other families with children a bit older than yours for fun outings, picnics, hiking, camping, skiing, etc.

Note: If your child's teacher voices concern or you notice poor eating, interrupted sleeping, or continued friendship problems, talk with a school counselor or your child's pediatrician.

See also: Bossiness; Sharing

# CAR, MISBEHAVING

*"My child misbehaves in the car. It's dangerous!"*

## UNDERSTANDING THE SITUATION

Children often choose the small arena of a car to pick a fight, whine, scream, throw things, or bounce around. Your child has you trapped. What a good time for her to get your full attention! When your child misbehaves in the car there can be serious consequences. Many car accidents occur because of a child's scream or distracting misbehavior. For the safety of each person in your car and others on the road, together establish the "rules of the road" and follow through with consistency. Ultimately, your only recourse with misbehavior in the car is to pull off the road, to ensure safety for all. It may interfere with your schedule, be terribly inconvenient, and anger you, but it is necessary. As with any attention-getting or power-seeking circumstance, it is best to act, not overreact. You need to stop, but do not give your child the social gratification of ranting and raving. At neutral times, be sure to catch her being good and tell her what she is doing well. Begin implementing the "rules of the road" with your preschooler, and she will show more self-discipline and responsibility when she is older.

## WHAT TO SAY AND DO

Establish a program for the car, "rules of the road," and be very consistent.

1. Be prepared. Check before departing to make sure you have drinks, food, books, batteries, blankie, etc., and that nobody

needs to use the potty. (Needs will change according to circumstances.)
2. Check seat belts and car seats. Never start the car or drive without them!
3. Be safe. Use words, not screams. Work to stay out of a problem, not in it. Never drive with escalated fighting, yelling, screaming, or throwing.

Post the "rules of the road" in the car on your visor. Post a "seating chart" next to it for older children.

Sample:

| | Mon. | Tues | Wed. | Thurs. | Fri. | Sat. | Sun. |
|---|---|---|---|---|---|---|---|
| Front Seat | Roy | Sam | Les | Roy | Sam | Les | Roy |

Check the agreed-upon rules occasionally with your child before departing. Questions with *how* or *what* or *why* will help her think. *"Holly, what are the rules of the road? How can you help keep us safe? What did you do to be prepared? Why do we use car seats and seat belts?"*

Refer to the agreed-upon rules. When you see her being good, compliment the specific effort: *"Rachael, thank you for helping us be safe. You told me you dropped your bear; you didn't scream."* Or *"Mark, good preparing. You went potty before we left with no reminders!"* When a meltdown begins, *"Mindy, how can you help us be safe? Right, tell me with words what you need."* Or *"Ryan and Leslie, tell me rule #3. Please work to stay out of a big problem. When we stop for gas, tell me how you resolved it."*

Never drive with bad, distracting behavior in the car. Use *action with few words.* Pick a safe shoulder, pull off, and turn on your hazard lights. Remain calm, use a *poker face,* and appear unimpressed by the escalating behavior. If you cannot ignore the behavior inside, stand outside the car. Policemen have been known to stop and talk to children in such a situation (one mom arranged it). That is very effective. Even a two-and-a-half-year-old will be impressed.

When your child is testing, sometimes a consequence is obvious. Tell her what you will do. Do not say it in anger; remain calm. *"If we are not safe I will pull off the road. You will miss gymnastics if we have to wait. You choose." "Angie, we won't have time to go to play at Evan's if I have to stop the car. We will go home." "Mary, you took fifteen minutes of my time to settle down. When we get home you will have to give me fifteen minutes of your time helping me with the dishes."* Even a three-year-old will learn to understand a reasonable, related consequence and become more responsible for his actions. Be respectful with a *poker face* and *action with few words*. Do follow through.

### PREVENTIVE TIPS

- Notice your child being good and comment on specifics!
- Let your child know what to expect each time you get into the car.
- Keep expectations reasonable. Do not expect a tired, hungry, or cranky child to hold up.
- Have fun things to do in the car. Catch your child before she melts down with a favorite story or song. Children's tapes with stories and music; a "happy box" with crayons, paper, stencils, and surprises that you add occasionally; and snacks are all helpful.
- Have fun with your child and sing and talk together. Take advantage of these moments together to stimulate thinking and show that you really enjoy being with her!

*See also: Car seats; Car, seat belts*

# CAR, SEAT BELTS

*"My child refuses to put on her seat belt."*

## UNDERSTANDING THE SITUATION

If your child often puts up a fuss or resists putting on his seat belt in the car, he's likely asking for a strong reaction from you. You may grow frustrated and scold or threaten. Out of expediency, some parents give up and allow the child to go without. But it is essential that you insist he wear his belt, for safety and the law. Post the "rules of the road" in the car. *(See: Car, misbehaving)* Appear unimpressed with his resistance and be consistent with your rule. Do not argue or battle with him. Never start the car until you hear the click of his seat belt. Be sure to comment when he makes an effort to cooperate. Remember, *you* must wear your seat belt too!

## WHAT TO SAY AND DO

By checking his understanding of the car rules, you show faith and may win his commitment. Refer to the posted rules: *"'Morgan, what is rule #2? Right, thank you for buckling up."*

Use a chant with a five- or six-year-old. *"Sam, climb in, buckle up, I'll start the car and drive! Climb in, buckle up, I'll start the car and drive!"*

Lighten up with fantasy and humor. Sincerely, with a little smile, say, *"Rachael, you wish you didn't have to wear a seat belt. I bet you wish you could jump to any seat in the car whenever you wanted. I bet you wish you could drive the car too!"* This lighter approach often mellows the child. Then kindly, *"Please be safe. Buckle up."*

If possible, give a *choice.* *"You may choose the front or back seat. You must wear a seat belt."*

When a reasonable consequence comes easily to you, use it: *"Andy, if I'm late for the grocery shopping, you may miss gymnastics. Buckle up or be late."* Or *"You may wear your seat belt or stay home."*

### PREVENTIVE TIPS

- *Encourage* with enthusiasm and sincerity. *"Thank you for being ready to go in the car."* Or *"I really enjoy being with you. We will have time to stop at the park because you cooperated."*
- Many children refuse seat belts because when they're buckled in, they can't see out of the car well. Choose a safety-approved seat that allows comfort and good visibility.
- A posted seating chart is a help when arguing over seats. *(See: Car, misbehaving)*
- Use an authority figure. Visit the local police station, where an officer will explain the law and the consequences of not wearing a seat belt.

## *"My child unbuckles his seat belt while I'm driving."*

### UNDERSTANDING THE SITUATION

This is a surefire way for your child to get your attention and elicit a strong reaction. You must be calm and consistent, with no exceptions!

### WHAT TO SAY AND DO

Stop the car at the side of the road as soon as it is safe to do so. Set the brake and hazard lights. In a calm voice say, *"Billy, I will not move the car until you are back in your seat, with your seat belt fastened. It's the law. Please let me hear the click of the seat belt."* Say it only once, and be patient. He will do it eventually. You may be late to your destination, but this is much more important.

**PREVENTIVE TIPS**

• If unbuckling is a constant problem, plan a car trip with no particular destination in mind so you can stop the car as long as necessary, without worrying about being late.
• Make a special trip to the police station, so your child can discuss safety and seat belts with a policeman. One mother called the police to have an officer meet her and her car pool on the road. She pulled over and he spoke. Very effective!
• Be a good role model. Always buckle up. If your child has to remind you, thank him and do it!

See also: Car, misbehaving; Car seats

# CAR SEATS

*"My child refuses to get in the car seat."*

## UNDERSTANDING THE SITUATION

Getting your child into his car seat gives him a perfect opportunity to assert his independence and say, *"No!"* A squirming toddler is practically impossible to put in a car seat, and he knows it! You may get angry, but your job is to appear cool and not get caught up in a power struggle. Be clear about the limits—the law requires car seats for this age. Be consistent and never give in!

## WHAT TO SAY AND DO

Post and point to the "rules of the road" in your car. *(See: Car, misbehaving)*. Do not assume your child understands what she needs to do, and why. Be short and direct; it can even become a chant: *"Hilary, rule #2, buckle in, be safe, it's the law."* Never drive until everyone is fastened in.

Let your child hop into his seat himself and buckle the belt if he can. *"Marc, show me how you climb into your seat and buckle up."* Be patient, take time! Cheer! *"Marc, you will be safe because you are following the law. You are terrific."*

Give him a warning. Tell him five minutes before it's time to get in the car: *"Peter, after 'Sesame Street' we will buckle you into your car seat and go to the store."*

Offer your child a *choice: "Peter, you have a choice. You may climb into the seat yourself or have me put you in."* If he struggles against you, remain calm and with your best *poker face* fasten him in. Later, when he is calm, say: *"It is more comfortable for you if I do not have to put you in the seat with a struggle."*

Use an authority figure. *"The policeman will be watching us and will stop us if your seat belt is not fastened."* Taking your child to a police station with a friend or a small group is worthwhile.

Distract your child. Leave a special toy in the car, a small bag of Cheerios, or a pad and crayons. Then you can say, *"Peter, as soon as you are in your car seat you may hold Muffin."* *"Hey, Peter! You can color this as soon as you hop into your seat!"*

## PREVENTIVE TIPS

- Make sure the car seat is comfortable. Use towels to cover hot seats or straps. Make sure that the straps are not too tight.
- Keep your expectations reasonable. A bad time to expect co-operation is when your child is tired or hungry. If you must take him with you at these difficult times, be understanding. *"Ryan, I know you are very tired. Thanks for hanging in there. I'll get you home to bed as fast as I can."*
- Use lots of *encouragement. "I love riding in the car with you! I just like being with you!"*
- Make riding in the car fun. Point to animals and familiar objects. Sing to tapes or rhymes or songs.

## *"My child refuses to stay in the car seat."*

### UNDERSTANDING THE SITUATION

Your child may test you by wiggling out of the car seat. Even though her behavior is dangerous, don't let her intentional disobedience evoke an emotional reaction from you!

### WHAT TO SAY AND DO

Stop the car on a safe shoulder. Set the brake and put on the hazard lights. With a *poker face,* say, *"Mary, either you hop back in your seat or I will put you back in."* Allow her a minute to decide. If needed, buckle her back in with *action with few words* and resume driving. When she is calm, say, *"I'm glad you are safe in the car. Thank you."*

Before you start the car, check with her about the rule for staying in her car seat. *"Hilary, we have to drive ten minutes. What is our rule about staying in your seat? Right, you do not get out. Thank you very much for cooperating. Tell me if you need something."*

Put a doll on the seat next to her and go around a corner and let her see the doll fly off the seat onto the floor. Ask, *"What happened to Mary Jane? What would happen to you if you weren't buckled in?"*

### PREVENTIVE TIPS

• Plan a car ride just for car-seat training. Leave yourself plenty of extra time to stop at the side of the road, so you always stay calm!
• Be sensitive with your demands. Toddlers can't always sit for a long time, especially near mealtime or naptime.
• *Encourage* with enthusiasm when she is being good: *"Mary, great riding!" "Wow! I like how you are sitting in your car seat!"*

*See also: Car, misbehaving; Car, seat belts*

# CARELESSNESS

*"My child doesn't seem to think. She is so careless."*

### UNDERSTANDING THE SITUATION

Do you find it hard to trust your child when she carries a cake or a box of glasses? Do you feel you have to tie everything she owns to her body so she will come home with what she left with? Do you check schoolwork and constantly find mistakes? Do you tire of taking the forgotten lunches or band instruments to school or the forgotten dance shoes to lessons? Carelessness may be a problem at any age, and your nagging and coaxing are discouraging and invite more of the same behavior. When you criticize your child you belittle her and lower her self-esteem. *"You will never learn, will you? Why are you so clumsy? When will you grow up?"* This creates a lack of confidence, which will make matters worse. She needs clear guidelines, your understanding when she makes a mistake, and your *encouragement* to find a solution to the problem. Children do not flourish in an environment of perfectionism. Your child will learn to think ahead and be more careful as she gains confidence and experience. Be patient. This is an ongoing process that takes years. Keep the faith.

### WHAT TO SAY AND DO

Don't vent your anger on your child when an accident happens, but be honest with *I* messages and separate what she does from her self-worth. Your child will know you are angry; let her know why. *"Jenny, I loved that plate. I'm sick it is broken. I need time out, and then we can talk about what we should do."*

Instead of coaxing or reminding, ask your child what he might need or do to prevent a bad situation. Encourage thinking. Before he goes out the door, say, *"Matt, it snowed last night. What do you think you might need to wear outside?"* Before you leave him at school, *"Rob, what will you bring home with you today?"* As she picks up the cake, *"Anne, the cake is heavy. How will you need to carry it?"* Say, *"What could you do that would help you to remember?"* One eight-year-old girl thought of making lists for herself. Before leaving for school and before leaving from school, she checked her lists.

Let natural consequences teach when possible. Shoes on the wrong feet will become uncomfortable. A forgotten coat will be missed if it is rainy or cold.

Apply a logical consequence to a problem when a natural consequence won't work. For example, your young child will have to sit in the stroller or hold your hand on your walk if he can't manage to stay on the sidewalk. Your school-age child will need to have his homework checked before bringing it to school. Your child will need to spend his allowance to replace the window his ball went through.

When a problem repeats itself, establish guidelines so that he will know what to expect. This will teach responsibility. *"Michael, you have forgotten both your lunch and your band instrument too many times. I will not be able to bring them to school anymore. I know you will learn to remember. If you forget, you go without."* Follow through. This may seem very hard to do, but you must not overprotect.

Be sure to notice all effort and improvement. Do not attach improvement to your child's self-worth with *"I'm so proud of you."* Instead, say, *"Heidi, I noticed you brought your coat home from Mary's. Good remembering!"*

## PREVENTIVE TIPS

• Your child's carelessness may reflect stress. Try to simplify his world as much as possible during this period of time. Too many activities can be overwhelming. Keep him on a regular eating and sleeping schedule when possible. When a child begins school or any new situation, it causes stress.

• Find time to hug your child for no reason, when she isn't

doing anything to win your approval. When she knows you love her all the time she won't be afraid that you won't love her when she makes a mistake.

- See that significant, positive adults spend *special time* with her as much as possible. All caring reinforces and builds confidence.

# CHEATING

*"My child cheats to win."*

### UNDERSTANDING THE SITUATION

If your child often cheats at games, you may feel concerned. Every parent wants his or her child to be honest and happily adjusted. You may feel threatened, believing that cheating is a reflection of your parenting. Cheating or playing unfairly is common behavior in childhood. It reflects a child's need to be first, right, or the best in order to be important and feel good about herself. Do not label her a cheater in your thoughts or out loud. *Your child is not a cheater.* Think positively. She's persistent, intense, and determined, characteristics often found to be strongest in only children or older siblings. *Encourage* a cooperative climate rather than a competitive one, and she will feel less pressure to defeat others. Focus on the preventive tips to encourage a basic feeling of security. You are the loving parent. Let her know she needs to play fair and follow the rules and require her to do just that. Be patient and allow time for her to mature and give up the idea that she must be number one.

### WHAT TO SAY AND DO

Supervision is important for a child who tends to play unfairly. Consider it *time for teaching*. Stop the cheating in a calm, matter-of-fact way. Children are not born knowing proper social skills, and some need more experience and guidance than others.

Address what he is doing, identify what he is feeling, and give him a *choice*. Do not label him a cheater. *"Randy, you are not following the rules. You seem to just want to win. You have a choice: Please either play by the rules or leave the game."*

If children complain about your child cheating in the middle of the game, talk to the whole group. Say, *"What do you all want to do about this? Do you want to stop playing? You all want to keep playing. What do you want to do if anyone cheats?"* The group's decision will make it possible for your child to choose to play fair or not. It is now her responsibility.

Do not challenge her with the question, *"Did you cheat?"* You most likely know whether she did, and questioning her may trigger lying to cover up her mistake. Instead, say, *"Andrea, you aren't playing fairly. We will try again another day."* Your child needs to know mistakes are for learning; they are okay. She should always have another opportunity to try again.

Try to limit competition and comparing her to others at home and at school. She will do enough of that on her own.

**PREVENTIVE TIPS**

- Catch her having fun and comment specifically on what she's doing when she is playing nicely.
- Socialize with other families. Find opportunities to work and play in groups involving moms or dads as well as other children and adults.
- Play games that do not stress competition and that have no winner or loser. "Friends Around the World" (Aristoplay, Box 7645, Ann Arbor, Mich., 48107) is a fun, cooperative board game. Other games like flashlight tag, baseball (everyone gets to bat), building with Legos or blocks, and bean-bag tosses are all ideas for win/win fun. When playing board games have everyone win when everyone gets to the end.
- Model good sportsmanship. When you play games, play fair and keep the emphasis on fun, not winning. As your child grows older, watch sports together live and on TV and comment on rules and referee calls.

• Encourage team sports such as soccer, basketball, or baseball. Seek a coach who will emphasize having fun, building skills, and teaming instead of winning.

*See also: Winning and losing*

---

# CHORES

*"My child refuses to help around the house."*

## Ages 2½–5

### UNDERSTANDING THE SITUATION

When a three-year-old refuses to help, it grows frustrating and tiring. You may nag and complain, even try to bribe your child, but find it easier and more expedient to do the chore yourself. Many parents don't require much of their young child because they don't understand how capable a young child is. They fall into a terrible trap of doing too much for the child and not expecting enough. This common mistake leads to bad patterns in later years at home and at school. Your child will be exposed to the cooperative learning approach in school; give him a head start by teaching him to work with you as a team to make a happy home. Begin healthy habits at age two and a half when your child is most excited to help, and increase the challenges and expectations reasonably with maturity. You'll find that much of your child's whining and babyish behavior will stop when he assumes more responsibilities. Many personal responsibilities such as potty training and learning to dress are big tasks for a child. Your job is to set guidelines, take the *time to teach*, and then create an atmosphere in your home conducive to your child wanting to help. Your child is very capable. Never do for him what he can do for himself, even when he says, *"No, Mama!"* or *"I can't."* ("I can't" usually means "I won't.") Take care of yourself for the energy you need to maintain your sense of humor and

enthusiasm. Your *encouragement* is vital to winning his cooperation.

## WHAT TO SAY AND DO

Select chores at a *family meeting*. Post all chores your child can do
and let her choose. By age five your child will be joining in the
family's bigger decisions and choices if you begin inviting partic-
ipation now.

Take *time to teach*. Do not assume your child will know how
to do what you expect. Let go of your perfectionism. Let her
feel good about how she did the task; later, when she is not
looking, do what you need to do to correct or finish the job.

Children of all ages enjoy music. Use it as a motivator. Turn
up the stereo with peppy marching music or other favorite tunes.
Have a sing-along as you do the task. Your three-year-old will
love working while singing.

## Suggested Tasks and Responsibilities

Remember, your child can do anything listed for his own age or
younger, and some of the tasks suggested for older ages. This list
is a guideline. Be creative and flexible.

**Ages 2½–3:** Wipe up own accidents, put away groceries on
lower shelves, pick up toys, stack newspapers and magazines,
sweep floors, dust, help set table, run hand-held vacuum over
crumbs after eating, help with hygiene (use toilet, brush teeth,
wash and dry hands and face, brush hair), choose own clothes,
and dress.

**Age 4:** Empty wastebaskets, take out garbage, help make
lunches, help with grocery shopping, prepare breakfast, set and
clear table, make bed, pick up room, hold electric mixer, bring
in firewood, clear table, help serve dessert, help add ingredients
to a simple recipe, mix juice, make Popsicles, get the mail, polish
silver, help do yard work, follow schedule for feeding pets, polish
shoes and clean up afterward, hang own towel and washcloth,
shop, and choose own clothes.

**Age 5:** Help with meal planning, make own lunch and simple breakfast (frozen waffles, cold cereal) and clean up afterward, pour own drinks, tear lettuce for salad, cut vegetables with supervision, clean mirrors and windows, wipe counters, play with pets, make own bed and clean room, choose outfit according to weather, dress on own, separate white and colored laundry for wash, sweep porch, answer phone and dial friends, pay for small purchases, help clean car interior, learn to tie shoes, join in family decisions, put away indoor and outdoor toys.

Post a chart of the chores your child chose for the week. She may choose initially to mark each item with a sticker as she completes the task. For example, here is a chart for Jamie, age 4:

**MAKE OWN BED**

| Sunday | Monday | Tuesday | Wednesday | Thursday | Friday | Saturday |
|--------|--------|---------|-----------|----------|--------|----------|
|        |        |         |           |          |        |          |

**PICK UP TOYS**

| Sunday | Monday | Tuesday | Wednesday | Thursday | Friday | Saturday |
|--------|--------|---------|-----------|----------|--------|----------|
|        |        |         |           |          |        |          |

**FEED FOOFIE**

| Sunday | Monday | Tuesday | Wednesday | Thursday | Friday | Saturday |
|--------|--------|---------|-----------|----------|--------|----------|
|        |        |         |           |          |        |          |

SET THE DINNER TABLE

| Sunday | Monday | Tuesday | Wednesday | Thursday | Friday | Saturday |
|--------|--------|---------|-----------|----------|--------|----------|
|        |        |         |           |          |        |          |

## PREVENTIVE TIPS

- Your child needs to know what to expect. Some children need to hear every hour what they will be doing next, and this can ease the hassle of getting chores done. *"Jeremy, this morning you can watch 'Sesame Street' and play some. We are meeting Auntie Cheri for lunch at the mall, and you can play on the tugboat."* Then later, *"Jeremy, as soon as you pick up your toys we will go to the mall and have lunch with Auntie Cheri."*
- Take short moments in the morning, afternoon, and evening to hold your child, squeeze him, giggle and have fun together. When you break your child's routine with hugs and positive attention, he will be much more cooperative.
- Thank your child for his efforts. Personal responsibilities are a big deal to him. Comment with enthusiasm on specific efforts such as washing face, brushing teeth, combing hair, etc.

## Ages 6-10

### UNDERSTANDING THE SITUATION

A common household scenario with an eight-year-old:

Parent: *"Johnny, please set the table."*

Johnny: No response.

Parent: Repeats request several times, finally yelling, *"Johnny, set the table now!"*

Johnny: Sighs that 'what's the big deal' sigh and says, *"I will."*

Parent: Growing angry, yells, *"You never help me when I ask for it. You are lazy and spoiled! Just go to your room!"*

The child goes to his room, and the parent sets the table himself. The parent feels terribly exasperated. The child feels resentful and more uncooperative. The child succeeds in avoiding the chore, but everyone loses. Motivating your child to do chores is a challenge. However, with a plan for team effort, encouragement, and consistency you can improve the situation. This takes a limitless amount of energy and time as kids are kids. Testing is their job, and yours is to follow through. Your positive attitude will make a difference as to whether your child feels these tasks are a drag or a contribution. It is easier for an efficient parent to do it all or pay for it to be done, yet your child needs to be given the responsibility, the opportunity to personally contribute and to work cooperatively with you. You will be glad you made this effort.

**WHAT TO SAY AND DO**

Read "What to Say and Do" for ages 2½–5.

Avoid the "chore wars." Develop a program. At a *family meeting*, list all the meaningful tasks and responsibilities involved in running the household. Use a blackboard or an easel. Each week your child will select the chores she will do.

Draw a "family wagon," with one wheel for each family member, and explain: *"Our family wagon works only when everyone works together as a team. When the wagon goes forward we have time to do more fun things. The wagon moves forward only with everyone's help. What happens if one person decides to be a big wheel and boss everyone?*

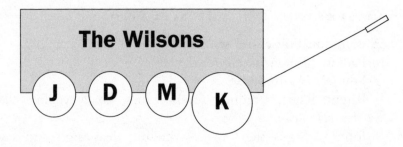

*What happens if someone wants to be a little wheel and not work at all?*

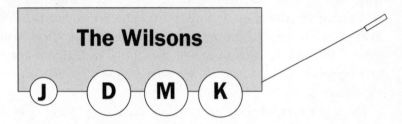

*What happens to our family if someone wants to be really different and just do his own thing his own way?"*

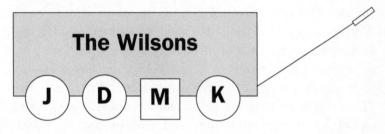

Be creative and make this a team effort. Have everyone jump in and work together. A three-year-old can help Dad set the table and make a salad, a seven-year-old can make a pizza, and Mom can do dishes. Be a team: *"I'll fold laundry with you, and you carry garbage out with me."* Be positive; make it fun.

Ask for your child's verbal agreement about the tasks she is to perform, and about what will happen if she doesn't follow through. Be consistent and check to see that each task is done as agreed. *"Holly, you agreed to pick up the family room before you made any other plans. It seems that you have decided to miss Jessie's birthday party."* Remember, do not lecture; make just one statement, *poker faced.* If she bugs you, say, *"You may go as soon as you clean the family room."* Or *"Betsy, you agreed to empty the garbage before dinner. Your dinner is waiting."*

Note: If you are in a heated power struggle, no consequence will work (your child would rather starve and drive you nuts). Let the issue go. Work on building a cooperative relationship at other times. Rather than engaging in a power struggle, discuss feelings at a time that's conducive to good listening. *"What's going on? You seem angry and resentful when I ask for your help lately."*

Reflect what your child says. Chances are when you take the time to listen to her, over time she will try harder.

Timing your request is important. Use an incentive: *"As soon as the patio is swept, I can start the barbecue, and we'll eat outside tonight."* Or *"Molly, as soon as you clean the bathroom you can go play at Virginia's."* Or *"When the toy room is picked up you may turn on the television."*

Give your child a choice when possible. *"Jessie, you have a choice. Sweep the patio today before soccer practice or tomorrow before you go to Mary's to swim."*

Do not bribe or pay your child for doing regular, necessary chores. Allowance should not be based on chores getting done. *"Lindy, living in our home is a tremendous privilege. We can have fun working together as a team while lightening the load for everyone. You do not get paid for chores. If you want extra money, we will discuss other, money-earning jobs."* Do not praise and then use "but," as in: *"I see you made your bed, but it still has lumps in it."* Absolute perfection is an impossible goal and seldom leads to improvement. Comment on what you notice done well and at another time suggest what you want to have done differently in the future. *"Ron, nice effort on your bed!"* Later, when you are helping him in his room: *"Watch this easy way to get the lumps out."* Be sure you are not using thirty-year-old expectations on a job your seven-year-old is doing.

## Suggested Responsibilities

Remember, your child can do anything listed for his own age or younger, and some of the tasks suggested for older ages. This list is a guideline. Be creative and flexible.

**Age 6, Grade 1:** Choose clothing according to weather or special event, water plants indoors and out, peel vegetables, cook simple food, prepare own lunch, hang clothes, gather wood, rake, pull weeds, clean scrapes or bruises, straighten or clean drawers.

**Age 7, Grade 2:** Care for own bike (wipe it off, put it away, use a lock), write down phone messages, wash pets, train pets, get up in the morning and go to bed on own, be in charge of lunch money and notes for school, iron simple items such as napkins, scrub bathtub and sink, clean toilets, wash plastic trash baskets, remove sheets to laundry, fold laundry, help put sheets on beds, put dishes into dishwasher.

**Age 8, Grade 3:** Fold napkins and set table properly, mop floor, run own bath, change into play clothes without being told, sew buttons on clothes, sew tears in seams, pick fruit from trees, pick wilted blossoms off plants, clean up animal messes in yard and house, help paint shelves or walls, write letters with help, rake yard, bathe a younger sibling, wax furniture.

**Age 9, Grade 4:** Operate washer and dryer, use grocery list and comparison shop, cross streets unassisted, prepare box mixes; prepare family meal, plan own party, learn banking, learn to sew, knit, or weave, make coffee, tea, or juice and pour it, clean car inside and out, be responsible for own pet.

**Age 10, Grade 5:** Take care of younger siblings (bathe them, prepare meals and feed them, and dress them), run errands on bike, handle small sums of money with honesty, stay alone at home, show self-control when in public with peers, mow grass, air-blow patio, wash pots and pans, clean kitchen, clean oven and stove, keep track of personal schedule with own calendar.

Post a chart of your child's daily routine. Include the chores she chose and other home responsibilities. She may choose initially to mark each item with a sticker as she completes the task. For example, here is a morning chart for Elizabeth, age 9:

| Morning: | 7:00 Wake up | Dress | Make Bed |
|---|---|---|---|
| | 8:00 Breakfast | Feed Woody | |
| | 8:30 Piano | Pack for School | |
| | | (lunch, notes, books) | |
| | 9:00 Leave for School | | |

**PREVENTIVE TIPS**

- Take *time to teach.* Before expecting a chore to be done, make sure your child's perception is the same as yours. Do not assume it is. Determine his understanding of the job to be done with *what, why,* and *how* questions.

- Be sure when you say, *"Please cooperate with me,"* your child doesn't think you mean *"obey me."* Jobs will be easier to sell to your child if you create an enthusiastic, team-spirit approach rather than a *"Do as I say because I said so"* atmosphere.
- Spend *special time* together often. Have fun together. Bike, take walks, play games inside and out. The better your relationship, the more cooperative your child will be.

See also: Evening hassles; Morning hassles

# CLIMBING

*"My child is a climber. It scares me!"*

### UNDERSTANDING THE SITUATION

Climbing is adventurous and challenging to your child. It's also a tremendous way to get attention. As you coax him down from a high fence or tell him for the fifth time to get off the back of the chair or off the top of the refrigerator, your nervousness grows into exasperation. Even negative attention is a social payoff to your child. Appear unimpressed with his climbing. Agility is something to encourage. Your fears may cause you to be over-protective. *Set limits* (for instance: if you climb up it, you must be able to get down from it), identify areas where climbing is okay, and be clear about where it's not. Try to evaluate each situation, and if you feel your child might fall but not be seriously injured, ignore it. Leave the room if you must. A minor fall is a great teacher, especially if you rush in not with an *"I told you so"* but rather with a caring *"Ow, that was quite a fall. What did you learn from that one?"*

**WHAT TO SAY AND DO**

Questions make your child think. Say, *"Ian, you have a lot of courage, but you are unsafe. What could you climb on that would challenge you and still be safe?"* If he is unsafe, remove him with *action with few words*, using a *poker face*. Do this as many times as it takes to stop his action. Be consistent and follow through. Alternatively, have him take *time out.*

Designate places he can climb in the house. When he climbs furniture to annoy you, redirect him with a *poker face* to places that are challenging but safe. Encourage his adventurous and courageous character. *"Alex, you are very brave, and you do enjoy climbing. You can climb the ladder up to the top bunk. Dad added more boxes against the fence that you can climb. The table is for books only and not for boys to climb on."*

Distract your child from an unsafe spot and verbalize what he might be thinking. Try a little humor. *"Chris, you are a good climber. You seem to want to climb very high and get my attention. The refrigerator is not for climbing, and I certainly don't want to join you up there. Go climb the apple tree, and I will be happy to bring some juice out and join you."*


**PREVENTIVE TIPS**

- Children often climb just to reach something that they want. Kidproof your higher areas so that they are not appealing. Remove those tantalizing things from view. Keep stools up on the counter if necessary, etc.
- Spend *special time* with your child each day. Do not just sit and watch him; try to be active with him. Find an opportunity to visit parks and climb the playground equipment with him, hike the wooded trails, climb rocks up a creek bed.
- Give him your attention at positive times. Let him know you enjoy being around him. *"Alex, I really enjoy watching you build those tall towers of blocks. Here's a little man. Can he scale your building? He's a climber just like you."*
- Encourage climbing safely. Work together to build a tree house, a fort, or a slide in your yard.

• Ask a children's librarian or knowledgeable bookstore clerk for children's adventure books that you can read together.

---

# CLOTHING, CHOOSING

*"My child and I battle over what she will wear."*

### UNDERSTANDING THE SITUATION

Choosing clothes for the day is a common battle between parent and child. Many spirited children declare by age two and a half what they will wear, how it will be worn, and what they won't wear, and they want to feel that control forevermore. Many young children are sensitive to textures, and zippers, snaps, and buttons become either a must or an absolute NO! Older children become more conscious of style. Battles over what to wear often ruin a morning before work or school, ending with yelling and arguing. Your frustration is over the struggle to be a "good parent" whose job is to dress your child in appropriate attire and be sure he is neat and presentable. Let go of that frustration. Instead be a "responsible parent" whose long-range goal is to raise a capable, responsible person who thinks for himself. Organization and planning will prevent much of the hassle. Your limits about choosing clothes should be few and reasonable: *Be clean, and dress for the weather.* Let go of your perfectionism and your concern over what others are thinking. Choosing clothes is a wonderful opportunity for your child to begin making his own decisions.

### WHAT TO SAY AND DO

When your child is young, plan for success. Select and make available clothes that are appropriate for the weather, clothes that he feels comfortable in, that can be coordinated together, and that allow him limited *choices*.

*Encourage* your school-age child to select his clothes without your help. This is an opportunity to let your child think for himself and learn how to make decisions about his likes and dislikes. He may put his shoes on the wrong feet; if so, keep quiet. If they hurt him he will switch them. He may choose odd combinations. He may want to wear the same two items every day. These are not life-or-death matters, so relax and let him be.

Take short shopping trips with your child, selecting her playclothes one day, shoes another time, special-occasion wear another time, etc. Your very young child can select her own clothes with limited choices, and when your school-age child chooses her clothes she will be more likely to assume responsibility for liking them and wearing them. In the long run, this could solve the problem of those unworn clothes *you* worry about.

Take *time for teaching*. Make or buy her a weather chart for her room. *"Hilary, what is the weather like today? Based on the weather, what is in your closet or drawer you would like to wear?"*

Should she choose short sleeves on a blustery day, negotiate, compromise, and offer *choices*. *"Caroline, I know you want to wear that blouse. That will be fine if you wear a sweater. If you get too warm, put it in your pack."*

Let the needs of the situation dictate the decision about what to wear. This helps you remain the parent but removes you from the control seat that says, "Do as I say." *"Hannah, I know you want to wear your dress. It will be rainy and cold on the field trip. Choose some warm tights, and your dress will work fine."*

## PREVENTIVE TIPS

- Comment often on what good choices your child makes, what a good decision maker she is.
- Separate clothes you do not want her to wear from her everyday clothes. Clothes she will grow into, special-occasion clothes, or seasonal clothes can be put away, out of sight and mind.
- Read together children's books about self-esteem. Some have to do with dressing. Try *The Purple Coat* by Amy Hest (New York: Macmillan, 1986), *Amazing Grace* by Caroline Binch

(New York: Dial Books, 1991) or *The Mouse, the Monster and Me* by Pat Palmer (San Luis Obispo, Calif.: Impact Publishers, 1977). See a children's librarian or knowledgeable bookstore clerk for more suggestions.

*See also: Clothing, dressing; Morning hassles*

---

# CLOTHING, DRESSING

*"My child will not cooperate about getting dressed."*

## Ages 2½–5

### UNDERSTANDING THE SITUATION

Getting dressed is a common problem that can often lead to a tremendous struggle. Your child plays attention-seeking games; you coax and remind. He dawdles, you grow angry (perhaps with the pressure of being late), threaten, lecture, and perhaps forcefully pull his clothes on for him. The attention getting soon turns into a power struggle. Stop! With proper management, this hassle can be significantly reduced. *Encourage* him to cooperate. Develop a routine for dressing. Take *time to teach* your child. A two-and-a-half-year-old can dress himself if he is encouraged and outfitted in appropriate clothes. Your long-range goal is to raise a capable, responsible person who thinks for himself. Don't do for a child what he can do for himself. An occasional helping hand is kind, but when done on a regular basis it is discouragement. He needs to hear that you love him even if you do not dress him and fuss with him. Take this opportunity to show confidence in your child. Celebrate and compliment him on specifics when he does well.

## WHAT TO SAY AND DO

A good dressing routine begins the night before. Your child will feel secure with the structure and know what to expect. Have him select his clothes for the morning and put them where he can easily reach them.

Take *time to teach* how to dress. Have fun and remain light-hearted. Stand in front of a mirror to dress. Play a game, as in *"I'll do your shoe, you do mine,"* or *"I'll do this shoe, you do the other one."* Sing a song. Use the same theme as brushing hair or teeth: *"This is the way we put on our shoes, so early in the morning."*

A three-year-old can dress himself. Once he is taught to dress himself and you know he can, greet him in the morning with a hug and a kiss and spend a little loving time. Give him something to look forward to. *"Aaron, you are such a big boy now, and as soon as you dress you can help me scramble the eggs for breakfast."*

Your child may change clothes a number of times, come to you for unneeded help, or complain. Identify his attention seeking. *"Roger, you seem to want my attention. This is not a good time for me. If you will dress while I make breakfast, I will have time to spend with you. We can read together."* Give your attention at positive times.

Do not get sucked into a power struggle. Do not nag or coax. If you feel a battle beginning, sidestep it. With a *poker face*, say, *"Meg, I'll be in the kitchen. Let me know if I can help. Breakfast will be waiting when you are dressed."*

Decide what you will do rather than what you will make her do. Let her know what to expect. *"Meg, we have to leave to take you to preschool in ten minutes. When the timer goes bing I will need to have you in the car. If you are not dressed I will take you as you are and take your clothes in a bag."* If the needs of the situation require it, firmly and kindly put her clothes in a bag and take her in pajamas to school to dress. She may holler and be embarrassed, but it probably won't happen again.

## PREVENTIVE TIPS

• Keep your expectations reasonable. Know what your child can do independently and what he needs help with.
• Review how to dress when you are not in a rush. Use a doll and your child's outgrown clothes to teach what goes on first, and how it goes on.
• Dressing takes time. Get up earlier so that you can give relaxed and encouraging time!
• Together read children's books, such as *The Purple Coat* by Amy Hest (New York: Macmillan, 1986) and *Mama Do You Love Me* by Barbara M. Joossee (San Francisco: Chronicle Books, 1991). Ask children's librarians and knowledgeable bookstore clerks for other ideas.

## Ages 6–10

### UNDERSTANDING THE SITUATION

Your older child may hassle you with indecision about what to wear, dressing very slowly, or not staying focused on her task. Coaxing and reminding feed negative, attention-getting behavior, and threatening and scolding fuel a power struggle. Neither results in cooperation or a good relationship. Your child needs to know you love her even if you aren't nagging or fighting her to dress. Nagging criticism *("Why can't you ever be ready on time? You are forever making us late!")* is not helpful. Help her establish a routine to stay on task, *set limits*, and never do for her what she can do for herself.

### WHAT TO SAY AND DO

Decide together how much time your child will need for dressing and help him design a plan for success. A training chart of morning tasks is helpful in teaching organizational skills. Each day when he finishes dressing, he can check it off on the chart. At the end of the week evaluate the chart with him. Notice and comment on what went well. If he needs more work, keep dressing on the chart.

Teach organizational skills by asking him to plan ahead, selecting and laying out clothes the night before. *"Alan, tomorrow is church. Please lay out what you want to wear tonight so that dressing will be easy in the morning."*

Avoid power struggles. Decide what you will do and not what you will make him do. Calmly and kindly give him a warning: *"Jeff, breakfast is in five minutes. I will need to put all the food away by 8:15."* One day without breakfast will be a good reminder to make a different choice for himself next time!

Offer an incentive ahead of time. *"In the morning, if you can be dressed and have breakfast promptly, you will have time for Nintendo before school."*

**PREVENTIVE TIPS**

- Allow your child plenty of time. Organization and setting priorities help to avoid chaos and hassles. Some responsibility for his dressing is yours. Let him know what to expect and do not lose your temper with him because you are disorganized or running late.
- Work on strengthening your relationship. Spending *special time* helps prevent attention-getting or power-seeking situations.
- Read together in the evenings. *The Mouse, the Monster and Me* by Pat Palmer (San Luis Obispo, Calif.: Impact Publishers, 1977) is a fun book about self-assertion and self-esteem. Librarians and knowledgeable bookstore clerks will have other good ideas.

*See also: Clothing, choosing; Morning hassles*

# COMPLAINING

*"My child seems to complain excessively."*

### UNDERSTANDING THE SITUATION

It is very annoying when your child whines, *"I'm too cold!" "This is dumb." "I need better shoes." "He got more than me."* It is irritating to start your day with your child complaining about the breakfast you served or the fact that her brother got into her things again. Some children do complain and grouse more than others. There is a little Eeyore in all of us, some more than others. Do not feel your child is out to get you *("How negative can I be today to irritate Mom?").* Most children who complain excessively have an intense and sensitive nature. They may react more strongly to the environment and be less tolerant of change, temperatures, tastes, or smells. Your child may be very sensitive to disruptions in routine. Someone's actions may trigger a feeling of rejection or cause her to feel a lack of control over what happens to her or her possessions. These characteristics can be positive when managed properly. She does not need your negative labels. *"You are always such a grouch"* is not helpful. Try not to lose your temper when she complains. Work hard to show your own positive attitude about life and give less attention to your child's annoying behavior when it happens. Complainers typically blame bad feelings on someone or something else. Help her to identify her feelings and to understand how she is responsible for them. This process will take time, maybe years; be patient and keep the faith.

## WHAT TO SAY AND DO

Offer a distraction. One discouraged three-year-old complained on a long hike with family and friends. One bright adult offered him a whistle. *"Zach, whistle each time you cross a stream of water. That will help us know we are near water."* The whistle was all that was heard from Zach the rest of the hike. He felt important.

Help your child understand why she may be complaining and teach her how to take care of herself. *"Andrea, you are tired of being so close to your sister. You seem to need more space around you after fifteen minutes in the car. Please be patient; we'll be home in ten more minutes."* Suggestions may help. *"Would you like to hear a story or sing 'The Old Lady Who Swallowed a Fly'?"* Or *"Leah, you were up late at the slumber party. When you don't get your required sleep you complain. Nothing is right. When you feel like that, go lie down on your bed or go out into the backyard and blow bubbles and relax."*

Rather than correct her with your perfectionism, criticism, and advice, identify feelings, use questions, and invite her ideas. Affirm positively. *"You are very sensitive about your possessions, and you are frustrated that your brother got into your things How might you prevent that from happening?"* Or *"He likes your things. What ideas do you have for your brother?"*

Give the responsibility to her to think about what she needs. *"Becky, you seem unhappy. What do you need from me?"*

Do the unexpected, lighten up, and use a sense of humor. Complain back to your child in a lighthearted way about random things. *"Rebecca, my throat hurts, my foot is sore, I have fleas in my hair, and my letter got lost."*

*Time out* is an appropriate way for her to work through her feelings and come back when ready to be with others. Address the action. *"Maria, the complaining is unpleasant to listen to. Please take a time out. When you feel better, you may call Mary to play."*

Tell her once that you have heard enough complaining, then ignore. Walk away if you must with a *poker face. "Mindy, we talked about your complaint, we decided what you might do, and now I do not wish to listen to it any longer."* Be consistent and watch for her positive change.

Give little attention to the complaining and give lots of attention to positive behavior. *"Rachael, we have been together shopping all morning. You are terrific! I love being with you. You are as much fun as my best friend."* That should delight her.

## PREVENTIVE TIPS

- Keep a log for two weeks. Record both her happier moments and her times of complaining. You may see a pattern. Is she worse when you are rushed? Is space an issue? Does she hate changing activities? Is she better with more children or fewer? Does she complain more around mealtime? Is she overwhelmed by too many directions or activities? If you see a pattern, you can help her understand how she feels and help her to help herself. You may plan ways to prevent trouble, e.g., give her more time, let her know more in advance what will be happening, spend one-on-one time together, cut out some activities, etc.
- Work on a positive attitude. Notice what is right with your child and comment on it often. Be specific.
- Be a good model. Talk positively about yourself. If you feel negative, look for the brighter side and verbalize it. Instead of *"I'm so dumb, I broke the glass. Nothing is going right."* say, *"I dropped the glass and it broke. That isn't like me."*
- Spend *special time* together and have fun. Read together and play games. *Alexander and the Terrible, Horrible, Not Good Very Bad Day* by Judith Viorst (New York: Macmillan, 1972) and *Spinky Sulks* by William Steig (New York: Farrar, Straus and Giroux, 1988) are books that can open up discussions on sulky feelings.
- You need positive support from other adults. Seek out a parent group through a local hospital, school, or church.

# CRYING

*"My child cries much too easily and too often."*

## UNDERSTANDING THE SITUATION

Excessive crying may be due to tiredness or an impending illness. Some young children, when frustrated, do cry easily until they are old enough to physically do what they mentally want to. For example, Andrew cries with frustration because he cannot tie his shoe. Nick cries because he cannot speak well enough to tell people what he wants. This behavior takes extreme parental patience. It is very hard for a parent to see an eight-year-old in tears because of fear or disappointment. It is natural to want to help and enable, and parents often give in to the crying to appease or protect a child from pain. Crying is a healthy way to express emotion. It is an unhealthy, manipulative way to solicit coddling and protection. Help your child understand her feelings. Take *time to teach* her to be assertive, to get her needs met without crying. Teach her what to say and do when someone picks on her or when she is unhappy, tired or in need of something. We all grow in our most difficult times. Show faith that she can handle the situation. Believe in her. She can and will handle it.

## WHAT TO SAY AND DO

See your pediatrician in order to rule out possible physical reasons for the crying.

Never label your child a crybaby. Identify your child's feelings. Get down on his level, place your hands gently on his shoulders, and make eye contact. *"Ricky, you are frustrated because you can't have the toy."* Show understanding. *"I can understand that you really want it.*" If he will not stop, say, *"I'd like to help. I will understand what you are saying when you stop crying."* Use *action with few words*, with no more attention to the crying. When he stops crying, continue. Listen and explore his feelings without judging. *"Thank you for not crying. It sounds as though you feel* _____ *because* _____ *"*

Empower your older child by asking, *"Maria, what do you need from me?"*

Give a *choice*. *"Mark, if you stop crying we will shop for the birthday present. If you choose to keep crying, we will go home with no present."* He may have to go to the party without a present, and this may be hard for you. Have faith that he can handle it.

Do not say, *"Stop crying."* State what you will do. Be kind, firm, and calm. *"Nicki, I need to change your diaper. You may cry, but I will change it."* Or *"Jamie, crying will not help. I will put your clothes in the bag, and you will dress in the car or at school."*

Use the unexpected with your younger child. Sit down on the floor beside her and pretend to cry. Do this in a lighthearted way with humor. This is not to scare her, only to lighten the atmosphere.

Once you have said no, ignore the crying. Leave the room if you must with a *poker face*. If you are in public, use a *poker face* and *action with few words*, removing both of you to a private area until she stops. If you give in, she will learn that crying gets attention.

### PREVENTIVE TIPS

- Praise often when your child is not crying. *"Josie, we had such a good morning. You are terrific. I really enjoy being with you."* Or *"Jen, we have had a good week. I am really impressed that you are talking about your feelings so much more."*
- After a crying spell, when she has calmed down, teach her assertion. Ask her what she can do instead of crying to get her needs met.
- Read together *I Am Not a Crybaby* by Norma Simon (Morton Grove, Ill.: Whitman, 1989; Puffin paperback).
- Keep her on a regular schedule. The stress of insufficient sleep,

an interrupted eating schedule, or feeling no control over what happens to her often triggers excessive crying. Children need to know what to expect.

• Log the crying. Observe what times of day it occurs. What has changed in your child's world lately? Have you added any activities? Have you been expecting more of him than usual? Is anything new going on at day care or school?

• Spend *special time*. This may be a period when he needs more one-on-one with you or with other significant people in his world.

*See also: Sadness; Bullied child*

# DARK, FEAR OF

*"My child is afraid to be alone in the dark."*

## UNDERSTANDING THE SITUATION

Fear of the dark is one of the most exhausting issues you may deal with as a parent. Your child deserves to be comforted through his fear. But at the end of a long day or in the middle of the night, you need your rest and have the least amount of patience. Fears of the dark come and go with different ages and stages of development and experience. The dark creates a stage for other fears, whether it be monsters at age three, a kidnapper at age seven, or fear of fire or thieves at age ten. Those fears are real to your child. He needs your nurturing support balanced with confident, positive assurance that he will handle the fear. Too much coddling or undue attention says, *"You have something to fear, and I will protect you,"* and it will create more of the same behavior. Be patient. Your child may need to learn to cope in small steps, and this takes time. If yours is a two-parent household, decide on the same approach and share the load with your spouse. If you are single, find time to get needed sleep so that you have energy for the consistency that is required.

## WHAT TO SAY AND DO

*Initially*, turn on a dim light, identify the fear, hold your child, listen, show understanding, reassure her, and do not try to fix or negate the fear. *"Katy, you are afraid of the dark. You are safe."* Or *"Sometimes the dark does seem scary. You are safe."* Do not say, *"You're not afraid of the dark,"* or *"Come on, grow up, it's only the dark."* This is a first small step. Now work toward offering ideas to overcome the fear.

Use the phrase *"How can I help you?"* Acknowledge what she wants, tell her what you are willing to do, *set limits*, and firmly and kindly follow through. *"Missy, I know you want me to stay with you. I can stay with you for five minutes. Then I need to put Joey to bed. The new lamp is on, you are safe, you can go to sleep."* Limit the talk. Use *action with few words*.

Your young child may want to pick a stuffed animal to watch over her. *"Maggie, take turns. You watch over Pooh Bear, and he will watch over you."*

If she hears the noise of the wind and seems scared, say, *"Julie, the wind is doing its job. Your job is to stay in your bed."*

Provide her with a lamp with a dimmer switch. Each night dim the light a little more.

Give more time to bedtime. Rather than negating your child's fear, take *time to teach* her how to take control of it. Sit with her in her dark room and have her tell you what she fears around the room. With a dim light or a flashlight, illuminate what she mentions. *"Josie, tell me what scares you the most in your room. The windows worry you. We will put new locks on to keep the monster out. You need to see to go to the bathroom, so we will get a dimmer switch for your lamp to give you a little light. You worry about things on the floor that look like monsters, so we will put all your clothes away before bed and give you a flashlight to shine on lumps that worry you."*

Once a month have a house fire drill. Take *time to teach* your older child what to do in a situation she fears. *"Kelly, you are afraid of fire. You can be safe if there is a fire. If you hear the smoke alarm* [demonstrate what it sounds like], *close your bedroom door, drop your rope ladder out your window, and climb down the side of the house. We will meet you on the grass."* Run through a practice fire drill with her regularly, using a positive attitude.

Have your child mark his successes on a training chart. *"Mark, this week you stayed in your room four times. Great effort! As soon as you complete one whole week—that is, seven days—you can have your very own flashlight!"* If he slips into fear one night, *encourage* with a second opportunity. *"You will find it gets easier. Tomorrow night is a new night!"*

Leave a sleeping bag next to your bed. *"Lia, when you feel afraid and want to be near us, quietly come in and crawl into this bag.*

*Do not disturb us."* This discourages attention-getting behavior and provides a truly fearful child an opportunity to handle the fear on her own.

Give affirmations and comment on successes and positive efforts. *"You are very brave. I am noticing your efforts to be in the dark. It takes time to overcome fear of the dark. You will do it."* We all need to learn how to talk positively about ourselves. For a very young child, make up words to a familiar tune. *"I am brave, I am safe, I am very, very safe and brave."*

**PREVENTIVE TIPS**

- Keep your child on a regular schedule. An overtired child will get wound up over fears easily. Be available. Leaving her with different sitters and an inconsistent schedule can make her feel less secure.
- Have fun in the dark! Turn out all lights and eat dinner by candlelight. Build a tent or a tunnel in the house and crawl in to play a game with a flashlight.
- Take advantage of storms that cause power outages and have fun finding candles or flashlights with your child. Model enthusiasm, and teach her to count the seconds between lightning and thunder to tell how close the lightning is.
- Together read children's books on all types of fear. Use your good judgment as to their appropriateness. Try *Bedtime for Frances* by Russell Hoban (New York: HarperCollins, 1960), *Anna in Charge* by Yoriko Tsutsui (New York: Viking, 1989), *There's Something in My Attic* by Mercer Meyer (New York: Dial Books, 1988), and *Sheila Rae, the Brave* by Kevin Henkes (New York: Greenwillow, 1988). See a children's librarian or knowledgeable bookstore clerk for other ideas.

*See also: Bedtime, getting to bed; Bedtime, staying in bed; Sleeping with parent*

# DAY CARE, DROPPING OFF

*"My child clings and cries when I leave her."*

## UNDERSTANDING THE SITUATION

Leaving an unhappy child at day care can be the worst way to begin a day. Crying and clinging commonly create a tremendous amount of parental guilt and anxiety. Your crying child is dealing with change and separation. Your hesitation and concern is negative and will not give strength to your child. Be patient with his day care adjustment and muster up all the positive energy you can, knowing that it may take some time. Do not hesitate to ask for positive reinforcement from a mature day care provider or your physician. Children in day care on a regular basis do need *special time* with a loving parent to be a priority. Take this time, and you will help to prevent typical attention-getting behavior and angry power struggles at home. Do what you can and tell yourself that you are doing your very best with what you have and what you know. Should your child not settle in comfortably after several weeks and show behavior that concerns you, such as crying the whole time you are away, not sleeping at night, not eating properly, or suddenly acting clingy or belligerent, this may be an indication that the day care situation is not good. Listen to your fear. Be your child's advocate. Observe him for a day, and you will get a better idea about what is happening. Make a change if your gut feeling is negative.

## WHAT TO SAY AND DO:

Find the best situation you can for your child. Do not pick a day care provider because it is new and fancy with the best play equipment or because it's convenient. Take the time to observe.

Watch the other children. Look for a child that reminds you of your own, a child that perhaps has a similar temperament. Watch how the teachers and the other children interact with her. Does she move about the room happily? Is she engaged in activity? For example, say that your daughter is very active and spontaneous. At one day care, you observe an active little boy that has to be in time out most of the morning. At another day care you may observe one teacher taking two very active children outside to run around and climb. Which teacher, which setting would your child prefer?

Try changing your underlying beliefs. When your feelings of guilt and anxiety change, you will convey a positive attitude. Instead of the belief that *"good parents stay home with their children. I should be home with him,"* adopt the belief that *"I am a responsible parent. I love my child. I have found a warm and loving environment for him while I need to be away. He will be safe and have friends and caring, mature adults."* He may continue to cry when you first leave, but never for long, and you both will feel better.

*Encourage* with small steps. Before leaving your child for the first time, visit for an hour and help her to become acquainted with the children and the teachers. Stay with her the first day for thirty minutes and decrease the length of your stay by ten minutes each day for a couple of days if needed.

Be a good actor. If you do have anxiety, do not let it show. Say, *"Here's your teacher. You will have a great day together. I will be back after naptime."* Pass your child over to the teacher with a hug and a kiss and exit with no hesitation. You may feel better if you call in a half hour. Did she settle down?

If yours is a two-parent family, alternate taking her to day care with your spouse. Both of you should use the same consistent, positive approach.

Let her know exactly what to expect. Young children have no concept of time, so give specifics. Say, *"I will take you to day care after breakfast. I will stay for playtime until the morning story starts. I'll be back to pick you up after naptime."*

Give her something to look forward to. Say, *"When you get to school you will see Amy. You can ask her to come to play on Saturday."*

Or *"Let's cut some flowers for Mrs. Lee. You can take them to her for the room."*

## PREVENTIVE TIPS

- Your child may have a temperament requiring a smaller setting. If day care adjustment has been hard, start with a relative, a sitter in your own home, or a small day care arrangement in a family home.
- Offer to help in the classroom or stop in once a week to have lunch with your child.
- Encourage friendships. Learn the names of the children and have them over to play when you will be home. Your child will enjoy going to day care or school to see her friends.
- Encourage your child to take a favorite stuffed animal or favorite object with him. Laminate a small picture of him with the family and tuck it in his pocket or hang it around his neck.
- Read these children's books together at a happy time: *Mama Do You Love Me?* by Barbara M. Joossee (San Francisco: Chronicle Books, 1991), *Going to Daycare* by Fred Rogers (New York: Putnam, 1985), *Waiting for Mom* by Linda Wagner Tyler (New York: Puffin Books, 1989), and *Will You Come Back for Me?* by Ann Tompert (Morton Grove, Ill.: Whitman, 1988). See a children's librarian or a knowledgeable bookstore clerk for other book ideas.

*See also: Day care, picking up*

# DAY CARE, PICKING UP

*"My child begins whining and clinging when I pick him up at day care."*

## UNDERSTANDING THE SITUATION

Nothing is more frustrating to a tired parent than to have to deal with a fussy child at the end of a long day. Your child may be very happy to see you, greet you with a hug—and then the demanding behavior begins. Most likely he is as tired as you, and because you have been away he demands your attention for comfort and a sense of belonging. You may feel like turning around and leaving him there through the night. Muster all the energy you have to greet him with enthusiasm and be prepared to give him loving, patient attention right when you arrive. Five minutes of one-on-one time with him, walking through the room and talking about his day, may give you more time alone in the long run.

## WHAT TO SAY AND DO

Greet your child warmly and get down to his eye level. Say, *"Hi, Willy. I am so glad to see you."* Do not rush. He may want to pull you around the room to show you what he did that day. He may want to exit. Let him direct.

This normally is not the time to chat with teachers or other parents. Say, *"Can I call you later tonight? We need to head home for our time together."*

Catch him while he's happy and before the meltdown begins. Say, *"You look happy. I'm glad, because we are going to spend some special time together. I have a snack in the car for you."* Arrive with a healthful snack. He is likely to be hungry and tired, and a good, nutritional snack is sure to help his tolerance level. Say, *"I missed you today, and I brought you some good food to give us energy to have fun together this evening."*

In the car discuss what you will do when you get home. Offer choices. *"We'll have time to play ball or take a walk before dinner. You choose."*

Give at least fifteen minutes of your undivided time to snuggle and cuddle when you get home. Your child needs physical contact with you. Even if you feel pressure to make dinner, etc., take this time and you are more likely to get dinner on the table without a major meltdown.

### PREVENTIVE TIPS

- Prioritize your time. Take time for yourself each day. Exercise is a must for stress reduction. Your child's behavior will reflect exactly how you feel.
- In today's fast-paced world, a tired child is easy to lose patience with. Try hard to give him your best. It is difficult, but your child needs your energy and enthusiasm for his confidence building.
- If possible, plan ahead so that your child can have your undivided attention when you come to greet him. When possible, do errands and shopping at any time other than when you pick him up from day care.

*See also: Day care, dropping off*

# DEATH, QUESTIONS ABOUT

*"My child is asking questions about death and dying."*

## UNDERSTANDING THE SITUATION

Sooner or later your young child will question you about death, perhaps because she sees it on TV, finds a dead bird on a walk, or hears someone relate a story about it. If caught off guard you may feel surprised and inadequate, not knowing how to answer these important questions. Your job is to be calm and answer her questions as simply and honestly as you can. Entire books are written on helping children cope with the death of a loved one. This is a big topic. If your child is experiencing a loved one dying, seek professional advice. You can help eliminate potential future fears or anxieties about death with a positive attitude. If you are caught off guard, tell her so in a sincere, matter-of-fact way: *"Jenny, I haven't thought about how to talk about that. Give me a little time."*

## WHAT TO SAY AND DO

Reassure your child when she asks with worry, *"Will you die? Will I?"* Say, *"You need not worry. We all will die someday. But you'll have me around for a very long time! And you'll be here much longer than that!"* Don't feel you need to give an elaborate explanation involving your deepest religious convictions. Give short, age-appropriate answers.

If you feel unequipped to answer your child's questions, tell her so. *"I don't understand all that you are curious about. Let's talk to someone who might."* Seek out someone who might be experienced with children's questions on death, perhaps your minister, a teacher, or a counselor. Interview this person first before you take your child in, to make sure his or her philosophy is consistent with yours.

PREVENTIVE TIPS

- Be prepared for your child's questions before they arise. Your matter-of-fact answers will influence her beliefs. *"We all will die someday, but I'll be here for a long, long time"* sends a positive message. *"I'll never leave you"* is not direct and sends an overprotective message.
- Read children's stories together. There are many very subtle, good stories about animals or the cycle of life that are good for all ages, such as *Fall of Freddie the Leaf* by Leo Buscalglia, Ph.D. (New York: Henry Holt, 1982), *I'll Always Love You* by Hans Wilhelm (New York: Crown Books, 1988), *The Tenth Good Thing about Barney* by Judith Viorst (New York: Macmillan, 1971), and *Death Is Natural* by Laurence Pringle (New York: Morrow, 1977).
- Use puppets or dolls to create a play with a younger child. You might play a bird that dies; let your child be who she wants to. Set the stage but let her create the story.

---

# DENTIST

*"I want to avoid hassles when we go to the dentist."*

## Ages 2½–3

UNDERSTANDING THE SITUATION

At two and a half to three years old, your child is a perfect age to introduce to the dentist. Your own family dentist may be good with children and a comfortable choice for you. Some families prefer a dentist with a pediatric specialty. Choose a dentist who is patient and enthusiastic with a warm, friendly office atmosphere. Have a friendly encounter that offers your child an opportunity to become acquainted with the dentist and his environment. This will provide the basis for a positive attitude in the event of an emergency or when routine work needs to be done. The more positive exposure, the less chance of later fears.

## WHAT TO SAY AND DO

Age two and a half is not too early for a "happy visit." Many dental offices offer your child (at no charge) a chance to visit, talk to the dentist, and see his or her equipment. Call your dentist and check it out. Then tell your child, *"Marni, Dr. Bud has time to show us his dentist chair. He has a big teddy bear in his office just as big as you!"*

Take your child along to observe a parent's, sister's, or brother's dental exam. Tell her what to expect. *"Jen, you get to go to the dentist today with Katie and Ryan. The dentist will look at their teeth, and the hygienist will clean them. You are a big girl now. Going to the dentist is a grown-up thing to do."*

Use friendly language. Words like *drill*, *needle*, *stick*, and *blood* are scary. Say, *"This is Dr. Bud. These are his tools. Here is his tooth cleaner."*

Many dentists recommend a routine cleaning by age two and a half. Do not insist on a thorough job. The goal is to let your young child have a happy experience.

## PREVENTIVE TIPS

*See: Dentist, ages 4–10*

# Ages 4–10

## UNDERSTANDING THE SITUATION

When your child cries and argues with you about going to the dentist, you may lose all patience for Positive Parenting. Lecturing and scolding won't win cooperation. Never ridicule or label your child a baby or a sissy. Do not argue. Do not bribe. Understand that though he is stubborn, behind his obstinate attitude is usually fear that the dentist will cause him pain. As with all fear, be patient, prepare him in small steps for his visit, and *encourage* with a firm, positive attitude; he is truly a grown-up boy now, and the dentist is someone to trust to help us. Choose a dentist that works well with children. He or she must care about your child's emotional needs as well as his teeth. Look for a warm, welcoming, child-centered office. Keep your own insecurities and past negative experiences to yourself. Your body language and tone of voice will make a difference. A very positive, matter-of-fact attitude builds confidence, and a questioning voice that shows fear and trepidation creates misery.

## WHAT TO SAY AND DO

Motivate. Use the *we* approach with enthusiasm and curiosity. Dental technology today is different from when you were a child. Let your child know you are just like her: You want to know what to expect. *"Elizabeth, this is exciting. You are growing up in an exciting time and lucky to be a child today. Going to the dentist is much better than when I was a child. I can't wait to see what the dentist has to show us."*

Go as a family if possible. *"Malia, we have a dentist appointment Friday."* Give her a sense of control with some choice. *"Would you like me to see the dentist first, or would you like to?"*

Give your child some advance warning that he has an appointment. Be direct and honest. *"Marc, you need to see the dentist today."* This is the time to listen to his fears and *problem solve.* Check your child's perception of who the dentist is and what he does. Do not assume he feels he is a friendly and helpful person. *"Marc, could it be that you are afraid he will hurt you? I understand you are scared. I remember when I was eight and I had a tooth filled. I held my teddy bear. When I was done the dentist gave my bear and me a sticker for being brave! You are brave too!"*

When he asks, *"Will it hurt?"* he wants to know what to expect. Be honest and brief. *"I don't know. I trust Dr. Bud. He will tell you exactly what you will feel and how long it will take."*

Never threaten your reluctant child. *"Brett, if you don't sit still he will drill through your face"* is disastrous. Be kind, clear, and firm. *"Brett, you need to have this done, and it is up to you whether you do it in one or ten visits."* Most dentists today do not believe in forcing a child through a procedure.

If the dentist is unable to accomplish all that is needed because of your child's behavior, leave with a firm, positive message. Say, *"Ryan, the dentist needs a little more time with you. We will come back tomorrow to have him finish the filling."* Because of modern dentistry and improved conditions of children's teeth today, it is often possible to modify or delay a procedure. Six months often makes a difference in how your child accepts the idea.

Do not bribe or reward your child with toys or prizes for going to the dentist. He needs to develop the understanding that he goes to keep his teeth healthy for his own good, not to please Mom or Dad. The dentist may pass out toy favors after the visit. This is recognition for effort, not a bribe. Even if the visit was not a great success, a toy is usually offered. *"Johnny, what a great effort. The dentist loves to see you. Pick out a toy!"*

## PREVENTIVE TIPS

- Take your child to observe other family members' teeth being cleaned. Do not have a fearful child visit while shots of novocaine are given, teeth are filled, or difficult procedures are undertaken.
- Read children's books together, such as *Going to the Dentist* by Fred Rogers (New York: Putnam, 1989), *My Dentist* by Harlow Rockwell (New York: Macmillan, 1973), and *Going to the Dentist* by Stacie Strong (New York: Simon and Schuster, 1991).
- Include brushing and flossing teeth in the morning and bedtime routines. Say, *"Our family motto is, healthy teeth make happy smiles and happy smiles make everyone happy."*
- Role-play, pretending to go to the dentist. Make up a kit for your child that includes toy dental tools. Your dentist may give you dissolving tablets, which are chewable tablets that leave a dark stain around areas that are not brushed well enough, a plastic mouth mirror, floss, a toothbrush, and toothpaste.

*See also: Brushing teeth; Doctor visits*

---

# DIRTY WORDS

*"My child repeats shocking and dirty words."*

**Ages 2½–5**

### UNDERSTANDING THE SITUATION

Many young children will use dirty or shocking words at some time, if only for the intrigue of hearing them, testing your reaction, and seeing if they cause great commotion. Often around potty-training time (which can take a considerable amount of time) you may hear silly and annoying "potty talk." Your child may hear you swear at another driver and later repeat it with the same zest that you used. Watch what you say. She is a mimic; you are her model. It is shocking when your four or five-year-old lashes out at you with angry, mean, or rough talk such as *"I'll slash your face."* This may indicate an underlying tension. Try to pinpoint what may be new in her world to cause this. Your reaction will help determine whether any of this behavior continues. Be firm; tell her such talk is not okay. It is no fun for her if she gets no emotional charge from you. If you are consistent she will soon stop. You may do all the right things and it may not seem to help, and then suddenly the language may go away as unexpectedly as it arrived. It may get worse before it gets better. Keep the faith and be consistent with your calm reaction. The behavior will pass, though it may return at a later age and stage of development.

### WHAT TO SAY AND DO

Don't laugh and encourage your young child to say bad words, even if it is cute. When a two-and-a-half or three-year-old spills out a dirty, four-letter word, he may get a rise of laughter from friends and family. The cute story of what he did may be repeated over and over. This fun usually ends abruptly when he repeats the same performance at a later age and is reprimanded because he isn't so cute anymore.

When your child uses a startling word, appear unimpressed, remain *poker faced*, and respond kindly and firmly. *"Heidi, that's interesting."* Then ask, *"What does it mean?"* Help her learn what the word means. *"That is bathroom talk. It means poop. Do you want to use that word now that you know what it means?"*

Bad words that are repeated by an attention-seeking child are best ignored. If you cannot ignore with a *poker face*, leave the room. If he is distracting in public, remove both of you to a space away from others. *"Roger, we will go back in when you stop the potty talk."*

Relax and lighten up. When your child lashes out with anger using bad words, give *time out. Cool off.* Then explore other words to use instead, with humor. *"Hilary, you were very angry. You used bad and hurtful words to tell me how you felt. We need new words for angry times."* Brainstorm together. *"How about jumpin' toadstools! Blisterin' bottoms! Plucked puckered pigeons!"*

Direct your child to the bathroom for *time out. "Ian, bathroom words belong in the bathroom. Say them in there by yourself."*

### PREVENTIVE TIPS

- Keep a log for two weeks of the times your child uses shocking words. Keep track of the circumstances under which he is using these words, what reactions he gets from others around him, and how you feel when he uses the words.
- At a neutral time, open a discussion about your child's use of inappropriate language. Cover what is appropriate, what is not. Let him know the action you will take if you hear him use inappropriate words.
- Discuss with him where he might be hearing these words. Ask yourself if any of these words are used at home by you or others in your family. If so, stop using these words at home.
- At neutral times, read children's stories together about bad

words. *Elbert's Bad Word* by Audrey Wood (San Diego: Harcourt Brace Jovanovich, 1988) is a fun and humorous fantasy and a great teaching tool.
• Play with rhyming words, silly words, and long words. These create fun and appropriate reactions from others.

## Ages 6–10

### UNDERSTANDING THE SITUATION

It is very shocking when your older child experiments with profanity or rough talk. Your reaction is to feel angry, yell back, scold, or punish. As with the younger child, these are strong words and do create quite a commotion. The child's goal at this age, if not to gain attention by being rude or showing off, is often to get control or revenge. Rather than simply ignoring bad language at this age, it is best to act unimpressed, stay cool, do not appear hurt, and consistently follow through with logical consequences using *action with few words*. Do not forget *encouragement*. Notice all the positive behavior you can, explore what might be discouraging your child, help him find ways to feel better about himself, and comment on his efforts to stop using bad language.

### WHAT TO SAY AND DO

Remain lighthearted. Act unimpressed with the annoying behavior. With a *poker face*, hand him a bottle of liquid soap. *"Randy, use this."* Do not expect him to use it; it is a suggestion in jest.

As with a younger child, give *time out* in the bathroom. *"Larry, those are bathroom words."*

Never talk about consequences when you are angry or hurt. Take *time out* to *cool off*. When you have cooled off, discuss the matter. Tell your child what action you will take if he uses bad words again. *"Trevor, you use bad language more after being with your friends. The next time you talk like that you will lose the privilege of being with friends. You will come home from school and spend more time alone, reading or building with your Erector Set. I'm sure your language will improve."*

When your child is disrespectful to you, it is extremely hard to remain cool. Let him know you are angry or hurt, but do not take your anger out on him. Calmly say, *"Miles, I am amazed you spoke to me that way. I'm really angry and hurt. I need to think about this. We both need time out."* Vent your anger someplace else, cool off, and then work on your relationship. Discuss his feelings and problem solve. *"Miles, I heard you use some very rough language. You were very angry because you felt I was unfair. Am I right?"* Do not judge or criticize. Pause and listen to his feeling. Reflect what he says. *"It sounds as though you feel . . ."* Show understanding and explore. *"I can understand that you were angry. You may not say those words to anyone even if you are angry. What can you do instead?"* Come up with ideas together and pick one. Let him know what you will do if the bad language continues. Notice and comment on improvement.

### PREVENTIVE TIPS

- Watch for the good times and comment on your child's efforts to not use bad language.
- Check out his world. Is someone in his life using these words a lot? Is he around older children? His peers may use similar language, in which case restricting play with them would be in order.
- Have a *family meeting*. List the family guidelines:

  1. We use words to tell others how we feel. We do not name call or use bad language.
  2. We do not hurt others physically or emotionally.
  3. We do not hurt each other's property.
  4. We work to get out of a problem, not stay in it.

- Increase *special time* together. Even if your child seems resistant, tell him you need more time with him. Make an effort to be available for him. Try to find things to do together you both enjoy.

- Join a club with good leadership such as Indian Princesses or Boy Scouts. Find an opportunity to have your child work in a group that involves Mom or Dad.
- Encourage team sports such as soccer or basketball. Seek a coach who will emphasize having fun, building skills, and teaming before winning.
- Talk with your child's teacher and other caregivers. Is this problem happening outside of home? Encourage all those who work with him to use Positive Parenting techniques.

See also: Anger, parent's; Meanness; Talking back

# DISABLED PEOPLE

*"My child embarrasses me by pointing at disabled people and asking questions loudly."*

## UNDERSTANDING THE SITUATION

It is very common for children to be curious, to point boldly and ask questions about a handicapped person. Others are afraid and may stare and shy away. Any overt action is embarrassing to a parent as well as to the stranger, and often no one knows how to react. As the population ages, there will be many more disabled or physically challenged people in our world. More handicapped children are being mainstreamed today into the schools. Your child will see many handicapped people, and you need to take the opportunity to explain about them to dispel any fears. It is important to stress to our children that even though someone may look or act differently, they are people just like us. Learn more about what to say and do and address the issue with confidence and a nonprejudiced attitude.

## WHAT TO SAY AND DO

Do not be embarrassed when your child points and asks questions. Judge the situation and look for eye contact from the person to tell you whether he might want to respond. Many disabled people enjoy talking to children and answering their questions. If he seems approachable, speak to him—using *we* to not single your child out. *"Excuse me. We had some questions about why you are in a wheelchair. Would you mind answering them?"*

Acknowledge your child's feelings. *"Kelly, you are afraid of the man because he looks different. He was injured in the war."* Reassure her he is very human. *"He is probably a very nice man. He may even have his own children. Maybe he is a grandpa."*

This is a wonderful opportunity for you to explain that all people are different, and all have feelings. *"Hilary, that man is in a wheelchair because he cannot walk for some reason. He has feelings just like you or me. He probably doesn't like being pointed at. Would you like to be pointed at?"*

## PREVENTIVE TIPS

- If possible, have your child experience sitting in a wheelchair, moving it or perhaps playing a game of tag in it.
- Play a game leading your child around blindfolded, to experience and thereby understand being blind.
- Wheelchair sports, e.g. tennis and Special Olympics, are becoming more popular and are sometimes televised. Take the opportunity to comment on them. *"Ricky, do you think it is harder to play tennis in a chair?"*
- Point out the special building arrangements for handicapped people when you are out. *"See the ramp the store added for people in wheelchairs? And the bathrooms are bigger too."*
- Visit a center for the handicapped with a scout troop or another group. Many questions can be answered there.

# DIVORCE, QUESTIONS ABOUT

*"My child is curious about divorce and is asking me questions."*

## UNDERSTANDING THE SITUATION

Your child may be exposed to a playmate or a relative whose family has experienced divorce. She may observe a friend of hers going back and forth between two homes. You may be uncomfortable discussing this emotional issue matter-of-factly, but your positive attitude is important. Your child is not asking whether divorce is good or bad; she does not want a moral lecture from you on the topic. She's observing that divorce is very hard for children. Show compassion and understanding from a child's point of view. Her questions may be based on an underlying concern for her friends experiencing divorce and possibly a concern that it might occur in her own family. Entire books are written on divorce; it is a big topic. If it is happening in your family, seek professional advice.

## WHAT TO SAY AND DO

Answer your child's questions about divorce as honestly and matter-of-factly as possible. Do not go into lengthy descriptions of tragedy or lecture about the morality of the world. Ask your child what he is observing.

Your child's questions about divorce may stem from an unconscious concern that this may happen to her family. Affirm your family's security. Say, *"Renee, David's mom and dad decided that they needed to live in separate houses. Your dad and I are very happy in one house with you. Dad and I are not getting a divorce. We love each other, and we will stay married."*

Confirm that your child's friend was not the cause for the divorce. Say, *"Jody, divorce is a grown-up decision. Ryan is not responsible for the divorce. He did not cause it."*

Your child's friend may act out and show changed behavior. Show understanding and compassion. *"Laura, Pam is very upset about her mommy and daddy's divorce. She hits you because she is so hurt that her daddy left. You are not to blame. You are her friend and very important to her. When she hits you, what can you do to try to help her?"* Take *time to teach* your child ways to work with difficult behavior. Brainstorm. *"Tell her you like her but do not like the hitting. Try to distract her or go play something else. You may have to leave if she keeps hitting but go back later."*

### PREVENTIVE TIPS

- Spend family time together. Taking walks, riding bikes, reading, and playing games are all ways to have fun together and reaffirm to your child that your family is healthy and happy. Instead of watching TV, be active together.
- Work on good family communication. Good relationships take work. Model settling arguments with compromise. Share hugs and positive messages, listen and share feelings. Model good anger control. Your child will gain confidence from your positive attitude. She will observe your efforts and mimic them.
- Single parents and their children need outside support. Include divorced friends or relatives in your family activities from time to time. Your child will benefit from your help in creating a community of caring.
- Read with your child *All Kinds of Families* by Norma Simon (Morton Grove, Ill.: Albert Whitman, 1976).

# DOCTOR, SHOTS

*"My child is afraid of shots."*

### UNDERSTANDING THE SITUATION

No one enjoys shots. However, it is the ultimate frustration when your child kicks, screams, and practically has to be hogtied when he has his routine shot, and then begins worrying about when the next one will be. Your threatening, scolding, or punishing will not win his cooperation or build his self-confidence. When you overprotect or pity him, he feels more anxious and sorry for himself. He needs your understanding combined with structure and direction. We must have shots, but we can choose how we take them. Plan his appointment in advance, give him a short warning, and go without haste or hesitation. Tell him he can handle it and celebrate with him when he does. Be sure you have worked through your own past negative experiences and personal fears about shots so that you can shine with a positive attitude. You may have to be a good actor. Being scared is real, and we make choices about how we handle our fears. You are raising a child who is developing courage to be responsible for his own wellness.

### WHAT TO SAY AND DO

Do not be locked into a traditional schedule. Your child may do better to get the shot out of the way first and then see the doctor. Many doctor's offices will allow you to separate the shot from the doctor's exam, though it may cost more. Waiting for the shot increases fear and sometimes ruins the doctor's ability to establish a good relationship. Make an appointment with the nurse or lab just to have the shot and get it done as quickly as possible!

Talk about what your child can do to help reduce her fear before she melts down. *"Elizabeth, it helps to relax and not keep your muscles tense. Let's think of ways you could keep your mind on happy thoughts instead of fear. Close your eyes and squeeze Mom's finger. Count out loud. Use headphones and listen to your favorite music."* Take a favorite stuffed toy along as a friend.

Talk about *choices* before going in. Be firm and kind. *"Tony, you may sit on my lap or on the table. You need the shot today. Try to relax and have it done quickly."*

Celebrate whatever positive effort your child made, whatever she showed improvement on. *"Megan, you struggled far less than you did last time. You are growing up and becoming quite brave! Let's celebrate and go to the park with a picnic."* Do not reward her with toys or candy for getting the routine shot; we all have to have shots to be responsible and take care of ourselves. Have some fun together after the visit by going out to lunch or to the park.

### PREVENTIVE TIPS

- Get acquainted on a happy visit when your child is not getting a shot. Look at the equipment, shot needle and syringe included. Have the nurse explain how the shot works and what it does. One nurse demonstrated on an orange, showing the needle going into the skin.
- Ask a children's librarian or knowledgeable bookstore clerk for books that talk about shots.
- A doctor's kit is a recommended toy. Your child will love giving pretend shots to her dolls or playmates.

*See also: Doctor, visits*

# DOCTOR, VISITS

*"Going to the doctor is a hassle."*

### UNDERSTANDING THE SITUATION

Doctor appointments are very stressful when your child won't cooperate and go willingly. The struggle and hassle is usually based on a fear that the doctor will cause pain. Your threatening, lecturing, and scolding won't win cooperation. Never ridicule or label your child a baby or sissy. Be patient, prepare her in small steps, and encourage with a firm, positive attitude to trust the doctor. Give your child a chance to experience the visit without your own insecurities and past negative experiences influencing her. *"Oh, you're not going to like this one"* is not helpful. Be a good actor if you must. Check your body language, facial expression (if your eyebrows are up you will not be frowning), and tone of voice. Shine with a positive attitude; be matter-of-fact and reassuring. You are raising a child who is developing courage to be responsible for her own wellness, and overprotection with a pampering attitude does not build courage and good coping skills. *Encourage.* Planning for successful doctor visits takes extra time and energy. Be patient!

### WHAT TO SAY AND DO

A good first step for a hesitant child is to become more familiar with the doctor and his or her staff. Call for a get-acquainted "happy visit." Visit again when another family member has an appointment.

Give her warning. You be the judge as to how much time she needs to adjust to the idea that she is going to the doctor. Some children need to know days in advance; some do better just knowing that morning. Be direct, matter-of-fact, and honest with your child. *"Jody, we have a doctor's appointment today. No, you do not need a shot this time. The nurse will have to poke your finger."* Here is where you shine with positive attitude. *"Jody, the new little bandages for fingers are fluorescent. If you bring bear, I'm sure he can have one."*

Do not negate her fear. Do not say, *"You have nothing to be afraid of."* Recognize the fear and be honest. *"Marci, you are afraid that you will have an 'owie.' It is normal to feel afraid."* Sharing a positive personal experience shows understanding. *"I remember feeling afraid to go when I was your age. I took my teddy bear and my little sister too. We all came home with Band-Aids on our arms."* Help her problem solve. *"You do need to go to the doctor. That is not a choice. Let's think of some ways to help you feel more comfortable going to see Dr. J."* Give her time to suggest ideas before you add your own. *"You could bring Tigger. You could bring your friend Brian. You could bring your tapes and listen to stories and songs to help you think happy thoughts."*

Tell the office staff as you arrive what you need. *"Mindy needs a bit of reassurance."* This is good training for your child to be assertive and ask for what she needs. The staff is experienced. Ask for their helpful suggestions. They are very busy, so be patient.

Never slip into bribing or rewarding with toys or prizes. She needs to develop the understanding that she goes to keep her body healthy for her own good, not to please Mom or Dad. Instead, suggest that she bring her favorite stuffed animal on the visit with her.

Comment on what your child is doing well. *"Julie, I'm glad you brought bear along. That is good thinking. You are growing up!"*

Try distracting her with fun things in the office. Rather than sink into an article in a magazine, spend time with her. *"Meg, let's count the tropical fish!"*

Offer choices and remain firm and kind. *"Dr. J. is going to look at your ear. You need to have this done now. You have a choice. You can sit on my lap or sit on the table."*

Never threaten with more fear, as in *"Stacey, if you don't sit still the doctor will give you a shot right now! Then you will have something to cry about."*

**PREVENTIVE TIPS**

- Your child may help participate in choosing the doctor you see. Many clinics have more than one physician to choose from, both male and female. Look for a warm, welcoming, child-centered office. Your physician should care as much about your child's emotional needs as her physical needs.
- Read to your younger child these children's books (some older children like them too): *Going to the Doctor* by Fred Rogers (New York: Putnam, 1986), *Going to the Hospital* by Fred Rogers (New York: Putnam, 1988), *My Doctor* by Harlow Rockwell (New York: Macmillan, 1973), and *Going to the Doctor* by Stacie Strong (New York: Simon and Schuster, 1991). Your children's librarian or a knowledgeable bookstore clerk may have other book ideas.
- Children love playing with a toy doctor's kit. Older children are fascinated with the real equipment. If you are lucky you may be able to locate a real stethoscope, blood pressure cuff, or other authentic instruments and have fun learning with the real thing.

*See also: Dentist; Doctor, shots*

# EATING, HEALTHFUL FOODS

*"My child has poor eating habits."*

## Ages 2½–5

### UNDERSTANDING THE SITUATION

A common struggle for many parents is over what and how much their child eats. Attempts to overcontrol his diet will only create power struggles. Your child's eating patterns will vary as he grows. At times he may appear to never eat; at other times he may appear ravenous. Your long-range goal is to *encourage* your child to be sensitive to his hunger and to be responsible for what he physiologically needs, rather than to eat because he is told to or because he feels a certain way. Supply healthful food at home and structure a regular routine for mealtime, snacktime, and exercise. Take *time to teach* about what our bodies need, and rather than concentrating on forcing him to eat, suggest he eats the healthful food first because that is what he needs. Your consistency and healthy, positive attitude about food are important to provide good modeling, since your child will mimic your habits.

### WHAT TO SAY AND DO

Supply your cupboards with nutritional food. Foods such as chips, cookies, candies, and soda pop are fats and sugars and are not categorized in any healthful food group. Your child may learn by the terms, "Sometimes foods" and "Everyday foods." "Sometimes foods" should be available only occasionally and sparingly to avoid a battle at home.

Take *time for teaching* proper foods. Your pediatrician's office may have a poster of the government-approved pyramid of healthful food groups. The base of the pyramid is the largest food group and makes up the largest part of our diet: grains, breads, potato, pasta, cereal. The next row up contains two groups on one level: fruits and vegetables. The next level finds two groups: milk, cheese, dairy; and meats, poultry, fish, beans, and eggs. The next level is the tip . . . not a food group at all, with no healthful relevance: fats and sugars.

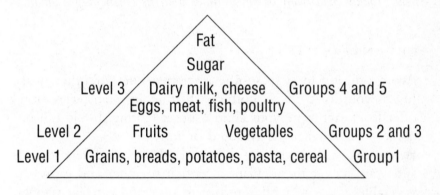

"*Jenny, what do you see on the poster that you ate today? Right! You are helping your body grow and to be strong and healthy.*"

It is important that your child learns to manage the availability of the "sometimes foods." Do not deprive them; children always go after the "forbidden fruit." Occasional exposure at home will help your child be familiar with them and handle them when away from home. Do not nag or threaten, set your *limits* so that he understands your reasoning. Use questions to make him think. "*Ben, Auntie Robin left the cookies. What would happen if you ate all of them today? Right, your tummy would be angry with you! I think your tummy could handle two a day until they are all gone. You are a good decision maker. You decide when you want to have your two cookies today.*"

Model good eating habits. Prepare food and eat together. Studies show that children who eat family meals together eat more nutritiously. Include your child in decision making by offering *choices. "Jamie, we need to eat a healthful breakfast. Would you like pancakes or oatmeal?*" Be creative to avoid confrontation. Pancakes can be made with whole wheat flour and in the shape of Mickey Mouse.

Organize snacks. Because of limited stomach capacity your young child will need to eat small amounts more often than you in order to meet his nutritional requirements. Plan together and prepare healthful snacks in small, sealed containers he can reach in the cupboard, drawer, or refrigerator. Juice can be kept in small containers he can learn to pour from. *"Matthew, if you feel hungry tell me. You may have your snack anytime before 'Sesame Street.' Daddy will want to have dinner with us when he gets home."*

PREVENTIVE TIPS

• Avoid offering food to soothe a scraped knee or other hurts. Just as you don't offer a bottle each time an infant cries, don't offer food each time your child is upset. Eating should not become a habit when he is bored or hurt.
• Be creative with a younger child and offer many different foods and ways to eat them. Plant a garden together and grow the vegetables you eat. Children love to pick and eat raw veggies.
• Establish a regular mealtime routine realistic for your child's age. He may need to eat before the older family members do. If your child is overtired or overstimulated he won't eat well.
• *Bread and Jam for Frances* by Russell Hoban (New York: HarperCollins, 1964), *Yummers—Starring Emily and Eugene* by James Marshall (Boston: Houghton-Mifflin, 1973), *What Happens to a Hamburger* by Paul Showers (New York: HarperCollins, 1985), and *Seven Kisses in a Row* by Patricia MacLaughlin (New York: Harper Trophy, 1988) are great books to read with your child.
• *How to Get Your Kid to Eat . . . But Not Too Much* by Ellyn Satter (Palo Alto: Bull, 1987) is an excellent adult book on children's eating.

## Ages 6–10

WHAT TO SAY AND DO

Encourage your child to help plan meals and even prepare one a week. At a *family meeting,* say, *"Jim, Wednesday night is your night* to prepare dinner. You have great ideas. Decide what we will have and make a list of what we will need to buy when we shop on Tuesday."

Include your child in the shopping and selecting of food for meals and snacks. "Tony, please help me choose the foods we need for our meal plan this week." Increase responsibility as he is ready by giving him a budget when you grocery shop for snack foods.

Self-esteem issues are reflected in your child's eating habits. Discuss feelings openly, and when she is bored or hurt redirect her from food to another activity or discussion about her feelings. A children's librarian or knowledgeable bookstore clerk may suggest children's stories you can read together that convey the message "I like myself unconditionally!"

Offer fruit desserts on a regular basis and not as a reward for a "clean plate." Have cakes and cookies once a week or for a special occasion. If they are not around they won't be tempting.

Encourage your child to listen to his body's cue. If he says he is feeling full, trust him.

## PREVENTIVE TIPS

- Your child needs a routine schedule of regular meals with good food, exercise, and sleep, and he needs you to model this as well.
- Comment when you observe your child using good judgment. She will want to put the candy away until after dinner when you comment on her good decisions.
- Take *time to teach* your child in the kitchen and then trust him alone to prepare food without your critical eye. Let go of your perfectionism. Learning takes place with mistakes.
- Hang a poster showing the pyramid of five food categories and information regarding the amount of calories, fats, carbohydrates, and protein needed daily.
- See book suggestions in Preventive Tips, ages 2½–5.

*See also: Eating, overeating; Eating, picky eating; Mealtime*

# EATING, OVEREATING

*"My child overeats."*

## UNDERSTANDING THE SITUATION

When your child is overweight and overeats, you are likely to worry. Thinness is in! If you have had a weight problem yourself or are close to someone who has, this may be an issue that pushes your button, and you may give it undue attention. Many children go through growth spurts, with a pattern of eating, gaining, and then growing! Children, just like adults, often eat when they feel bored or unhappy. Experts agree that when communication in the home improves and children begin hearing what they do right instead of criticism and judgment, their self-esteem grows and overeating may cease being a problem. Diets are not generally recommended for children. Instead, doctors recommend trying to maintain the weight until height catches up with it. Your child does not need your worry, he needs your unconditional love and *encouragement*, and your show of faith that he will make healthful choices.

## WHAT TO SAY AND DO

Do not call attention to your child's overeating. Fix and serve reasonable portions. He will not overeat if it is not there to eat. Have crisp, fresh vegetables and fruit available for snacking. He may ask for it and have an unlimited amount.

The combination of healthful choices plus increased energy output is most successful in decreasing weight. Keep nutritious foods available and avoid buying foods high in fats and sugars. Make a conscious effort to build exercise and activity into your child's day. Younger children enjoy simple calisthenics, jumping jacks, or running in place in a game of Simon Says. Most children love dancing to music or creative movement. *Encourage* walking, jumping rope, swimming, biking, and other noncompetitive activities.

Overeating is often a symptom of other stress; we eat when we are bored or unhappy. Allow time to discuss your child's day and listen to his feelings. At bedtime say, *"Rob, what was the best part of your day? What was the hardest?"* This often leads to *problem solving*, and you can help him brainstorm solutions.

### PREVENTIVE TIPS

- If your child expresses unhappiness about weight or you have concerns, see a pediatrician and, if he or she recommends, a registered dietitian.
- Model good eating habits. When you have junk food available and you overeat, your child will likely do the same.
- Get in touch with your own issues about eating and self-image. Separate your problems from your child's.
- For your own reading, try *How to Get Your Kid to Eat . . . But Not Too Much* by Ellyn Satter (Palo Alto: Bull, 1987).

*See also: Eating, healthful foods; Mealtime*

# EATING, PICKY EATING

*"My child is a picky eater."*

### UNDERSTANDING THE SITUATION

Many children drive their parents crazy with the few acceptable foods in their diet and the tiny amounts they eat. If you have a "picky eater" and worry about his nutrition, bribe with rewards to get him to eat, or grow angry and lecture and scold, you will surely create problems! Selective eating is a way for your child to learn his likes and dislikes. Have faith that your child has the ability to make good choices. Studies show that even selective eaters get their nutritional needs met without parental advice. Do not get sucked into power struggles with your child by insisting what and when he eats or by permissively letting him control you by preparing just what he demands. Your responsibility is to provide foods that meet nutritional needs, to model eating a variety of foods, and to encourage healthful choices.

## WHAT TO SAY AND DO

Plan together a structured mealtime and snacktime routine. Your selective eater may eat small amounts but be willing to do so more often.

Try to serve some food she will eat at each meal but do not prepare special meals to please her. Provide opportunities to try new foods at mealtime using a "just one bite" agreement. *"Julie, please have just one bite of the sweet potato. You are a good taster."* Do not make an issue over her eating the one bite. She may spit it out onto her plate; that is okay. If she fights or argues with you, it may reflect other issues, so let it go. Food should not become a battleground.

If your child is antsy at mealtime and hops down from the table, have him put his food away until he is ready to sit and eat. This should not be saved as a punishment or put on the menu for the next meal. It is reasonable that it be eaten before any nonnutrional food. *"Brett, put the food in a sandwich bag, and if you are hungry later, come eat it."*

Stop nagging and making negative comments such as *"You don't eat enough to keep a bird alive"* or *"Think of all the starving children."* Be positive. *"You are very sensitive to taste and texture. Some day you may be a famous cook and you will enjoy many foods!"* Over about a week's time, if not nagged, your child will likely eat enough for a balanced diet.

When your child seems to take forever to eat, decide on a reasonable time for the meal to be finished. Allow at least ten minutes more time than you need. Set the timer. When it goes off, tell her the meal is over.

Talk with friends and family privately and let them know you are not concerned about your child's habits. Explain your "just one bite" policy and ask them politely to back off. Say, *"David is a selective eater at this time. He's learning his likes and dislikes."*

*Encourage* your child by looking for times she eats well and makes new choices. *"Julie, you tried the olives! Alright!"*

**PREVENTIVE TIPS**

- Offer raw vegetables. Plant a vegetable garden together. Children often will eat a raw or frozen vegetable before a cooked one, and eating freshly picked food is fun. Be sure to grate or chop it fine for your very young child.
- Read together *Bread and Jam for Frances* by Russell Hoban (New York: HarperCollins, 1964).
- *How to Get Your Kid to Eat . . . But Not Too Much* by Ellyn Satter (Palo Alto: Bull, 1987) is an excellent adult reading choice.
- If you have worry or concern, direct questions to your family physician, not your child!

*See also: Eating, healthful foods; Mealtime*

# EMOTIONS

*See: Feelings*

# EVENING HASSLES

*"Evenings are tiring and frustrating!"*

### UNDERSTANDING THE SITUATION

The worst demands on parents are often at the end of the day—a busy, seemingly nonending time for cooking, dinner, dishes, whining, yelling, homework, fighting, bedtime, up and down and up, etc. Many parents end the day exhausted, feeling pressure to give special time and commitment to the family or community and wondering what could possibly be left for themselves. Many evenings end with tears and battles, an unhappy way to end a day. Evening hassles will never entirely disappear, but if you plan for some peace, designing a routine suited to you and your child's current needs, you both can have a positive, loving ending to the day. *Children do take time, and they need time with a significant adult in the evening after a long day.* You are a wise parent to slow your pace and let go of some of your commitments. Do not forget to take time for yourself. This may be difficult and take tremendous organization and energy. It's worth it. Do it!

### WHAT TO SAY AND DO

Maintain a positive attitude and be honest. If you are tired, tell your child so; don't make him guess or think you are tired of him. Nagging or complaining says to him, *"You are in my way. Just leave me alone."* and causes attention-seeking behavior and lower self-esteem. *"Ronnie, I am very tired this evening. I'm not grouchy because of you. I love you, and I have looked forward to being with you all day."*

Before reading the paper, watching the news, or beginning dinner, sit with him and share some relaxed time. He will do

better after he has had his share of time with you. You are creating a cooperative situation.

Let your child know what to expect. Design a chart together
with daily and evening responsibilities and post it. Draw pictures
for your young child if she does not read. Discuss what she
might do with her free time other than fill it with television.
These are good times to read, play games, and have quality time
together. Redo this chart weekly or as schedules demand.

*Katherine, age six*

5:00:    feed dog Rufus
         set table for dinner
5:30     free time
6:00     family dinner
         clear table
7:00     free time
8:00     bedtime routine

Vary the traditional routine according to needs. Be creative
with your schedule. Some ideas:

1. Hunger can be an obvious reason for your child to melt
   down at the end of the day. A healthful snack prevents nib-
   bling and irritating hounding. Very young children need to
   eat smaller quantities, more often. Prepare snacks of fruit,
   crackers, cheese, and veggies, enough to sustain until dinner.
   Instead of *"Save room for your dinner,"* let the snack be healthful enough to be dinner.
2. Hire a middle-school-age child to come play and help you in
   the late afternoon. Do not attempt to do it *all*, every day.
   Children are exhausting, and you need your energy to be a
   true encourager. A break for you between four and six o'clock
   may make all the difference to you for a successful evening.
3. Baths are very relaxing, a good activity for a tired, very young
   child in the late-afternoon, fussy time. Dad can help at the
   tub while Mom fixes dinner. Have the family dinner and then
   a relaxed bedtime routine.

4. Say no to TV until the end of the evening. Television makes some children very irritable and less involved in contributing. Don't use it as a sitter so you can finish what you need to do. Try having activities at your fingertips so that you do not depend on TV. Make Play-Doh available or set your child up at the sink for water play. Have your older child read aloud to you. Use TV as leverage. *"Hilary, as soon as we do evening chores, have dinner, do homework, and get ready for bed, we'll watch TV."*

Your preschooler will enjoy making an activity out of having a healthful snack while you prepare dinner. For example, let him string Cheerios onto spaghetti.

**PREVENTIVE TIPS**

- Keep your expectations reasonable. What you can expect to get done in an evening with a two-year-old is quite different from what you can do with an eight-year-old.
- Get rid of thinking "the shoulds": *"I should be going to that meeting, I should be cleaning the kitchen, I should have called Grandma."* Talk to yourself assertively and positively. *"I choose first to spend some time with Brian. He is my priority."*
- Transitions are hard for some children, especially when they are tired at the end of the day. Allowing extra time to help your child move through the evening routine will help eliminate hassle. Spend five minutes with him talking or sing a song as you move him from one activity to another.
- Schedule *family meetings*. The weekly agenda should deal with each family member's schedule and needs for that week. Age three is not too early to be involved in planning and decision making. When children participate in family decision making, they are more responsible. They like knowing what to expect. Post a chart of evening schedules for the week, good for a busy family.

*See also: Bedtime, getting to bed; Chores*

# FANTASY

*"My child tells whopping untrue stories."*

### UNDERSTANDING THE SITUATION

You may be frustrated and perhaps worried when your child begins to fantasize to the point where truth and fiction become the same to her. Many children tell tall tales and actually do believe them. This is not to be mistaken for lying. Do not label her a liar. Most experts seems to agree that understanding the difference between fact and fiction develops in stages and that fantasy is extremely important in the development of a child's creative thinking. Fantasy will mean something different to your child at different ages, and it is a wonderful opportunity to use humor with her and share hers as well. The trick is to teach her the difference between truth and fantasy according to her level of understanding without denying or forbidding her the fantasy. Children use fantasy in order to reenact life as they see it, helping them to understand how it works or to reinvent life as they wish it were. Many children use fantasy to deal with stressful situations and find it a good way to handle a sometimes serious and scary world. Lighten up, use humor, and when appropriate, greet your child's stories with pleasure. She needs your loving enthusiasm.

### WHAT TO SAY AND DO

When your child tells a tall tale and you want her to distinguish between the truth and fantasy, do not cross-examine. *("Annie, is that really the truth?")* This causes denial and lying. Say, *"That sounds like a pretend story. You have quite an imagination."* Use humor (but not mocking or sarcastic humor). *"Oh, I see. And then the monkey ate the tree and fell on his knee."* Use "You wish." *"Anna, that is an amazing story. I bet you wish that you did have a horse."*

If she is telling a story and exaggerating the truth, do not scold or admonish, but do not ignore the issue either. *"Slow down, Jana. I need to know what part of your story is the truth and what part is pretend."*

Take *time to teach* your child the difference between truth and fantasy.

1. When the TV is on point out what is real and what is not. *"Joey, the scary monster is only pretend. It is a person in a fuzzy suit."*
2. Pretend play with him. Fantasize stories and plots. *"Jim, I'll be the hurt lion and you be the vet at the zoo. What is my story, how was I hurt?"*
3. Make up stories with your child. Fantasize all you want; make your story big and bold and have him add to it. This is a great way to pass the time on car trips.

### PREVENTIVE TIPS

- If your child observes you embellishing your stories, she likely will mimic you. Watch your own exaggerating.
- Keep a record of the wonderful things she has said or imagined as a child. She will love hearing or reading about what she used to call a "spider," or learning that she used to imagine she could sit on the clouds and look down on everyone.
- Bring short, humorous stories to the dinner table. Riddles are fun. Tell your child what happened to you that day and have her tell you what happened to her. She will likely tell the truth if she feels you care to listen. She won't feel she must embellish.
- Use the fantasy in children's stories to explain emotions, values, or important lessons. *Jessica* by Kevin Henkes (New York: Greenwillow, 1989) is about a child with an imaginary friend. Many such children would identify with this story and be interested to know that other children have imaginary friends.

Talk about the wolf in *Little Red Riding Hood* and explain why we don't talk with strangers; discuss Goldilocks, who enters the bears' home when they are not there. Or talk about Pippi Longstocking, a self-reliant little orphan girl who lives alone with her horse and pet monkey. Though Pippi is fantasy, her characteristics make for thoughtful discussion about capable children in today's world. Read about heroes who are brave and moral and encourage your child to discuss the details and perhaps add her own endings.
• Provide a variety of puppets, dolls, and costumes for creative play. Play is necessary to your child's understanding of the world.

Should she become too immersed in fiction and you become concerned that she is not facing reality, consult your pediatrician or a school counselor.

*See also: Lying; Santa Claus*

# FEAR

*"My child is very fearful, more than most other children."*

## UNDERSTANDING THE SITUATION

Some children seem to face life fearlessly, while others have changing fears all through their childhoods. A truly fearful child can be very demanding and exasperating. We all want our children to be self-confident, and how much easier a child is who tackles life with zest and courage. Your fearful child will gain courage. Do not nag, ridicule, or label him a sissy or a baby. Lecturing or punishing will not make him less stubborn or more cooperative. Do not yell at him or reject him. Though it is very hard to remain patient, take ten deep breaths and *encourage*. Identify the fear and then prepare him in small steps to gain courage and to be assertive. This takes time. Keep your own insecurities and fears to yourself. Research indicates that adults today are quite fearful and easily pass their own fears on to their children. There is a fine balance between teaching your child what he needs to know to be safe and telling him more than he needs to know and scaring him in the process. Think positively, verbalize, and teach him to believe he can handle his fears. Empower him, and in time he will become confident.

## WHAT TO SAY AND DO

Initially, identify the fear. Your child's behavior is only a symptom of what she feels. Hold her, make eye contact, and show understanding. *"Margie, you are afraid you will not be safe if I am not with you."* Reassure her. *"You are very safe. How can I help you?"*

Understand there is a fine balance between empathy and overattention. If you begin to feel very annoyed by a repeated procedure it's likely you are overattending. Appear unimpressed by the fear. *"Lisa, I know you want me to stay. I will stay five minutes, and then I need to go. I know you can handle it because you have done this before."* Limit the explaining. Use a *poker face* and *action with few words.* Do what you say you will do.

Do not overprotect. If you say, *"Joey, I know you are afraid. Come cuddle with Mommy,"* this makes your child feel he has something to fear and that he needs you to protect him. Take *time for teaching* assertion and control over each of his fears. Use role-playing to show him how he can feel safe. *"Scott, we will walk to school together and decide how to be safe the whole way. See the houses you could run up to and ask for help if you needed? Here is a whistle to fasten to your jacket."* Help brainstorm solutions to fearful situations.

Give affirmations and comment on positive efforts and successes. *"You are very brave. I am noticing your efforts to find someone to play with when I leave. You will learn not to mind my leaving. You will learn to trust that I will always come back."*

**PREVENTIVE TIPS**

- Read books on child development to become familiar with the fears common to certain ages. Louise Bates Ames, Ph.D. and Frances L. Ilg, M.D. have written good books on child development.
- Stay on a regular routine. An overtired or stressed child will be more fearful. Have regular, familiar sitters when you cannot be at home.
- Read together children's stories about all kinds of fears.
- Play and have fun pretending. Have your child be a monster while you run away.
- Involve her in physical activities such as swimming, gymnastics, bicycling, soccer, skiing, etc. She will feel stronger and more confident with each accomplishment.
- Make opportunities for her to perform. She can hold a tea party for the family, act in a play for friends and family, learn a musical instrument and give a recital. Performing in front of small audiences is a great way for some children to build self-confidence and feel better about themselves.
- Broaden your child's world. Broaden her experiences with you and other families and other mature adults who enjoy sharing with her and teaching her. Her self-confidence and feelings of self-worth will grow from sharing with people who value her ideas and enjoy being with her, as well as from her hearing their ideas.
- Television can promote a fearful imagination. Limit TV and videos during this stage or eliminate them entirely.

*See also: Baby-sitters; Dark, fear of; Feelings; Strangers*

# FEELINGS

*"My child's feelings seem to control her."*

## UNDERSTANDING THE SITUATION

It's normal to feel tension when your child screams or breaks things in frustration, cries and carries on over disappointments, or yells and races around the room with excitement. The dilemma of wanting to control him but not wanting to squelch his personality can leave a parent feeling helpless. For example, persistence is a quality much needed in today's world, and Eric is a very persistent three-year-old. When he wants something he begs tenaciously, and if begging won't work he cries and carries on; his "water power" usually works to get him what he wants. Eric's mom is reluctant to be too strict—she's afraid she may hurt both his feelings and his spirit—and now Eric has learned to manipulate with his emotions to get his way. While emotions add an important dimension to a personality, no one should use them to manipulate or control. Your goal is to help your child learn the steps to self-control, which is necessary for his self-esteem. This is a process you can begin with a two-and-a-half-year-old. First, you can teach him about his feelings, to identify and begin to understand and not to fear them. *"I feel excited, my friend came to play." "I feel angry, I don't want to share."* Next, you can teach cause and effect, the associations among his feelings, his actions, and the consequences of his actions. *"I was so excited that I knocked the lamp on the floor, and I had to go to time out." "I was frustrated and broke the window, and now I have to pay for it to be fixed."* Next, you can help teach your child that he has choices about how he reacts. He might then decide what he can do differently next time and to be responsible for his actions. *"I'm so mad. But I'll get into trouble if I punch my sister so I'll hit my punching bag. Next time I won't leave my toys where she can get them."* Have patience. Your child will be more emotional when feeling tired, hungry, or stressed, and slip into younger behavior. Developing emotional control is a process; do not expect a finished product in a lifetime. Appreciate and celebrate your child's efforts and progress. Children mimic what they observe at home. You are his best teacher. You're not perfect—no one is—but if you work on understanding your own feelings and communicating openly and honestly to get your own needs met, he will follow.

## WHAT TO SAY AND DO

It is easy to deal with your child's happy feelings such as love and joy, but the bad feelings such as sadness, fear, or frustration need your patient understanding. Never forbid your child his negative feelings. It is not helpful to say, *"You shouldn't feel that way."* Don't ever tell him how he should feel. Your goal is to help him understand how he feels, and then he can choose what to do.

Identify your child's feeling. One little girl called the lonely feeling she had when her sisters were gone the "missing piece feeling." Use *you* messages. *"You feel _____ when (or about) _____ because _____"* Sometimes you can add a helpful suggestion: *"So. . . ."* Relax and be sincere. *"Ryan, you are frustrated because the lid will not fit. Try this one."* Or *"Mary, I know the bees scare you. Hold still, be calm. They will leave you alone."* Or *"Zack, you are afraid you are not safe in the boat. This is a very safe boat and it will never tip over. You are safe!"*

Feelings sometimes are confusing when several come at once and conflict. For example, when a new baby arrives your older child may be excited but also jealous. Or, when your child is very tired and you insist he go to bed, he may feel relieved, but he also would like to be out playing with the older kids. When you explore his feelings with him, you help him understand his confusion.

Don't give in to manipulation. Identify the feeling and state what you need. Do not nag or talk too much. *"Kelly, I know you love the fruit. What you may have is one more apricot."* *"Karen, I*

*know you are hurt. When you cry I cannot hear what you need."* Hold
her and wait for her to calm down.

After recognizing the feeling, help your child design a plan.
You cannot solve his problems for him, but your suggestions may
be helpful. Use *problem solving.* *"Bill, you are nervous about reciting
at school and your tummy feels upset. Let's think of some ways to help
you be less nervous. How about tucking the feeling away in your pocket?
If you want it you can pull it out anytime."* Or, if he is too emotional, let him *cool off* and at a happy time discuss what he might
do differently next time. *"Andy, I know your sister makes you very
angry. Shouting and name calling is not okay. Let's come up with some
ways you can keep from yelling bad words at her when you are angry."*
(Tell her you are angry with your words. Use an old mattress to
jump on, or punch a punching bag. Go into your room and listen to music or blow bubbles.)

If you are unhappy with your child's emotional behavior, remain *poker faced,* use *action with few words,* and leave the room.
*"Jenny, I will come back when you tell me you are ready."* One mom
removed her plate from the dining room to the kitchen and finished dinner there. It may be necessary to give your child *time
out* to deal with his emotions and *cool off.* If you are in public, remove yourself and your child to an isolated area; for instance,
step outside or sit together in the car. One dad put his son in his
car seat and stood outside the car until his son calmed down. Always try to avoid embarrassing your child in public.

After a difficult emotional outburst hold your child and reassure him that you love him. *"I always will love you, though I may
be frustrated with what you do."* Discuss what happened using questions, not a lecture. *"You were excited. What did you do? What happened? Why did that happen? What could you do differently next
time?"* This helps him with the process of learning to be responsible for his actions.

### PREVENTIVE TIPS

• During a late-afternoon talk or at bedtime, your child might
  like to tell you about the happiest and then the saddest or most
  frustrating times in his day. Ask him what he would have

changed. Share the ups and downs of your day with him as well.
- Share with your child a similar experience that you had at his age and the feeling you had at the time. This is a wonderful way to show your understanding of his feelings.
- Model emotional control. Use good communication skills. When you blow it, admit to it and apologize. Have the courage to make mistakes.
- Read together children's books about feelings. Try *Feelings* by Aliki Brandenberg (New York: Morrow, 1984), *Temper Tantrum Book* by Edna Mitchell Preston and Rainey Bennett (New York: Viking, 1988), *Double-Dip Feelings* by Barbara S. Cain (New York: Magination Press, 1990), or *Sometimes I Get Angry* by Jane Werner Watson, Robert E. Switzer, and J. Cutter Hirschberg (New York: Crown, 1986). For an older child, try *The Mouse, the Monster and Me* by Pat Palmer (San Luis Obispo, Calif.: Impact, 1977).

See also: *Anger, parent's; Fear; Temper tantrums*

# FIGHTING, BETWEEN PARENTS

*"My child is upset when I argue with my spouse."*

## UNDERSTANDING THE SITUATION

When you and your spouse argue with loud, irritated, and forceful tones, words, or actions, you may worry your child. Your child is likely a good observer but, like other children, a very poor interpreter. He observes the argument but does not understand what it is about. At this point think of him as a good friend. Would you fight like this in front of a friend? Would you want others to have this argument in front of you? Your child may cry or cling to you for reassurance or retreat to a quiet spot feeling anxious or even guilty that he has done something to cause the unhappy situation. Fighting parents who lose control and possibly say and do things they regret later is unhealthy. Learn respectful ways to deal with conflict in your adult relationship. This is important modeling for your child.

## WHAT TO SAY AND DO

Decide to follow guidelines for dealing with conflict with your spouse. Notice how similar this is to dealing with conflict with your child. Essential tools:

1. Show mutual respect. *Cool off* before dealing with issues.
2. Understand the belief or feeling behind the argument. You may be arguing over money while the real issue is control or fairness.
3. Avoid blaming and focus on solutions. Brainstorm. Hope to reach a win/win decision.
4. Do not try to make the other person do anything. Decide what you will do.

Let your child know what you are upset about. Make it clear he is not involved and it is not his fault. *"Mikey, Dad and I had an argument about the fence. I'm upset, but this is not your fault. It's about the fence. I love you and I love Dad."* Give him a reassuring hug.

Tell your child that you are angry, and separate what you are angry about from the person. *"Jason, I'm angry that your dad was late. I love him and yet I do not like his lateness."* Muster up all the energy you can to *cool off* and then deal with the problem.

## PREVENTIVE TIPS

• Your modeling is your child's number-one teacher. You need to value yourself and model respect for all family members.
• If you blew it and yelled and lost control with your spouse, apologize to your child afterward. Say, *"You don't like me to yell at Mom. I am sorry that I lost my temper. I was upset, but it isn't your fault. There was nothing you could do. I'll try not to do that."*

- Acknowledge that we all make mistakes. They are okay!
- Extreme verbal or physical fighting between parents is abusive and never good for your child. Seek counsel if it is happening.

# FIGHTING, BETWEEN SIBLINGS

*"My kids fight with each other constantly."*

## UNDERSTANDING THE SITUATION

Fighting for the number-one position in the family is a common hassle; every child wants to be the one most loved and noticed. Children compete over everything from who gets out the door first to who sits in the seat by the window. Children begin at birth to observe their world and decide where and how they will belong. For example, Jana at age two and a half watched as her brother Gary, age four, read a book with Mom. She observed Mom's delight that her four-year-old seemed so bright. Jana tried to pick up a book and win the same response but obviously was not able to read and gain the same recognition. She decided her brother was smarter and tossed the book across the room. Another child, possibly more intense, might pull a book from her brother's grasp, slash a book with scissors, or scribble in it to get some recognition, even if negative. Jana became the family clown and was more outgoing than her brother. She danced to music, played ball, and made Mom and Dad laugh as they shared rhymes and stories out loud. With Mom and Dad's help, she found a unique and positive way to feel important to her parents.

Sibling rivalry is affected by:

1. Age and development: How young are your children? How close in age? Are there any disabilities?
2. Gender: Do you have all girls, all boys, or both?
3. Temperament: Is one or more of your children very active,

very intense, more sensitive, or more persistent? Do you have introverts or extroverts? What is your temperament?

4. Placement in the family: The placement of children in the family influences the way children win attention. Often the youngest is babied or spoiled and the older child is assumed to be more responsible. The middle child often becomes the peacemaker.

5. Parent influence: Listening to your kids fight is tiring. Do you constantly nag, nag, nag, or scold and punish with spanking or a lecture? No one is perfect at all times. Do you try to be a Positive Parent?

Encourage your children to resolve their own disagreements. You will need to talk with them about negotiating, sharing, compromising, etc. at good listening times and intervene when safety or values are a concern, but your goal is to help each child feel special and unique so no one has to compete for a place in the family. Clarify the family guidelines and create an atmosphere for positive interaction. Creating loving relationships is a lifelong process. Be patient and keep the faith in your children and yourself.

### WHAT TO SAY AND DO

Most fighting is for your attention. Ignore it if possible. At a good listening time, let your children know what you will do. *"Zack and Zoe, when you bicker it annoys me. I will leave."* Then follow through; step outside and water the lawn, or vacuum the living room. One mom peels carrots with her Walkman on listening to soothing music.

Use humor. Play a popular song and come in lip-synching or dancing. Good, sincere humor can prevent a bad situation.

You will need to curtail emotional hurting such as name calling, ridicule, or rejection, and certainly physical hurting such as biting, hitting, punching, shoving, choking, or unwanted tickling. Refrain from taking sides and with a *poker face* give each child *time out* in separate spaces. Even a one-year-old can go to a time-out area for thirty seconds while an older sibling goes to his room. *"Time out for each of you to cool down."*

At a *family meeting*, establish guidelines. Children do better when they participate in the agreement process.

1. We use words to tell others how we feel. We do not name call or use bad language.
2. We do not hurt each other physically or emotionally.
3. We do not hurt each other's property or our own.
4. We work to get out of a problem, not stay in it.

Intense children need anger control. Thinking stops with intense anger, and at such times they cannot be reasoned with. Take *time to teach* what to do. At a good listening time, say, *"Justin, your anger is real. You need to express it but not on your sister. You may calm yourself by blowing bubbles, kicking the ball out back, or punching your punching bag. Music may help soothe you."*

Ideally you may prevent the meltdown by redirecting the children before a crisis. (Offer another activity, a snack, etc.) You will need to assist at very angry moments. Use your *poker face* and *action with few words* to separate your children. Your consistency is an important teaching tool. Your children will be able to separate themselves eventually.

Disputes are normal and your children should be allowed to work through their arguments when possible. You cannot be the judge and jury fairly. Treat all children in the fight together. A bench works terrifically. *"Jenny and Jess, sit on the bench together. Hop down when you both decide that you can play nicely."* Or, put them in a room together and ask that they draw up one plan that will help them both resolve their problem. Children too young to write can draw a picture. *"You two can work this out in this room. Let me know one solution that will work for both of you."*

A great prescription for fighting siblings is to require they spend more time alone with each other. When friends are along, showing off, teasing, and fighting often occur. Say this with sincerity; it is not meant to be punishment. *"Jenny and Mike, you two need some family time to be together to remember how nice it can be to have each other. This weekend we will spend quality time together to have fun. No friends, no sports. Just us!"*

PREVENTIVE TIPS

- Young children have short attention spans. Change their activities before fighting occurs. It's tempting when they are having a good time to leave them alone, but they will learn to play nicely by your positive reinforcement if you change their play before it erupts.
- Labeling and comparing breed competition, which breeds sibling fighting. Don't refer to your children with labels such as, *"He's the athletic one. He's the fastest of all the kids. She's our clown."* You will always have a concern over some child in your family, but it should never be the same one all the time.
- Your family needs time alone together. The process of planning a trip or an activity encourages team play and is as valuable as the event. Your children may argue through the planning, but they are learning negotiation and compromise. Set aside one night a week to play noncompetitive games, read a short story and discuss its values, listen to older children play musical instruments, let the children plan a talent show or a puppet show, play charades. Go on fun adventures such as bike rides and picnics and let the children help plan and prepare together. Include difficult tasks as well as fun ones. Work together in the yard, lifting and hauling and sharing the effort. A rugged hike or camping experience builds closeness and trust.
- Help strengthen each child's private world. Encourage friendships, and let each child choose school, sports, or musical activities based on individual strengths and interests. (These choices should be based on true preferences, not on a child's fear that he can't do something a sibling can do.) Talk with your children about their differences. Help both the older and the younger remember that they are of different ages, that they will learn at different rates and according to their own learning styles.
- Spend special time with each child in the family. Make lists so that you have ideas about what to do for fun together when

the time comes. With proper planning it can be done. Give separate naptimes when they are little, hire a sitter for one and take the other with you, have Dad take one out on a date, etc.
• Reassure each child often. Tell him that you love him, especially when he has done nothing special to deserve it. Unconditional love for each in the family means *"I will always love you, no matter what your actions are."* Do not assume this is automatically understood. Say it.
• When you talk with friends or family, let your children overhear you compliment their relationship and comment on the fact that they often play together and think of each other.
• Read together children's stories such as *Angelena's Baby Sister* by Katharine Holabird (New York: Crown, 1991), *I'll Fix Anthony* by Judith Viorst (New York: HarperCollins, 1969), *Mama Do You Love Me?* by Barbara M. Joossee (San Francisco: Chronicle Books, 1991), *Bailey the Big Bully* by Lizi Boyd (New York, Puffin Books, 1991), and *The Pain and the Great One* by Judy Blume (New York: Dell, 1985). *Bailey Goes Camping* by Kevin Henkes (New York: Greenwillow/Morrow, 1985) is great for the youngest in the family.
• *Keeping a Head in School* by Dr. Mel Levine (Cambridge, Mass.: Educators Publishing Service, 1990) is adult reading about learning abilities and learning disabilities. This may help you in your talks with your children about their own learning styles. This does relate to their comparing and competing.

*See also: Bullied child; Bullying; Friends, fighting; New baby*

# FLATULENCE

*"My child 'passes gas' on purpose to get my attention."*

### UNDERSTANDING THE SITUATION

Passing gas to show off to peers, or to annoy anyone of the older generation, may be humorous a first or second time, but usually becomes irritating and embarrassing to a parent. This is generally an attention-getting issue that you do not want to emotionally react to. Set clear *limits*. Tell him ahead of time what you will do. Work on building a positive relationship with him at neutral times when he is not misbehaving. Help him win attention for more mature behavior. Remember, the behavior you model will be the behavior you get.

### WHAT TO SAY AND DO

Don't make this too serious! Maintain a sense of humor without encouraging the behavior. *"Scott, you win the award for being the most original this evening. Now seriously, no more!"* If he persists, do not overreact. Give *time out*. With a *poker face* say, *"You may be excused for a time out. Come back when you can be polite."*

If you are in public, excuse yourself and your child and take him to a bathroom. Do not get sucked into a power struggle. If possible, offer a *choice: "Randy, you may go back with the others and be polite, or we will have to go home."* This could ruin your plans, but your follow-through could mean that it won't happen again. He'll begin to believe that you say what you mean and you do what you say you will.

Logical consequences are best discussed ahead of time with your child. *"Zoe, your breaking wind has become annoying and embarrassing. If it doesn't stop, you'll need to come home after school for a week. No friends, no activities, no public places."* Or *"We will leave you home tomorrow night when we go to the movies if you can't be polite tonight."*

## PREVENTIVE TIPS

- Spend special time weekly with your child. He needs to know from you and other significant adults that he is worthwhile and enjoyable to be with.
- Watch for what your child does right; comment on that and ignore annoying behavior. When you talk to other people in front of your child, let him hear a positive comment about himself.
- Explore outside activities such as sports, art, music, etc., in which he may feel successful.
- Do fun things with other families and their children, such as hikes, barbecues, etc. Seeking negative attention may become less important when your child is part of a fun group of children and their parents.

# FRIENDS, CHOOSING

*"I do not like my child's friend."*

## UNDERSTANDING THE SITUATION

You will be able to choose your child's playmates when she is very young. As your child grows older she may from time to time choose to play with someone you would not have chosen. This is normal, though it can be troubling to a parent. She is learning who she is and who she wants as her friends, and it will be a process of trial and error. Do not be openly critical with negative comments. When you judge or criticize her choice of friends, you are criticizing her wisdom and judgment, so important to her self-esteem. As hard as it may be, these are the years to let her experience many types of people without your criticism and judgment. Your hands are not tied, however; you are the parent, and you need to *set limits* on her behavior. Encourage many different friends. Encourage independence from any one peer group and teach your child to be assertive and feel good about herself! Show her you trust her to make good decisions for herself. Think about what you learned from different friendships you have had and ask yourself, am I trying to control her learning? You may hear criticism from friends and family. Do not treat your child differently because of what others may think about your parenting. Listen to all positive support, think for yourself, and do what you believe is best for your child.

### WHAT TO SAY AND DO

When your child is of preschool age you still have control about which children she invites to play. Take *time to teach* her your values regarding friendships and still allow *choices*. *"Holly, he is a very rough boy and breaks toys. He needs a lot of my attention when he comes. I haven't time this week. Parker plays nicely, and you always have fun with Kate. Who would you choose today?"*

Do not criticize the friend. Rather than blame or accuse with *you* statements, say "I feel . . ." and explain to her kindly. *"Rosie, I'm very upset because when you play with Jill you talk back to me with rough talk that we do not use in this family."* Try hard to separate what she is doing from her self-worth. You love her; you just don't like what she is doing.

*Set limits* on the unwanted behavior and together establish the consequences if the behavior continues. Ask your child to state the rule. *"Rosie, what is our rule about using bad language?"* A possible consequence would be *time out* from the friend. *"You will not be able to play with Jill at her house or here for two weeks if you choose to continue to use rough language."* This choice allows her a way out of the friendship if she needs one.

*Encourage* good choices. *"Rosie, today when I was at your school I watched you work with Marti. Would you like to have her over sometime to play? You two seemed to be having a great time together!"*

**PREVENTIVE TIPS**

• Take time to be alone with her. At bedtime give her an opportunity to talk about her day. *"What was happy, what was sad?"*
As she talks about her feelings, you may learn why a child you
dislike appeals to her. Low self-esteem may be a reason for
latching on to this friend.
• Read together a delightfully illustrated book, *Edward the Emu*
by Sheen Knowles (New York: Angus and Robertson, distrib-
uted by HarperCollins, 1992), and an old classic, *Best Friends
for Frances* by Russell Hoban (New York: HarperCollins, 1969).
These are children's books that all ages enjoy.
• Make a wish list of all the children she would like to have as
friends. Discuss what she likes about them and what they may
have in common. Encourage her to think of ways to make
friends with them. She needs your vote of confidence.
• Encourage other friendships. Have her invite other friends over
and plan activities to help her establish good relationships. Join
other families for activities such as picnics, camping, or biking.
Close bonds develop with children of families you enjoy and
respect and prevent peer pressure later.
• Volunteer in her class, drive car pools for field trips, and actively participate in getting to know the children in her class
and in her activities.

*See also: Friends, lack of*

# FRIENDS, FIGHTING

*"How do I stop my child from fighting with her friends?"*

## Ages 2½–5

### UNDERSTANDING THE SITUATION

It is normal but disturbing when your young child fights with playmates. It is very hard for a parent to know when to step in and how to resolve the fight. Very young children do not interact with other children much; playmates are important, but most play alongside one another, not with each other. Between three and four your child will begin to have fun playing with other children and will need your help with socialization. Fighting between friends at this age is often over *"what is mine and what is yours,"* or *"who got the most,"* or *"who will be first."* Comparison and competition are significant issues at this age. Some children with strong temperaments are quite territorial and fight with others more on their own turf; some children are more intense and have trouble with transitions and sharing. Some children have a competitive home environment and are used to fighting with their siblings or have learned to win adult attention or gain control of a situation by fighting. Your child and his friend need your support to acknowledge each other's feelings and your help in finding solutions. Establish guidelines and create an environment conducive to having fun. Have faith in both children. Even though they are young, you do not have to mediate every situation.

### WHAT TO SAY AND DO

Your child needs to have her feelings recognized. When she learns to identify her feelings, she will begin to gain self-control. *"Rosie, that hurts Heidi. You seem very angry."* Next, give direction. Tell her what she can do. *"Rosie, you may not hit her. Tell Heidi what you need with your words."* You are beginning to teach both of them assertion.

Give *choices* to both children together. *"You two have a choice. Either you share the toy or I will put it away."* Very young children can learn from such an example the consequences of their actions; be sure you follow through.

No one reasons when angry. Give both children *time out* to *cool off.* Two three-year-olds who played together regularly were put on a bench and told, *"You two are angry. Cool off, and when you are ready to play together hop off the bench."* Very young children can find solutions together if this method is used consistently. Others, when intense, will have to be separated to cool off.

## PREVENTIVE TIPS

- Young children have short attention spans. Listen to voice tones as loud, irritated tones indicate that trouble is starting. Try redirecting the children to something different before this happens.
- Read Preventive Tips for ages 6–10.

# Ages 6–10

## UNDERSTANDING THE SITUATION

Listening to your school-age child argue with another child is frustrating. The noise is irritating, and occasionally you may see some behavior you used as a child that you hoped your child would not inherit. We all want our children to get along with others, to be thoughtful and accepted. This tends to cause us to jump at resolving their problems. Be a supportive parent by letting the children know the rules before play begins. Empower them by letting them know they can handle disagreements. Stay out of arguments unless they become emotionally hurtful or physically unsafe. Remain positive. Notice and comment on what they do right. Be careful not to compare children, because competition breeds fighting. Even good friends put each other down to make themselves feel better. Thinking stops when there is intense anger, and that is not the time to teach. If you need to intervene, give each child time to cool off before reasoning, understanding feelings, or coming to a solution. At good listening times, take *time to teach* your child people skills: making and keeping friends, assertion, handling anger, resolving conflict, and cooperating with others. Have patience. Teaching social skills will be ongoing. Fighting with friends is normal and one way your child will learn needed social skills that he will use his whole life.

See also: *Understanding the Situation for ages 2½–5.*

## WHAT TO SAY AND DO

Be unimpressed with annoying, attention-getting arguing. Show your faith and trust in the children to resolve their own problems. Leave the area if you cannot ignore it. When it is over, give *encouragement. "Wow, you two worked that one out well! You two are really something, you are good friends! How about joining me outside for a picnic lunch. You played so well that I had time to pack a good one!"*

When the children are very angry, their thinking stops and they won't reason. Identify their feelings and ask them to take *time out. "Hilary and Hank, you both are very angry. Please take time out to cool off."* Later, if you find a time when they will listen and talk with you, acknowledge their feelings, show understanding, and explore a solution. *"You were both very angry. I could see how much you both believed you were right."* Questions make them think. *"What could you do next time to resolve the situation without such a fight?"*

One alternative when fighting damages, either with bad words or actual violence, is to interrupt but not take sides. Speak to both parties together. *"Jenny and Josie, I didn't see who started this fight. It is out of hand. You two sit on this bench together. When you both agree to play together without fighting you may hop down."*

Give both a *choice.* Again address them together, placing no blame. Calmly and kindly say, *"Joey and Colin, you are fighting in a hurtful way. You both have a choice. I can take Colin home, or you two can agree on how you will settle the argument in a friendly way."* Wait for the two to decide. Do not get sidetracked resolving their spat, just focus on their decision about the choice you offered. *"Alright, you both want Colin to stay. Sit on the couch and decide how you are going to resolve the argument. Let me know."* If the fight continues, take Colin home. Tell them they can try to play again sometime soon.

### PREVENTIVE TIPS

- Set limits about your child's and his friend's play before it begins. Be clear about the consequences if they do not get along and identify something good that will happen if they can be a good team. (The friend can stay longer, stay for dinner, etc.)
- Bored children, tired of their own play, will fight. Supplement their play with an art project, charades, or a game of ball if you sense they are getting bored. This teaches them to change activities on their own.
- After the friend goes home, at a good listening time, comment specifically on what your child did well. Discuss the trouble spots; acknowledge your child's feelings and explore how the other child may have felt. This is when you teach assertion and *problem solving.*
- Join other families for activities such as picnics, camping, biking, etc. Your child will observe many people interacting and build bonds with children her own age as well as those who are older and more mature.
- Read together children's stories about friendship to stimulate discussion about people skills. *I Want to Play* by Elizabeth Crary (Seattle: Parenting Press, 1982) is a how-to-make-friends book to use together. *Manners* by Aliki Brandenberg (New York, Greenwillow Books, 1990) and *Communication* by Aliki Brandenberg (New York: Greenwillow Books, 1993) are two wonderfully illustrated books for all ages on the topic of interpersonal relationships. *Camper of the Week* by Amy Schwartz (New York: Orchard Books, 1991), *Old Henry* by Joan W. Blos (New York: Morrow, 1987), and *Because of Lozo Brown* by

Larry King (New York: Viking, 1988), and *Chester's Way* by Kevin Henkes (New York, Greenwillow/Morrow, 1988) are all lighthearted picture books about friendship and are fun for all ages.

*See also: Bullied child; Bullying; Feelings; Sharing*

# FRIENDS, LACK OF

*"My child has trouble making and keeping friends."*

## UNDERSTANDING THE SITUATION

*"Jenny wouldn't play with me." "Nick was captain in p.e. and didn't choose me for his team." "The kids moved to another table when I sat down to eat my lunch with them."* Distressing comments such as these commonly come home with children. *"They didn't invite me, she doesn't like me"* is very hurtful to hear from your child, yet very normal. No one wants a child's feelings hurt; old feelings of some rejection you experienced as a child may surface, making you even more sensitive to her hurt. You want your child to feel accepted, and you may feel a strong need to protect her feelings and fix difficult situations for her. Yet too much parent involvement can be very discouraging. Your goal is to help her feel she is capable of making and keeping friends. Listen, support, and give her the responsibility of working through her relationships. Help to prepare her for positive interactions in school years. This will carry over into adult life. She needs your sense of humor to help her learn give-and-take and not take life too seriously. She needs you to listen so that she will learn to understand her feelings in order to act assertively. She needs you to observe interactions when she invites others to play. She needs you to explore with her what she may do, rather than to bribe friends with treats or fancy outings. She needs your faith and confidence. Be

patient. This is a learning process that takes years. For some children, making friends is as easy as falling off a shelf, and for others it's like pushing against one headwind after another, but it is an issue for all children.

Note: Friendship problems are common and very normal. However, do not belittle your child's complaints about loneliness. If your child mentions this often, it is a signal. Listen, offer support, and watch for behavioral changes such as interrupted sleep, loss of appetite, or irritability, to name a few. Talk with her teacher about her behavior at school. Talk with the school counselor and, if suggested, seek counseling.

## WHAT TO SAY AND DO

Be careful not to assume your child is lonely because you see her alone. Being alone and being lonely are different. She may have a temperament that seeks more space and fewer people around. She may be an observer at this age and like standing back rather than jumping in. Inquire from her teacher if loneliness seems to be a problem, or listen for an indication from her that she feels upset about being alone.

Check your child's perception about how many friends he feels he needs. Some children feel everyone in their class must like them, then feel bad when they don't.

Encourage friendships with younger children. Playing with a younger child often builds confidence. Invite a younger playmate over. Some school-age children play at recess with children a grade or two younger. The older child often feels more skilled and less intimidated at play.

Your young child needs supportive adult supervision, as well as exposure to other children. Ideally, find an intimate playgroup or day care where children are encouraged to work out their own differences, with adults reinforcing proper behavior when necessary.

Take *time to teach* people skills to your older child. Do not assume she knows how to go about making and keeping friends. Talk with her at a good listening time. *"Mattie, the best way to make a friend is to just be yourself! Act like yourself. Find someone who*

*likes the same things you do. Ask questions to show an interest in her.
'What do you do after school?' Tell her about yourself. 'I like trolls,
and I made a big house for my collection.' If you get along and have
similar interests, invite her over to play."* Role-play if she shows interest.

When she is discouraged, do not try to fix the situation. Help
her identify her feelings and show understanding. This leads to
self-evaluation and will help her decide what she can do. Listen
and reflect back what she is feeling with a *you* message. *"You
feel . . . when . . . because . . ."* Be sincere. *"Suzanne, you feel
afraid when Kate doesn't invite you over to play because you feel you
will be left out."* It is natural for you to want to give advice, but
what she needs is for you to assist her to explore and discover.

She needs your understanding. *"Margie, I remember when I was
eight and my best friend Molly invited someone else to the fair. I felt really hurt!"* Help her to problem solve. Ask questions. *"What
would you change if you could? What could you do differently next
time?"* Or *"What could you do to feel better?"* Suggest that she
brainstorm ideas and decide on one or two. Do not be too quick
to think for her. When you *encourage*, you help to build her confidence, and assertion will follow.

When your child invites a friend over, have one or two organized activities to warm up the atmosphere and then let them
play alone. Be inconspicuous observing her interaction with others. Too much of you and your interfering is pressure. Take *time
for teaching* later; point out something she does well. *"Brianne, I
noticed you shared your candy with Molly. You are very generous."* Is
she bossy, timid, too aggressive? Are her feelings hurt too easily?
*"Jessie, Molly will want to play with you more when you learn to share
your toys."* Or *"It is no fun to come to play when you tell her what
to do. Try asking her what she wants to do."*

*Encourage* her to make an effort. *"Jen, pick up the phone and call
Leslie to play."* Do not give up. She may not do this easily. Be
flexible and persistent. *"Okay, this time you dial and I will talk.
Next time you do the talking."*

Try not to embarrass your child by correcting her in front of
her friends. If possible, wait until later. Or leave the friend with

an activity and excuse yourselves to work through the problem privately.

## PREVENTIVE TIPS

- If you have an only child, provide many opportunities for social interaction. If you have two or more children, encourage sibling friendships. All friendship thrives on cooperation. Comparing your child to other children will not promote strong friendships, only competition.
- Do not worry your child with your concern, but do use your resources:

  1. Ask her teacher for observations. Are there indications she is having academic or social problems?
  2. Volunteer in the classroom. Observe her with other children and become acquainted with her peers and their parents.
  3. Keep in mind that tutoring boosts academic performance, which in turn builds self-esteem and social confidence.
  4. Talk with the school counselor. He or she may be willing to talk with your child and offer support. Some school counselors have a "lunch bunch," a small group of children who eat lunch together once a week and discuss social issues at school. Children need support groups with qualified leadership.
  5. Gain insights from coaches involved with your child's activities.

- Spend fun, quality time with other families. Bonding with other adults and their children strengthens a child's self-esteem and enhances the ability to interact with peers.
- At good listen and talk times, such as bedtime, offer to listen about your child's day. *"What did you feel happy about? Was there anything sad?"* This is a good time to share feelings and discuss what it feels like to have and be a friend.
- Read children's books together. *I Want to Play* by Elizabeth Crary (Seattle: Parenting Press, 1982) is a how-to-make-friends

book to use with your child. Also try *Making Friends* by Fred Rogers (New York: Putnam, 1986), *Chrysanthemum* by Kevin Henkes (New York: Greenwillow/Morrow, 1991), *George and Martha* by James Marshall (Boston: Houghton Mifflin, 1972), *Fat Fat Rose Marie* by Lisa Passen (New York: Henry Holt, 1991), and *Earl's Too Cool for Me* by Leah Komaiko (New York: HarperCollins, 1988).

- Begin when your child is age six or seven to teach her journal writing as part of the bedtime ritual. *"Jill, this is your own private book. Write about what you did during the day, and some of your thoughts and feelings. When you read it over time you will see how you've changed and grown."*
- Spend *special time* together. Plan to do something you both enjoy, such as taking a bike ride or going to the zoo, or do something unexpected that you've never done, like having breakfast on a ferry boat. Have fun together! She needs to feel you enjoy being with her as much as you enjoy being with your best friend.
- Become involved in the school community. Meet other parents and help with school functions.
- Find outside groups for children that have excellent leadership, such as a scout troop, an athletic team, an art or music class, etc. Team sports such as baseball, soccer, or basketball with good coaching encourage good interaction.

*See also: Bossiness; Sharing; Shyness*

# GRADES

*"My child's grades aren't what I expect."*

### UNDERSTANDING THE SITUATION

When your child brings home a report that shows poor marks he most likely feels like hiding it, or giving it to you and running. Poor grades are discouraging to both parents and children. Unfortunately, too many parents base their child's "success" on a grade, whereas his progress should be based on his effort and understanding. Do not use *any* grade as an absolute indication of his progress. Be a supportive parent, aware of his learning process and progress on a regular basis. His grades are secondary to this and most likely will improve with your continued interest and *encouragement.*

### WHAT TO SAY AND DO

Grades too often become the labels that reflect the child's identity. Your child should never be labeled, "Our *A* child." That sets her up to believe she is worthwhile only when she is perfect and makes *A*s. Then, how does she feel when she gets a *B*? The child who receives *C*s may decide that's all she can do, why try for better? This surely could limit her from reaching her potential. Your child may do *Unsatisfactory* work with one teacher one year and yet the following year, because she matures, listens, and understands better, *or* relates to another teacher better, raise her grades to *Satisfactory* +.

When your child brings schoolwork home, regardless of the grade, look and comment on what was right and what she learned. *"Sally, seven words are spelled perfectly."* Many teachers mark wrong answers. Children do better when the mark is about what is right; that gives something concrete to help them improve on.

You will be more encouraging if you let go of your perfectionism and not push your high expectations on her. Let her grades be hers, not yours. Ask her how she feels. *"How do you feel about these grades? What are you most happy with? What would you like to change?" "What is your goal for this quarter in this class?"* And offer support. *"I'm here in the evenings to help. I am always happy to drive you to the library."*

When stating how you feel, separate the work or the grade from her and be specific. A good format; "I feel ____ about ____ because ____ ." *"I am frustrated with the grade because I did not see you put much effort into learning the material."* Or *"I am excited about this grade because I know you worked very hard and learned your facts."*

Confer with your child's teacher anytime you have a concern regarding school. Do not feel you must wait for the scheduled conference time. Conferences held with your child, you, and the teacher are most effective. This is about your child and she will feel more responsible for her actions if she is asked to participate.

Teach your child that mistakes are okay. Stimulate with thinking questions. *"Bill, mistakes are often the way we learn best. What will you do differently next time?"*

Work for overall improvement rather than perfection. Comment specifically on what she has learned. *"I noticed you are now up to eighty on the times test."* Instead of *"I'm so proud of you,"* say, *"How does that make you feel?"* Encourage her effort. *"You are really putting a lot of energy into this. Nice work!"*

Do not compare good grades or bad grades with any other child, especially siblings. Each child's learning is unique to her. Children will automatically compare themselves.

### PREVENTIVE TIPS

• Be a good observer. Watch your child at home following directions, observe his interests, watch as he learns new skills, tackles new situations, or plays with other children to get an insight into how he learns. Share your observations with your child's teacher. Some children are not ready to read until third or fourth grade. Should a child have *D*s or *Unsatisfactories* shoved in his face because he isn't developmentally ready for the school's schedule? Your child may be a kinesthetic learner, needing to see and do an activity to learn. The teacher may lecture, using a more auditory approach. One child may learn numbers with quick lessons from a text. Many others need rods or cubes to count and measure. An active child may do better sitting at the front of the room to help him focus.

- Take *time for teaching* him about the system. At the beginning of the school year show him a blank report card, the areas for comments and grades. He will apply more effort when he knows what to expect.
- Be home to help support a homework program in the late afternoon or early evening. Show him learning is a priority.
- Hire outside tutoring to encourage learning and help with areas that need reinforcement. This may be costly, but in the long run it is a wise investment. If you are financially unable to, talk with your child's teacher, principal, or counselor. Some schools have volunteer tutors. Children given extra needed help show an increase in *self-esteem*.
- Take an active role in your child's learning. Check with the teacher about a way you can visit or volunteer in the class. Many working parents find time to go on a field trip, or read with children just thirty minutes a week.
- Invite children over to play and encourage friendships. Encourage outside activities, such as athletics, music, art, or drama. These areas will strengthen his self-image and help make school a fun and interesting challenge.

*See also: Homework*

# GRANDPARENTS

*"My parents criticize my parenting."*

## UNDERSTANDING THE SITUATION

A common, frustrating parenting issue is conflict with grandparents over discipline. Many grandparents say that the parenting approach today is too permissive. (They may be right.) A frequent comment: *"She will be a brat, never spanked or punished as you were. Why, you turned out all right."* They remember the authoritarian style: children seen and not heard, "Do as I say because I said so," no choices, and all discipline from without. Other grandparents tend to spoil their grandchildren, showering gifts, candy, and treats on them, feeling that discipline is your responsibility. Positive Parenting and Positive Grandparenting are one and the same. Ideally, your child needs both sets of loved ones to use the same positive approach to discipline. Children today are very fortunate if they have active grandparents who are willing to learn new parenting styles. The world is not the same as when you were young. Your child will be exposed at a very early age to more choices than you ever were. Today, any significant adult in your child's world needs to set limits with him and follow through with the Positive Parenting basics.

## WHAT TO SAY AND DO

No one wants to be criticized. Your body language, facial expressions, and tone of voice will show disapproval even if you say nothing about what you are feeling. Blaming statements are hostile and put others on the defensive. *Cool off*, then identify the grandparent's feeling. *"Mom, you feel frustrated that I do not spank Eric. You feel afraid that he will grow up with no self-control."* Use questions. *"Would you like to know our thinking about discipline?"*

Explain why you handle a situation the way you do. *"Mom, parents are learning today that children need choices to feel capable and gain self-control, which is important to healthy self-esteem. I do not make Ricky eat. I offer him a limited choice of foods. He can sit at the table and eat or hop down and wait until 3:00, when I'll offer a healthful snack. He is learning responsibility for his actions and how to make good choices for himself."*

A certain amount of spoiling with gifts and attention is good for your child in today's stressful world. Spending the evening one-on-one, being read to, going on a special outing, getting some new clothes or a toy can be wonderfully special to your child and helpful to you.

Watch for what your parent does well with your child. Comment on it often. Be specific about what you like. Encouragement works wonders at all ages! *"Dad, you have a sense of adventure that Johnny really enjoys. He loves to fish with you. You encourage him when you have him bait his own hook. He learns self-confidence with you."*

Your parents may not agree with all your parenting ideas. That is to be expected. However, all caregivers should support Positive Parenting. If your parent refuses your suggestions and continues to criticize, spank, etc., tell him how you differ. Refrain from asking him for baby-sitting help.

### PREVENTIVE TIPS

• Offer good Positive Parenting material for the grandparents to read. Today, excellent videos, audio cassettes, and books are available.
• Classes for parents and grandparents are often offered at hospitals, health centers, schools, senior centers, etc. Check your local newspaper and invite your parents to attend one with you or on their own.
• Spend time together without your child and show an interest

in and appreciation for your parent. Everyone needs appreciation.

• Spend time with your child and your parent and model Positive Parenting techniques.

# HEAD BANGING

*"My child gets so angry he bangs his head."*

### UNDERSTANDING THE SITUATION

Head banging and breath holding are common forms of temper tantrums. When your child is so angry or frustrated that she bangs her head, most likely you intervene. This behavior usually gets a lot of attention, which makes it worthwhile to your child. Your long-range goal is to help your child understand that she cannot control or manipulate with this action, and to help her learn to deal with her anger without hurting herself or others. You will achieve this in small steps. Be patient; it will take some time. Not every technique will work with your child. Pick one and be very consistent. The behavior may get worse before it gets better. Have faith in her and do not give up in frustration.

### WHAT TO SAY AND DO

Appear unimpressed with the head banging. Take away the social advantage; if no one attends to it, what fun is it? Let her know what you will do when she bangs her head. Do it and be consistent. If you can, remain *poker faced* and ignore her behavior or leave the room.

Alternatively, stay with her, *poker faced*, and hold her and rock her and hum. Even if she kicks and screams, your calmness will pass to her.

When she is calm, hold her and help her identify her feelings. *"Laura, you were very angry. You wanted me to take you to Sam's. Sometimes you want to be the boss. You want to control and when you can't, you get frustrated and bang your head."* Show understanding. *"I understand how you feel. When I was five I got so mad that I slammed the back door and broke the glass. Everybody feels that frustrated sometimes."*

Brainstorm ways she can handle her anger differently. Ask for her ideas before you offer yours. *"Shelly, head banging can hurt you. What else can you do when you feel that frustrated? You do not want to hurt yourself or others."* Some children learn to use a punching bag, jump on an old mattress, or kick an old cardboard box. (Note: Some children get *more* wired when venting anger this way. These are not good activities unless they are timed and stopped.) Some children do better with a more calming activity such as taking a warm bath or shower, listening to music, walking around the block with you, or blowing bubbles. Help her decide on one, and help her to follow through.

## PREVENTIVE TIPS

- Discuss what causes your child's anger and help her to understand strategies that might prevent it. *"Cheri, you do not want Kevin to have your toys. Let's choose the ones you want to keep from him, and we will put them in your own private place. He can then have the ones that are out."*
- Read together children's books about control and anger. Ask a children's librarian or knowledgeable bookstore clerk for up-to-date titles.
- Catch your child getting what she wants in appropriate ways. When she asks nicely, comment on that. When she handles disappointments, compliment her. Notice her efforts. *"Carli, you have not banged your head for two days. When you were angry with me you told me in words. Nice effort! How does it feel?"*

*See also: Temper tantrums*

# HITTING

*"My child hits other children and adults."*

## UNDERSTANDING THE SITUATION

Hitting is often due to frustration. Some young children who cannot talk well hit to get what they want. Hitting may be a bid for attention or control. Your child may think, *"I belong when I hit. Mom gets worried and spends time with me."* Or *"I can make Johnny give me what I want."* Or *"He cries when I hit him."* Many children hit when their boundaries are invaded. When other children get too close or push or shove, even if by accident, some children feel exasperated and hit. This behavior is embarrassing to a parent. We all want our children to be accepted and well adjusted, and no one will want to play with a child who hits. Act immediately when he hits, kindly and with a firm *poker face*. Other people may tell you what you should do, and you may feel terribly guilty in public. Kids will be kids, and some kids hit. Your child needs your unconditional love. *"I love you very much, though I do sometimes get frustrated with what you do. Hitting is not acceptable behavior."* It may take some time to remedy this behavior, but do not give up the faith. It can be done. Be consistent with your follow-through at home, at school, and in public.

## Ages 2½–5

### WHAT TO SAY AND DO

Never slap your child for hitting. Do not take your anger out on your child, even to teach him a lesson. When you spank or swat your child you are only teaching him to hit when he wants attention, when he is angry, or when he feels hurt.

Remove him with a *poker face* to *time out.* *"Nick, you are very frustrated. Take time out to cool down."* When he is calmer, say, *"Nick, when you hit other children you will have time out."* Help him learn other ways to get what he wants: Use words, trade or negotiate, ask an adult for help.

Provide adult supervision to help him identify his feelings, understand what he wants, and learn new ways to get it. Before he hits, say, *"Gary, you want the truck. Let's find a toy to trade with Mark."*

If hitting has been a persistent problem with your child, give him warning. *"Morgan, we are going over to Michael's. If you hit anyone, we will have to come home."* If he hits, follow through. *"I'm sorry that Morgan hit you, Michael. I see that you have decided to go home, Morgan."* Leave even if he kicks and screams and promises never again to hit. Let him know that he will get another chance. *"Morgan, we will try again tomorrow."*

When he plays well with no hitting, notice and comment. *"Lex, you played with no hitting. That is terrific! How do you feel?"*

**PREVENTIVE TIPS**

- *Set limits* at home. Post your family guidelines. Young children will learn them when you read them often and will remember them when away from home. Some parents illustrate them for younger children.

  1. We use words to tell others how we feel. We do not name call or use bad language.
  2. We do not hurt others physically or emotionally.
  3. We do not hurt each other's property or our own.
  4. We work to get out of a problem, not stay in it.

- Simplify the play situation. Your child may do better with fewer children, or there may be children with whom she plays particularly well.
- Keep play sessions short and successful. Leave before she gets frustrated and hits.

• Talk about feelings and together read children's stories about them. Try *Sometimes I Get So Angry* by Jane Werner Watson, Robert E. Switzer, and J. Cutter Hirschberg (New York: Crown, 1986), *The Temper Tantrum Book* by Edna Preston and Rainey Bennett (New York: Puffin Books, 1976), or *Feelings* by Aliki Brandenberg (New York: Morrow, 1984).

## Ages 6-10

### UNDERSTANDING THE SITUATION

Please read the above section, for ages 2½–5. The intensity increases with this age group. Remember, your child is discouraged and may not know why. Be a good observer. Watch her play with other children, interact with her siblings, and talk with her teacher and other caregivers. Be patient and very consistent in *setting limits*. Most important, *encourage*! If you reach a point of frustration and wonder *"What more can I do?"* seek help from your pediatrician or a school counselor. Anger management is an issue for all school-age children today. You and your child may need outside help. Ask for it. You will be glad you did.

### WHAT TO SAY AND DO

Some children vent anger with hitting. At a calm talk time, identify his feeling and brainstorm to identify what is okay to hit. *"Mark, you seem to release a lot of frustration with hitting. That is okay. It is not okay to hit other people or their property. Here is a punching bag we will hang in your room, and an old mattress for hitting, and a pillow you can hit when you need to."* Some children get *more* wired when they hit. You may want to suggest a more calming activity such as listening to music, walking with you around the block, blowing bubbles, or taking a warm bath or shower.

Your child is old enough to learn cause and effect. *"Ryan, you were angry with Alex."* Ask, *"What happened? Why did that happen? What could you do differently next time?"* Do this consistently when he has cooled off. He will learn more self-control.

Let him know ahead of time what the consequences will be when he hits others, and follow through. You might limit his TV viewing. *"Jonathan, you are hitting. Perhaps it is because you are watching violence on TV. No TV for one week."*

Notice the moments when your child plays nicely. Build on those moments. Celebrate. *"Marie, you played so nicely this morning. Would you like to invite Leslie to the movie?"*

### PREVENTIVE TIPS

- Your child needs *special time* with you. Provide good listening time to hear what is in his heart. He is discouraged. He needs time to discover and share what is causing him to hit others.
- Show your child what his boundaries are. Walk up to him and have him tell you when to stop. That is where he is naturally comfortable with people. Explain to him that when people are too close he feels his boundaries are invaded. He may feel like hitting. Brainstorm what he may do instead. Some children learn to move away to avoid confrontation.
- Karate or Tai Chi are good activities to help your child work through bottled-up aggression. These are good activities for increasing concentration and tolerance as well. He needs an activity that allows him to feel good and do well.

*See also: Fighting, between siblings; Jealousy; Temper tantrums*

# HOLIDAYS

*"Holidays are supposed to be fun, but we end up exhausted with my child in a heap of tears."*

## UNDERSTANDING THE SITUATION

Holidays can complicate an already hectic and stressful lifestyle for most young families. Added to the stress of work and daily tasks come decisions and anxieties about present buying, dashing to parties, overloading daily routines with late nights, and traditional family obligations. Your child will react to this stress at any age. In addition, the holiday atmosphere is a true setup for disappointments that come from too high expectations. Halloween costumes go on sale in September, and Christmas often shows up in stores before Halloween is over. Order and structure provide security and safety. Evaluate your holiday traditions and activities and make adjustments according to the needs of your family. Traditions are very important to your child's healthy self-esteem, yet not all traditions that you grew up with will continue to work for your family. A feeling of identity and solidarity comes when extended family and friends are brought together, yet life may be different for you from life in your grandmother's day, when there was time to bake, to sew, and to have large, lengthy family gatherings. Set priorities and make a holiday plan based on what are the most workable, enjoyable, and meaningful traditions to keep for your family. Do not get sucked into believing you must do it all. You can modify the plan each year according to the needs of your family.

## WHAT TO SAY AND DO

Traditions are important to your children. Decide as a family which old traditions you will keep and which new ones you will begin. Don't discard the holiday; make your own new traditions. For example:

1. If Aunt Mabel's dinner table will be surrounded by people you hardly know, decline her invitation. Instead, take Aunt Mabel out to dinner with those you are close to and love.

2. Seek out the alternatives to trick-or-treating offered by many schools and churches.

3. Go to professional fireworks displays on the Fourth of July. Don't suffer watching your children light fireworks because you feel they should observe a tradition that you observed as a child.

4. Order presents from catalogs. Do not get caught up in the frenzy of entertaining and gift buying to the point of getting crazy.

5. Stay "underwhelmed." Try to stay at home more and avoid the hype of the stores. Reduce the pace. Plan quiet time with your child each week, and for very young children each day. Enjoy your time together without the holiday noise. Read and listen to music together and make time for some loving peace and calm.

6. Help your child identify possible trouble spots before the holiday. Tell your child what to expect and take *time for teaching*.

- Gift giving: *"Jessie, what do you say when someone gives you a gift? What do you do if you are disappointed in a gift? What will you do if you do not get the car you want? Aunt Sally is coming to dinner and will be bringing gifts. What will you do if you like Michael's gift better? Last year you thought I liked your sister's present better than yours."*
- Visitors: *"Grandma is coming to stay with us for a week. She talks a lot to Mommy. When you want my attention, what will you do?"*
- Planning: Involve your child in the plan. *"We're having dinner at Aunt Mabel's this year. It is a long time to sit at the table. Let's pack a small box of things to do to help you sit longer."*

- Plan a short trip of trick-or-treating and then have a small group over for some games. Talk to your child before Halloween about how much candy he may have and about giving some of the candy to the needy, perhaps to children at a shelter or day care center.
- Talk about the trouble spots that you remember from previous years. *"The fireworks are very noisy. You didn't like them last year. We can take earmuffs this year. You'll be ready for the noise, and you always enjoy the parade."*

## PREVENTIVE TIPS

- Let go of your "shoulds" and do not try to be perfect. *"I should bake the fruitcakes, make the gifts by hand, give at the office, attend holiday parties, have the entire family for dinner. . . ."* Instead, choose what you want to do based on knowing that parenting is your number-one priority.
- Keep your expectations reasonable for you and your child. Your child will be older next year; do what is reasonable this year.
- Keep your routine and your child's as normal as possible. With the excitement of a holiday, she will need a good amount of rest and regular, nutritious meals. If you are stressed, she will pick up on it and be more demanding.
- Share appropriate gift ideas with your spouse, the grandparents, or significant others in your child's life. More toys may not be the best idea. Suggest a traditional ornament, a contribution to a dollhouse, an addition to a train set, clothes for the one special doll, etc.

# HOMESICKNESS

See: Separation

# HOMEWORK HASSLES

*"My child complains and won't do his homework."*

### UNDERSTANDING THE SITUATION

Some children act discouraged, whine, and complain about homework and entice a parent to do it for them. Others ignore homework until the parent nags, lectures, or threatens, *"No friends, no TV, and no sports for three weeks."* Do not get caught up in your child's success to the point you nag and push him or, worse yet, do his projects for him. Separate your need to feel like a good parent from your child's need to succeed or fail on his own efforts. Kids are kids; they do argue and procrastinate. Homework issues often complicate family life and stress both you and your child. Keep the faith! With Positive Parenting, develop good coordination between home and school and let your guidelines dictate your actions. Do not give in, be supportive, and be consistent with your follow-through. Homework is given to reinforce and extend what is taught at school, and it is a good way for you to keep up with what your child is learning. Research shows that grades and achievement improve dramatically when homework is signed by a parent and returned and reviewed by the teacher. Be patient and maintain a positive attitude. Your child's success in school will require time and effort from you. In the long run, you will be glad that you invested the understanding and the energy!

## WHAT TO SAY AND DO

Eliminate daily hassle by structuring a specific homework time. Post a chart listing homework time. Try to be home and available during this time.

1. Check with the teacher about what will be expected and ask to be informed of daily and long-term assignments. For example, when you know that every Friday is a spelling test and every month a book is to be read, you can reinforce studying at home.
2. Homework time is for learning, even if no homework is due. Your child can spend the time reading, playing educational games, etc. Use a logical consequence if you must. *"Kelly, as soon as you finish thirty minutes of reading you may watch a half hour of TV. If you argue there will be no TV this evening."*

Avoid power struggles. Remain unimpressed with your child's ranting or complaining. Avoid getting sucked in. Lighten up and keep a sense of humor. Show understanding, offer help if she needs it, and leave the room if she whines or becomes angry. *"Megan, I know you are upset about having to do homework. Let's see what you need to do before TV time."*

Give limited choices. *"Marnie, your homework is to read for thirty minutes tonight. Do you want to read to me or read by yourself?"*

Encourage daily! Reward efforts with enthusiasm. *"Joe, this has been a week of great effort on your part! You have done a lot of work! Let's spend time together building with the Lego set that you got for your birthday over the weekend."*

Show interest in your child's work. Check her understanding of the material. This is a chance for you to see the warning signs of a possible learning problem. *Do not do the work for her.* Do work through a problem with her if she does not understand. *"Marnie, I love you and I will be happy to help you. I know you will feel good when you accomplish this. I don't want to do the work for you and rob you of this opportunity to learn how to do it yourself."* Contact the teacher if you don't understand or if your child has a special problem. This is common, so do not hesitate to call.

Sign and date the homework and ask to see it after the teacher corrects it. Read the teacher's comments to see if your child understood the assignment and if the teacher is communicating helpful information to your child.

If your child cheats on schoolwork, this may be a sign that she's lacking confidence, that she feels threatened with the work and is afraid to make mistakes. Parental pressure may be a reason she's cheating, and your concern may make it worse. Work with the teacher and school counselor if this persists. She may need a different placement or individual tutoring.

**PREVENTIVE TIPS**

• Establish a fun family learning time daily when your child is very young. Limit TV, read, draw, play board games, etc. Visit museums, aquariums, zoos, plays, and musicals. Travel and encourage your child's curiosity!
• Provide an inviting space for her to use. Ask for her ideas in arranging a comfortable and efficient space with good lighting. Be enthusiastic, as if it were your own office.
• Participate in the classroom and at school functions. You are an important advocate for your child, but you must be informed. Research shows children do better in school when parents take an active interest and participate.
• Consequences for not doing homework should be between your child and his teacher and handled at school. Involve the teacher if you become concerned that the homework isn't being done or that your child does not understand assignments.

*See also: Grades; School, won't go*

# HOSPITALS

*"My child is afraid of hospitals."*

### UNDERSTANDING THE SITUATION

Today most hospitals provide programs for children to familiarize them with the setting, to help eliminate their fears, and to correct any misconceptions. Before you have to deal with a medical emergency, introduce your child to the hospital. Take every opportunity you can to visit. This will help to minimize any fears in the event he should need medical treatment there. Hospitals are scary to many children. Whether he will be going to the hospital for his own treatment or to visit a friend or relative, he needs to be prepared in as positive a way as possible.

### WHAT TO SAY AND DO

Drive by the hospital in your area with your child and comment about what happens there. Do this often and offer new and different positive information about the hospital each time. *"Cory, there is your hospital. That is where you were born." "There is our hospital. People go there to feel better." "There is our hospital where many people take classes. When you start baby-sitting, you can take their baby-sitting course."*

If your child is to be treated at the hospital, ask your doctor to arrange a positive visit before the day he is admitted. Children do better when they know what to expect. Your child should be able to see where he will be staying and have his questions answered honestly. Point out the positives: the TV, the ice cream on the menu, the friendly nursing staff, the wheelchairs in the long hallways, etc.

Visit a friend or relative in the hospital if he or she is not in critical condition or in pain. The nursery is especially fun for children, and visiting someone with a new baby is a treat. Prepare your child for what he will see before visiting the hospital. Do not force him to go if he refuses. As above, point out the fun, interesting aspects.

### PREVENTIVE TIPS

- Call the education office of your local hospital and ask what programs they have for children. One hospital had a "birthday open house" for the children who were born there. The children and their families were invited for cake and ice cream and a tour of the nursery.
- Buy hospital toys (Playmobil has an entire operating room) that encourage role-playing among young children.
- Read together children's books about hospitals. A children's librarian or a knowledgeable bookstore clerk can give you good ideas.
- Visit a hospital with a scout group. Prepare the children for what they will be seeing.

# INTERRUPTING

*"My child rudely interrupts me."*

## UNDERSTANDING THE SITUATION

You are likely to be bugged and interrupted by your child (at any age) when you are on the phone. It is also a given that when you are involved in a conversation for any period of time with another adult you will surely be interrupted if your child (at any age) is with you. She's got you. This is a most frustrating issue for most parents. All children need to be taught not to interrupt and to take turns and be polite. Older children may need a review from time to time. This will take some time and persistence on your part. Do not nag, nag, nag *("Hannah, I'm talking. Hannah, wait your turn. Hannah, just a MINUTE!")*. She will become "parent deaf" and continue to bug you as long as you react to her bugging. Take action. It may get worse before it gets better, but do not give up. Be consistent and she will learn respect. Keep your faith, and celebrate when she observes that you need her to wait.

## WHAT TO SAY AND DO

Give her opportunities to be heard and help her know when she needs to listen. Teach her to "wait and listen" with a gentle hand signal or a kind glance or simple phrase. *"Laurie, it will be your turn in a minute. Hang on to your thought."* Do not make her wait too long. She will forget what she wanted to tell you. Never say (if she forgets), *"Well it must not have been important."*

Identify what your child is doing at a time when he is not bugging you. *"Michael, when I am on the phone you seem to want my attention."* Brainstorm what he might do instead of interrupting. *"You have options when I am talking to get my attention. Pull my skirt, nudge my arm. When I raise my hand, you know I heard you. Then you must wait for me."*

Keep your expectations reasonable. A young child cannot stand around forever listening to your long conversation. Keep it short. Limit yourself to three minutes, and set a timer.

Take *time for teaching* your child not to interrupt you on the phone. Teach him a hand gesture that means *"Wait until I finish."* Let him know what you will do if he tortures you. Have some conversations on the phone that are not important while practicing ignoring his interruptions. Avoid scolding and getting angry at him with *you* blaming words: *"Stop it right now. You stop bugging and interrupting me. Use your manners."* Instead, remain calm and unimpressed. Give the familiar hand gesture. Use a *poker face* and ignore his interruption. If you have a cordless phone, go to the bathroom and lock the door. You may have to review this with him at different stages of his development.

Let your child know what to expect. Before you get on the phone or begin talking with a friend, tell him what you need to do and make a plan with him. Ask him what he needs from you before you make the call. *"Nick, I need to be on the phone two times. You watch 'Sesame Street,' and by the time it's over I will be done. Is there something you need before I get on the phone? We will have a snack after I make my calls."*

When appropriate, include your child in your conversation to show her importance. *"Jenny has lost a tooth. Jen, would you like to tell how it happened?"* Give her time to talk on the phone with friends or relatives who want to talk to her. Help her understand that she cannot participate in *all* your conversations.

## PREVENTIVE TIPS

• Teach with games. *"Greg, let's play the interrupting game. You tell Dad about the exciting camping trip coming up and I will be the interrupter. We'll take turns."* Demonstrate, then discuss how it feels to be interrupted.
• Be a good model. If you want your child to learn not to interrupt you, do not interrupt her. If you need to break into

her words, be polite and say, "Amanda, excuse me. . . ." Avoid interrupting her as she is concentrating on a task (such as dressing), even to give a compliment.

• Comment when your child does not interrupt you. Celebrate and cheer with enthusiasm. *"Michael, you are so observant. That was the doctor on the phone, and you did not interrupt. Thank you!"*

*See also: Showing off*

# JEALOUSY

*"My child seems to always want what other kids have."*

### Ages 2½-5

## UNDERSTANDING THE SITUATION

It is very normal for a young child to act jealous or possessive about everything from "my toy" to "my mommy." Typically he feels *"What is mine is mine and what is yours is mine also."* Leaving babyhood, he first learns the concept of ownership, the joy of possession. Now he must learn an unpleasant reality, *"Some things are not mine but yours,"* and he feels *"I'd like them to be mine."* This can be a tiring and frustrating issue. It can be the root of sibling rivalry. At times you may feel embarrassed in front of others because of your child's obnoxious behavior. It is hard but important to stop worrying about what other people think. Do not let their criticism affect your good judgment. With your Positive Parenting, your child will grow to be a responsible and thoughtful person. Be patient with the process. It takes time—years for some children.

## WHAT TO SAY AND DO

Jealousy is a feeling. You cannot tell your child not to feel jealous. Help her identify and understand her feelings. *"Hilary, you wish that you had a car just like Sam's."* Empathize. *"I do not blame you. I would like to have one just like it too."*

She needs her own possessions apart from those of her siblings. Before she can learn to not feel jealous, she needs to feel the joy of ownership. When you go to visit other children, have her bring one or two of her own possessions.

Introduce the concepts of sharing and negotiating. *"Michael, you would love to have Billy's truck to play with. If you share your remote-controlled car with him, he may share with you."*

If your child cries and carries on about wanting a toy, give her a warning and then carry through with a logical consequence. *"Carrie, the doll is Jenny's. You need to give it to her or we will go home."* Be prepared to do what you say you will do. Do not give idle threats. Use *action with few words.*

When your child shares or shows an effort to not be jealous, be quick to comment and celebrate. *"Alright, Mark. I know you wanted the ball and mitt, and you gave them up nicely. I know Tommy will share with you sometime too!"*

**PREVENTIVE TIPS**

• Take *time to teach* about ownership, the concept of yours and mine. Young children love games with humor like "Your nose, my nose, your truck . . . no, its Mommy's truck."
• Give your child a small locked box with a key. Give her a little treasure occasionally to be her private possession.
• Discuss feelings as much as you can. When you help her identify any feelings she may have (such as jealousy), she will begin to understand how to handle them and grow to be more responsible.
• Read together children's books. *Angelina's Baby Sister* by Katharine Holabird (New York: Crown, 1991) is about sibling jealousy. Talk to a children's librarian or a knowledgeable bookstore clerk for other good book suggestions.

# Ages 6–10

**UNDERSTANDING THE SITUATION**

Your school-age child may demonstrate jealousy by acting out with misbehavior or moodiness or by developing a bad case of the *"I wants."* Social acceptance becomes very important as children grow older, and jealous feelings are often noticeable. This can be very tiring to you. It is irritating to raise a child and feel you can't possibly do enough to please her. Do not get caught up in her controlling or hurtful ways. Be supportive, listen, and explore feelings but be careful not to rescue or overindulge. If you support your child's desire to keep up with everything other children have or do, she will never be satisfied with all that she has and does. You will need to *set limits*, help her separate her wants from her needs, and help her accept that she will always be blessed with more than some others and that there will always be someone who has more than she does. She can also learn to work for what she really wants. Developing this concept is part of the long process of maturing. Do not lose faith. Plant the positive seeds now and cultivate. Your child will grow to be a thoughtful, creative, and respectful individual.

### WHAT TO SAY AND DO

Listen and identify feelings. *"Randy, you wish you had a skateboard just like Michael's."* Empathize. *"I would want one, too. Everyone feels jealous sometimes."* Explore the concept of how others feel as well. *"How do you think Michael feels, knowing you want his board?"*

Do not be too quick to say no. Empower your child by giving him the responsibility to find a solution. *"Randy, if you want the skateboard, what could you do to earn it?"*

Give a logical consequence for acting out. There is a fine line between showing empathy and allowing bad behavior. *"Joey, I understand that you really wanted Nick's shoes. That is no excuse for taking and ruining them. Let's explore how you will pay for them."*

### PREVENTIVE TIPS

- Provide listening time. At bedtime ask your child what made him happy that day and what made him sad. Tell him your feelings.
- Have your child make a list of all the great things he has or has had. They do not have to be material items. *"Tony, you live by a park, Grandpa reads wonderful stories to you, and last summer you learned to swim at the lake."*
- Share memories with him about when you were his age and what made you feel jealous.

- Your child needs *special time* with you and other meaningful mature people. He needs to play and have fun with you. Kick a ball around, play games like hide and seek, or quietly play cards or board games. Children who feel they are a loved and essential part of the family are less likely to obsess over what they are "missing."

*See also: Feelings; Fighting, between siblings; New baby*

# LESSONS, ATHLETIC

*"Which athletic activities are best for my child?"*

## Ages 2½–5

### UNDERSTANDING THE SITUATION

There are so many choices for athletic activities for children today that a parent may easily feel overwhelmed. We can sign up our preschool children for skiing, swimming, dance, gymnastics, etc. By the time a child is five, team sports such as soccer, baseball, and basketball are available. It is easy to feel anxious or guilty, wondering, *"Am I doing enough?" "When should she begin?" "Which program is right?" "How hard should I push?"* Some effort in this area is definitely appropriate because lifelong patterns of eating healthful foods, exercising, and enjoying athletic activity are established in early years. Also, athletic lessons may help you to become friends with other parents and at the same time help your child to separate from you, learn to deal with other children, and listen to other adults. A well-chosen instructor or coach will provide skills in good listening, communication, and self-control that are necessary to your child's healthy self-esteem.

### WHAT TO SAY AND DO

When choosing an athletic activity, consider: Does your child have friends signing up with her? Is the instructor energetic, positive, and encouraging? Avoid a lecturing instructor and large classes that require a lot of sitting time. Is the equipment safe? Is the hour of the day good for your child? Some children are tired after school and need food and rest before an activity.

Do not overcommit your child. One activity at a time is enough. She needs free, unstructured time to play on her own or with siblings or other playmates.

Observe the class with your child before you sign her up. If her response is negative, don't push it. In six months' time she may feel eager. She will do better when she chooses her activity and commits to the full session.

If she complains about not wanting to go, say, *"Anna, you signed up for four weeks, and I paid the money. You need to go each time."* Depend on the instructor to handle her in class. A good instructor will never force a child. It will be good for her to be with the group, if only to watch.

### PREVENTIVE TIPS

See Preventive Tips for ages 6–10

## Ages 6–10

### UNDERSTANDING THE SITUATION

Please read the above section, for ages 2½–5. As your child begins school, the choice of activities increases. Both team and individual sports are available to most children. Boys and girls have such an advantage to have team sports begin at this age. Team play teaches cooperation. A child who is bossy or has trouble playing with other children may flourish on a soccer team. Winning and losing are equally important lessons in life. Team sports provide a healthy arena to learn competition. A positive coach is a must—one who concentrates on teaching basic skills well, who builds on what the kids are doing right, and who encourages working together. Parents are often asked to actively participate by coaching, assisting, etc. Be careful not to push your child into an activity for your own enjoyment. It needs to be his choice, his activity.

### WHAT TO SAY AND DO

Competition is a fearful experience for many children until they are older. The coach or instructor should be energetic, enthusiastic, and positive. At this age winning is not as important as the fun of the game: learning the skills, working as a team, and showing good sportsmanship.

When you are at your child's game, root for the whole team, not an individual. *"Go Blue Bombers! Good save! Alright team!"* When they win, say, *"What an effort! You really worked as a team!"* When they lose, say, *"Nice try. Someone will win and someone will lose. What will you work on next week?"*

Eliminate criticism even if you feel it is constructive. You may think your advice is helpful, but if it is not asked for or unwanted it is negative. Let your child receive information from a coach or an instructor instead.

### PREVENTIVE TIPS

- Play with your child. If you are a working parent, this is a wonderful way to spend fun weekend time together. Take the time to throw the baseball, toss the basketball, or kick the soccer ball with her. Keep it fun. Go light on the instruction.
- Instead of perfection, look for good judgment, good reasoning and thinking, effort, and improvement. Identify your child's skills and express how far she has come, not how far she has to go.
- Be a fun, active parent when you have time together. Bike, swim, ski, walk, or run with your child. Sitting in front of a television watching sports is not enough to teach her to enjoy activities and stimulate her thinking.

# LESSONS, MUSIC

*"My child won't practice her music lessons."*

## UNDERSTANDING THE SITUATION

The prestige of music lessons and the excitement of learning fun, familiar songs usually are the motivations for children to start playing a musical instrument. Practicing between lessons is tedious for most children, and it is easy to grow angry with your child for avoiding it. The more you want her to play the instrument, the more likely you will have power struggles about it. Do not nag, bribe, or threaten your child to make her practice. Begin lessons when your child is eager. She needs to buy into the program. Together make agreements with the teacher about the routine of lessons and practice. Her success depends on your enthusiasm. Your support and *encouragement* will carry her through learning the hardest of skills. Muster up all the energy you need to be patient with her. Do not just focus on the end result. Celebrate each step of the process of learning to play. The learning process helps to build your child's self-esteem as much as the finished product.

## WHAT TO SAY AND DO

Agree together about a routine for practice. When and how long she plays can be posted on a chart. When she finishes each day, she can add a sticker to the chart.

Refuse to battle over her practicing. *"Hannah, we committed to piano lessons until Christmas. You need to practice twenty minutes each day."* Use a logical consequence. *"You may play with your friends after you practice."* If you are willing to follow through, use this consequence: *"After you complete this session, taking lessons is your choice. No practice, no lessons."* If she decides to quit, let three to six months pass before you allow her to begin again.

Every once in a while, sit with her while she practices and provide her with an enthusiastic audience. *"Maggie, I love listening to you play. This is the best part of my day—I get to relax! Thank you."* She is a social being and most likely will enjoy her practicing more if she has company.

Communicate with the teacher. Say in front of your child what you feel is going well and what you would like support on. *"We have enjoyed listening to her play this week. She really liked the music."* At the sign of any stubbornness, use your teacher as the authority. *"Jen doesn't like to practice lately. Perhaps you can suggest some different music. Let me know how I can help."*

Make a deal with your child that shows her how important her playing is to you. *"Heidi, if you will play the piano for the next twenty minutes I will do all the dishes. I just love to hear you play."*

Once in a while, take time to listen as a family audience. Celebrate the performance, serve refreshments, and occasionally invite close family and friends.

## PREVENTIVE TIPS

- Shop for a music teacher with a personality and program suited to your child. A very competitive teacher with tough demands and many recitals may be great for one kind of child, while another child may want less push and pressure. All children do better with teachers who are enthusiastic, positive, and energetic and who send the message *"You are special, and I enjoy being with you."*
- Limit your child's outside activities. You can overcommit your child. One sports activity plus music lessons is plenty.
- Support her interest in music by taking her to concerts and playing a varied selection of music at home. If you have friends who play an instrument, take her to hear them perform or invite them over to play for her.

# LISTENING

*"My child will not follow instructions."*

## UNDERSTANDING THE SITUATION

Many parents complain that their child will not listen or do what is asked. Aggravated, you yell, *"I am sick and tired of you not listening to me."* And when that doesn't work, you yell his name: *"BRETT! DO IT NOW!"* Your blood pressure rises, and he looks at you as if you are crazy and are really losing it. We all want respect from our children, but we do not gain respect by demanding it. Your child may not listen because you nag repeatedly. He may know you are going to tell him five times before you'll yell. This could be a power struggle. Improving poor cooperation takes *encouragement* from you and better communication. Be very consistent with your follow-through.

## WHAT TO SAY AND DO

Give one direction at a time when your child is young and keep it simple. Observe her and judge when she is ready to handle multiple instructions.

Make eye contact with your child. Some very intense children are so deeply immersed in their thoughts or what is going on around them that they truly do not hear you. These children often respond to a touch as you tell them what you need. Do not shout a direction from another room.

Tell your child what you want once and mean it. *"Mary, you need to put your pajamas on and brush your teeth before you turn on the television."* If she turns on the TV, turn it off. Use *action with few words.* Check her understanding. *"Mary, what were you asked to do?"* Be consistent and follow through with what you say. *"You may watch TV when you are ready for bed."*

Give your direction with a motivating consequence. *"Mary, as soon as you brush your teeth you may watch television."*

Logical consequences work best if you let your child know what to expect before it happens. *"Randy, put your bike away tonight before dinner. If you do not put it away, I will hang it out of reach for two weeks."* Follow through with what you said you would do. Use *action with few words.*

Never argue with your child, and do not say, *"Do it because I said so."* Give a good reason for what you want her to do. That shows respect. However, you do not need to explain endlessly or repeatedly. Once is enough.

Your child may be "parent deaf" from your past nagging. Try leaving a note or a picture rather than using your voice. Have him follow a job chart to see what he should do next. Set a timer to tell him when his time is up.

Avoid interrupting him with your instructions. Too many times we throw another instruction out while a child is completing the last one.

Give him some warning of what you need and when. Children don't watch the clock as adults do, so provide some sense of time passing. *"Jason, after this television show, please set the table."*

## PREVENTIVE TIPS

- If you want your child to listen to you, listen to her. Be a good role model. Put down your book or paper, get down on her level, listen and reflect what she is saying to you.
- Be sure your child has had a recent hearing test. Most schools give them once a year.
- Look for opportunities to build a good relationship. Talk to your child about the importance of listening when you are having a good talk. Comment on his good listening when he does follow directions. Tell him and leave little notes that say, *"I love you."* Put a note on the napkin in his lunch: *"You are*

*very special.*" When you do leave a note with a direction or tell her to do something, she will feel like doing what you say.

• Take *time for teaching* listening skills. Tell stories and have her add parts as you go along. *"Once there was a little troll. Where did he live?"* Play listening games. Have a poem in mind. Say, *"Repeat after me. . . ."* or *"I'm thinking of something big and furry and it begins with B"* or sing a phrase of a song like "Row, Row, Row Your Boat" and have her echo it.

---

# LONELINESS

*See: Friends, lack of*

---

# LYING

*"My child lies to avoid getting into trouble."*

## Ages 2½–5

### UNDERSTANDING THE SITUATION

*"Boy, we'll nip this in the bud! We certainly aren't going to raise any liars!"* This is a typical parent reaction when a young child tells her first lie or two. You may overreact to this common childhood behavior, fearing you need to get the situation under control now, before it gets out of hand. Young children do occasionally lie. Your child's understanding of right and wrong is not on the level of consciousness yours is. A lie may be a fantasy, an attention getter, or, in a moment of fear, a method of staying out of trouble. Your child is not a liar and will not become one. Be a Positive Parent, relax, and have faith in your child. Maintain

your sense of humor. Set your limits, and consistently follow through. Please read the section below, for ages 6–10.

## WHAT TO SAY AND DO

Young children will fantasize. Some children do this to be noticed. Do not label your child a liar or call her story a lie. Most fantasy can be handled with fun, humor, or more fantasy in return. Calmly say, *"Annie, that sounds like a make-believe story. I bet you wish that really happened."*

If there is a problem, rather than concentrating on blame, look for a solution. If there is more than one child involved, rather than asking, *"Who did it?"* put them together to find the solution. *"Jessie, the cake is on the floor. I do not care about who did it. I care about how we will clean up the mess and find a new dessert for the family dinner."*

Avoid asking your child, *"Did you do this?"* when you know the answer. That questioning style creates threat, creates fear, and invites lying.

## PREVENTIVE TIPS

- *Albert's Toothache* by Barbara Williams (New York: Dutton, 1974), *Rosie and the Yellow Ribbon* by Paula DePaolo (New York: Little, Brown, 1992), and *Tooth Fairy* by Audrey Wood (New York: Child's Play International, 1989) are children's stories with a fantasy or telling-the-truth theme that are fun to read together.
- Compliment and celebrate when your child tells the truth.
- *Encourage.* Give your attention when he isn't demanding it. *"I love you!"* is great to hear when he is doing nothing specific to deserve it. He shouldn't feel he has to tell tall tales to win your attention or affection.

# Ages 6-10

## UNDERSTANDING THE SITUATION

When your child lies, initially you may feel shocked, and if she continues you feel angry or hurt. *"How could you lie to me after all I've done for you?"* Lies are only a symptom of a mistaken underlying belief, and whether the purpose is to avoid a consequence, protect oneself or someone else, or win approval, lying is a sign of discouragement. Do not get too serious and worry about this behavior. To lecture and admonish creates shame or guilt. If your child is lying often you need to examine your atmosphere of discipline. A critical or judgmental environment or angry confrontations and physical punishment create fear which may cause your child to suppress the truth. Ignoring the issue, pretending a lie didn't happen, is just as bad. She needs to learn limits and the difference between right and wrong. Take the *time to teach.* Look for and comment on all the good she does. Show your faith and trust in her. Never label her a liar. The behavior is unacceptable, but she needs to know you will continue to love her unconditionally.

## WHAT TO SAY AND DO

Accusing cross-examination will force more lying. Be direct about the lie, especially if you know the truth. Speak about the event or circumstance rather than blaming her. Say, *"Marnie, the gate was left open and the puppy is lost,"* not *"You left the gate open and you've lost the puppy."*

Do not focus on the lie, but let your child know you know the truth. Help him discuss a solution and to learn from the mistake. (If you are very upset *take a time out* to *cool off.* He needs to hear your feelings of concern or love, not of fear or anger.) *"John, you say that you were late because you and Kevin got lost. I know you were not lost and that you are afraid I am angry with you. I was worried about you because it was dark and I didn't know if you were safe. What will you do next time to make sure you are home on time?"* Apply a logical consequence if the situation happens again. *"John, until you know how to find your way home on time, you need to not play with Kevin. We will try again next week."* This consequence is not punitive; it does promote responsibility.

Do not punish for telling the truth. When your child tells the truth, especially when it may mean she takes a risk, compliment with enthusiasm. *"Julie, I thank you for telling the truth about the broken lamp. I appreciate your courage. You are growing up. We all make mistakes."* Your encouragement will help her face the consequences of the action, such as, in this example, helping to pay for the broken lamp.

### PREVENTIVE TIPS

- Be honest and truthful yourself. Your children will watch your behavior and do the same. If you lie about their ages to get them onto a ferry or into a movie for less money, or lie to a friend to protect your credibility, they will learn to do the same.
- Be a good listener. Give your child *special time.* Lying is often used to gain a feeling of importance or to get attention. Listen to his feelings.
- Be positive and let go of perfectionism. Mistakes are okay; we learn from them.
- He may lie to you so that you won't think less of him. Discuss at a good talk time how lying makes a person feel. *"How do you think others feel when you lie to them?"* *"Would you want a good friend to lie to you?"*

*See also: Fantasy*

# MASTURBATION

*"My child masturbates and embarrasses me!"*

### UNDERSTANDING THE SITUATION

It is very embarrassing when your child masturbates in front of you or, worse yet, in front of company. You may be terribly uncomfortable about how to address the matter with your child. Keep calm. Masturbation is normal and an early, pleasurable activity that young children usually learn by accident. It is a first experience in learning about their sexuality. Some children learn early on to masturbate in privacy, and others need *time for teaching.* Some children have more of an urge than others. This is an uncomfortable subject for most parents. We all need to learn how to address sexual issues. Shunning the subject or scolding and punishing will send a message of shame and guilt: *"You are not okay when you touch your private parts."* It is important that your child understand that it is not bad; it is normal to feel like masturbating. If you forbid the activity and her urges are strong, she may hide and do it anyway. She may feel more stress and increase the behavior. Masturbation does becomes a concern when it is done excessively or in public. This may be a sign of stress and indicate the need for professional help. Your pediatrician, your child's teacher, or a school counselor are good resources.

### WHAT TO SAY AND DO

Often you can distract a very young child without mentioning what she is doing. Masturbation sometimes happens with boredom. *"Emily, the squirrel is up in the tree. Let's go give him some peanuts."* Or if you are next to her, simply take her hand and hold it and keep doing what you are doing.

With an older child keep a lighthearted attitude. She may not be aware she is doing it. Kindly, without sarcasm or ridicule, give her a knowing glance and just say her name.

Be honest about how you feel. Ideally, as with all other sexual issues, it is best to use proper terminology, to be kind, and to be as matter-of-fact as possible. When addressing your concern be aware of your body language, facial expression, and tone of voice. You may say calmly with the best intentions, *"Jenny, that is your vagina that you are touching."* Your face may say to her, *"Stop, that is yucky!"*

If this subject is difficult for you to address, say so. *"I'm uncomfortable talking about masturbation. When I was five my mommy did not talk to me about my private parts."* If you do not address how you feel, she may sense that you are uncomfortable and feel bad about herself, or masturbate more to gain attention.

If this is a persistent habit or is done in public, *set limits.* Be kind and firm. *"Jes, it feels good to touch or rub your private parts. You need to do that in your own private space. Your bedroom is a good place for you to do that."* Or *"Jeremy, I understand touching your penis feels good. You may do that in the privacy of your bedroom, but it is not appropriate in front of others."* Be very consistent. If you allow it once or twice to perhaps avoid a confrontation, it will continue.

### PREVENTIVE TIPS

- Ask a children's librarian or knowledgeable bookstore clerk for reading suggestions for both you and your child. There are many excellent children's books about the body available to read aloud together. Encourage your child's questions.
- Introduce the concept of private versus public at a good private-talk time. *"Morgan, some things are done in private. Dad closes the door when he uses the bathroom, I like to close my bedroom door when I dress, Dad and I close our bedroom door at night to be alone. What are some times when you want to be private?"*
- If your child masturbates excessively and seems withdrawn from friends and activities at school, consult your family physician to determine if professional help is necessary.

# MATCHES

*See: Safety*

# MEALTIME

*"Mealtime is chaos! Sometimes we miss it altogether."*

## UNDERSTANDING THE SITUATION

Mealtime is a time to be together, share, have fun, and celebrate! In our fast-paced, modern society, with both parents active and working and children involved in sports and other activities, mealtime is often abandoned. Though it is very difficult, make mealtime together a priority at least once a day. Structure a meal plan each week. Your child will want to come to share at mealtime if you show genuine interest in her and what she is interested in. Try not to get lost in adult conversation and concerns; save that for another time. Manners can be suggested in a supportive way, but do not make manners the focus. This is a time to enjoy being together. Let go of perfectionism. Mealtime with family will always be somewhat chaotic.

## WHAT TO SAY AND DO

Mealtime is a very important family time. With very busy schedules it is easy to overlook it. Plan for a daily mealtime. At a *family meeting* determine when you will have meals together as a family.

Build mealtime into the chore chart for all ages. Your child will enjoy helping to plan menus with you and can assume some responsibilities for meal preparation for the week. *"Bobby* [age seven], *this week you chose to make salads and clear the table. Maria* [age four] *will help Mom make pizza Monday night and pudding Wednesday."* The structure is important; the choices can change each week. Be creative!

Establish a tradition of starting each meal hearing from each family member on a positive note. Try giving a compliment or telling about the best event of the day. Be creative and never put anyone on the spot. Give everyone the right to pass.

Lighten up and have fun! The day is serious enough, and everyone needs a sense of humor. Relate fun experiences and include everyone.

### PREVENTIVE TIPS

- This is not the time for Mom and Dad to discuss adult topics. This is time to include the children. Share compliments, happenings at school, activities outside of school. Be sure each child has a chance to be heard.
- Consider your table a place to entertain company. Treat your children as if they are your best friends and have stopped over for a meal with you. Put your best foot forward and be respectful.
- Include your younger child at mealtime. He may hop down sooner, he may have eaten some dinner beforehand, but he will enjoy being part of the group if he is included as a significant person.

*See also: Eating, healthful foods; Eating, overeating; Eating, picky eating; Mealtime, manners*

# MEALTIME, MANNERS

*"My child won't behave politely at the table and ruins meal-time."*

## UNDERSTANDING THE SITUATION

Mealtime at home is for sharing and for appreciating time with family. Keep adult conversation and problems for another time. This is good practice time for eating with others. It is not the time to lecture and instruct your child about manners. Manners can be suggested in a supportive way. Although you want to see certain standards of behavior met, don't be critical or judgmental about what and how your child is eating. Be positive and notice what he is doing right! Keep the family conversation interesting and include everyone; this will help eliminate attention-getting bad manners. Don't forget to model all the appropriate behavior you hope to see your child use in public.

## WHAT TO SAY AND DO

Bad manners at the table are best ignored as much as possible. A knowing glance will often put a stop to poor behavior. If you feel manners need to be addressed, make your request firmly and kindly. *"Heidi, please sit up straight and finish your bite, and then tell me about the dog."*

Lighten up! Use a sense of humor with a kind, playful comment. *"Roger, there has been a fly buzzing around the table looking for an open mouth to land in. Better close yours!"* Do not use sarcasm.

Give your child a *choice* to stay or leave the table. For example, if your child is very antsy and bounces up and down from his chair to the floor, say, *"Karen, when you're down you're done!"* This works best when your child understands that the kitchen will be closed until morning.

Use *action with few words*. One way to defuse poor behavior is to decide what you will do rather than what you will make your child do. For instance, if two children begin fighting, with a *poker face* leave the table with your food and place mat and eat in another room. Or you may remove a child from the table for *time out*. *"Erin, time out. Come back when you are ready to be polite."* Later discuss the behavior, how and why it happened, and what will be different next time.

### PREVENTIVE TIPS

- *Family meetings* are good times to discuss manners or mealtime concerns. Arrange a *time for teaching* good manners and celebrate success with a fancy dress dinner. Be creative. Older children can learn what to do and can teach as well as you.
- Keep expectations reasonable. A two-year-old cannot be expected to sit for more than ten minutes with you at a meal. Don't let meals drag on and on.
- *Never compare children*. Promoting the "clean plate club" only causes children to compete for your approval. Pointing out that Lauren is sitting quietly isn't going to improve Jason's behavior.
- *How My Parents Learned to Eat* by Ina R. Friedman (Boston: Houghton Mifflin, 1987) is a children's book to read together about manners and Japanese culture.

*See also: Eating, healthful foods; Eating, overeating; Eating, picky eating; Mealtime; Restaurants*

# MEANNESS

*"My child says cruel things, scratches, and hurts others."*

### UNDERSTANDING THE SITUATION

It is shocking when your child lashes out at others in a very mean way. It is hurtful if she lashes out at you. You want to punish her for rough language or cruel actions to make her behavior improve. Punishing with spanking, scolding, or lecturing will not help her to be better. She is definitely discouraged, and probably feeling hurt herself for some reason. One child was being teased by neighborhood children because she had a physical disability. She became so frustrated that she lashed out at the person with whom she felt safe and who would always love her: her mom. Try to find the source of the problem. Muster up all the energy you can to deal with this situation. It may take a lot of time and a lot of persistence, as it may get worse before it gets better. *Set limits* and be lovingly consistent. Your *encouragement*, and that of other significant adults, will be what makes her feel better and be better. Catch her when she is loving. Watch for the good and comment on it. Use all the Positive Parenting principles you can.

### WHAT TO SAY AND DO

Take your child to the pediatrician for a complete physical. Some children are found to have trouble hearing or seeing; others have developmental delay or underlying emotional difficulties. Some medications can cause irritability.

If your child hurts you, do not demand an apology. Do not say, *"You tell me you're sorry. Apologize!"* Do not overreact. You don't want to support the mistaken idea that because he feels hurt, he can hurt others. You may say, *"Jimmy, that hurt me,"* but try to remain cool. As much as you feel inclined, do not hurt him back. That only teaches him that you can be meaner.

Always separate what your child does from who she is. Hitting is mean. She is angry, but she is not mean.

Stop the behavior calmly with a *poker face* and *action with few words.* One way to help your very young child is to identify his feelings and hold him. *"Roger, you are very angry. I'll hold you real tight until you calm down."* Some young children are afraid of their anger. Holding and rocking is comforting. Use *action with few words* and a *poker face.* Your calmness will pass through to him. Wait for some time before exploring the solution to the situation.

Another way to help a child of any age is to stop the behavior calmly with a *poker face* and *action with few words* and give *time out.* *"Michael, you are hurting Hilary. Please take time out to feel better."* If possible go with him to time out and stay with him. If he hurts you, leave with a *poker face* but remain nearby. When he calms down, welcome him back and help him with the transition. *"I am glad you feel better. Let's have some juice."*

Wait for your child to be calm before you discuss her action. For some children this may take several hours, for others, a whole day. Your child probably will not be able to tell you what was wrong. Explore with her, be a good listener, and refrain from being judgmental or critical. Reflect what she says *("You feel ____ about ____ because ____ ). "Nancy, you felt angry with Meg because she seems to get everything first."* Wait for her response and repeat what she said. *"It sounds as though you feel . . ."* This is a remarkable method for helping children of any age to understand their feelings and reach solutions on their own.

When your child is calm, discuss what it feels like to be hurt by a mean action. Calmly and kindly, ask, *"Heidi, would you like it if I scratched your arm hard like you did to me? What do you think that feels like?"*

After reflective listening, *problem solve:* Explore what sets her off and invite her to think of solutions. *"Sally, you were frustrated because the children ran off without you. You can be frustrated, but you cannot hurt others. What could you do to soothe yourself when you feel frustrated or angry instead of hurting others?"* Offer your ideas only to supplement hers. *"How about going into another room and turning on some music, blowing some bubbles, taking ten deep breaths, or jumping rope?"*

Comment on the times she plays without using mean behavior and on the good times you have with her. She needs to hear lots of positive feedback about what she does well.

### PREVENTIVE TIPS

- Check with teachers and other caregivers to determine whether your child's mean behavior happens away from home. If so, ask for their help in using a Positive Parenting approach. Explain that your preferred method of coping with this behavior is to separate, cool off, discuss feelings, and problem solve.
- Spend two weeks logging her behavior. Observe particularly when she shows meanness and observe what may be the reason.
- Spend *special time* regularly. Have other times together to explore feelings. At bedtime ask, *"What was the best part of your day and what was the saddest?"* Tell her about your ups and downs as well.
- Provide opportunities for her to be in charge and in control. Give her limited choices and provide jobs she can handle and be successful with. Your young child can be in charge of a pet, make a dinner salad, toast bread for sandwiches, or make pizza.
- Read children's stories together. *The Hating Book* by Charlotte Zolotow (New York: HarperCollins, 1969), *Bailey the Big Bully* by Lizi Boyd (New York: Puffin Books, 1991), and *Feelings* by Aliki Brandenberg (New York: Morrow, 1984) are fun books that stimulate discussion. Talk with a children's librarian or knowledgeable bookstore clerk for other ideas.

Note: If you observe other disturbing behavior in addition to the meanness, such as poor eating, disturbed sleeping, sadness, irritability, etc., see your pediatrician or a school counselor for support.

*See also: Dirty words; Talking back*

---

# MEDICATIONS

*"My child fights me when she needs to take medicine."*

### UNDERSTANDING THE SITUATION

Giving medicine is often a battle. An antibiotic prescribed to be taken four times a day is inconvenient enough, but when it tastes awful to your child and she either blows it across the room or refuses it, medicine time becomes a dreaded ordeal. You can try all kinds of gimmicks: Mix in it fudge sauce on ice cream, follow it with a gummy bear. When push comes to shove (and it might), she will have to accept that the choice is not hers to take the medicine or not; she only has a choice about how she takes it. Take time to help your child understand that medicine is to help keep her healthy and that you are raising her to be responsible for her own health. Medicine should be respected and not overused. Be very matter-of-fact with no apologies given. Whimpering *"I'm sorry we have to do this"* is not supportive. *"This is just one of those things we have to do, and I know you can handle it"* is supportive.

### WHAT TO SAY AND DO

When possible give your child a *choice.* Remember that medicine comes in different forms and flavors. *"Marnie, you need to take the medicine. The doctor wants it to be as comfortable as possible for you. Do you want the liquid given four times a day or the chewable tablets given three times?"*

Medicines can be mixed with ice cream or other appealing foods. *"Steve, I crushed your pill in the chocolate syrup. One spoonful!"*

The medicine must be taken. If you have tried patience and understanding, the next step is to give the medicine. This is tough and no fun, but necessary. Use a *poker face* and *action with few words.* *"Billy, you need to take the medicine. You have a choice, to be brave and take the medicine by yourself or to take it with my help."*

If administering an over-the-counter medication, such as Tylenol or cough syrup, poses a tremendous challenge, let go of the necessity. *"Morgan, you have a bad cough. You would be more comfortable with this medicine."* If she says no, let it go! Save your energy for the dose of medication that is absolutely necessary.

PREVENTIVE TIPS

- Never indicate that medicine is like candy. It is taken only when needed and when supervised.
- Pill swallowing is difficult for some children. Practice swallowing small pieces of food. One doctor suggested swallowing an M&M with milk. Teach your child how to put the pill on the back of the tongue and swallow it down with liquid. This may take time, but do not give up!
- A doctor or nurse can be a good authority figure to support your giving medication. Take your child back for a consultation if needed.
- These children's books are not specific to the topic of medicine taking, although their themes may encourage a cooperative attitude and better understanding. If you'd like to address your child's complaining, read together *Alexander and the Terrible, Horrible, Not Good Very Bad Day* by Judith Viorst (New York: Macmillan, 1972). If you'd like to address what happens to swallowed medicine, read *What Happens to a Hamburger* by Paul Showers (New York: HarperCollins, 1985). Both *I Was So Mad* by Norma Simon (Morton Grove, Ill.: Whitman, 1974) and *I Am Not a Crybaby* by Norma Simon (Morton Grove, Ill.: Whitman, 1989) address common feelings when battling over medicine taking.

# MONEY

*"My child has no appreciation for money."*

### Ages 2½–5

#### UNDERSTANDING THE SITUATION

Most 2½-year-olds have learned that shopping trips are for coloring books, gum, candy, and other goodies artfully placed at the checkout counter. By age four and five the "I wants" increase, and it is assumed that with a little hassle, Mom or Dad usually will give in. *Set limits* before you enter the store; tell your child what you have to spend and what you are going to buy. Be consistent. If your child manipulates you at this age to spend money, you will surely have a price to pay when she is older. An allowance program may start at age three, especially if your young child has older siblings and sees how the system works. This is a good method to introduce an appreciation for money. She can learn to appreciate the value of money early. Begin now.

#### WHAT TO SAY AND DO

As soon as your younger child starts asking for this and that in the stores, begin her allowance program. Present her with her first piggy bank. This should be nonbreakable, designed so money slips in easily but is more difficult to take out. Use play money for playing. Her real money stays in her bank. Cheer as she drops money into her piggy bank to prevent carelessly losing it.

The amount of allowance is determined first by what you can afford and next by your child's needs and wants. Begin small. She is learning the concept of money at this age.

Begin talking with your child about the difference between needs and wants. *"Erin, I buy you what you need. You need a new jacket and shoes. You* want *a toy."* Do not buy something for him every time you shop either to bribe him or reward good behavior. Occasional treats are special. They should be the exception rather than the rule.

Let him occasionally experience taking money from his bank to buy gum or a toy when you go shopping. Take *time to teach* what will happen. *"Sam, you will give the lady your money and she will give you the gum. She will keep your money and you will keep the gum."* He may not want to give up his money to the clerk because he is just learning the concept of "mine and thine." He should have the chance to change his mind, and he may cry or have a temper tantrum over wanting both the money and the gum. Stay cool and firm. *"Sam, it's one or the other."*

Do not be too quick to either approve or deny a request. Use the opportunity to negotiate. When your four-year-old wants you to buy something that you are willing to buy, make a deal. *"Ryan, you really want the hamster. It will cost six dollars. As soon as you save two dollars of your own money for the pet food, I will buy the hamster."* At fifty cents a week, saving enough will take some time. Time and saving will determine how badly he really wants what he thinks he does.

**PREVENTIVE TIPS**

• Provide many opportunities for your child to work with money.

1. Play money games. Four and five-year-olds enjoy learning to count with play money. Purchase a toy cash register and set up a play store at home.
2. Take a calculator with you to the store. Your four or five-year-old can punch in prices as you collect items.
3. Let your child give the store clerks your money and receive the change. Be sure to discuss beforehand how it works, or your child may not be willing to give you back your change.

• Comment on how well he is beginning to understand how money works.

- Keep your comments about money honest but positive.
  Please read the following section, for ages 6–10.

## Ages 6-10

### UNDERSTANDING THE SITUATION

As your child grows older, those little "grocery store goodies" are replaced with more expensive wants. Generally we are quite inconsistent about buying this and that for our child until we feel a money crunch. Then the child is likely to get a negative, criticizing, blaming, *you* lecture. Do not do that. Instead, take *time to teach* her about the value of money. The allowance system is a good tool for training about money. Agree to allowance guidelines with your spouse or other significant adults and follow them with consistency. Your long-range goal is to teach her to make money work for her instead of being controlled by it. Start as early as possible and expand her understanding and responsibility for money as she grows. When she is eighteen, leaves home, and receives her first Visa card, she will understand that a credit card is not a license to an unlimited amount of money, and she will be financially more responsible.

### WHAT TO SAY AND DO

Keep chores and allowance separate. Chores are done for the needs of the family. Allowance is a tool used to teach how money works. *"Molly, you help with the dishes because you are part of this family. We do not get paid for family chores. If you need more money than your allowance pays, we have jobs you can be paid for. Washing the car or pulling weeds is a good way to earn extra money."*

Develop a family allowance system. Give your child three banks:

1. Short-term savings, for immediate wants and needs. She makes decisions with this money.
2. Long-term savings, deposited by her into a bank account in

her name. This is not a college account but is for items to be decided on with parental guidance.
3. Savings for a charity—perhaps church, a community charity, or an environmental fund. Help her be involved so that she knows where her contribution goes.

Decide on the amount of allowance to be given according to what you can afford and the needs of your child. If your child needs more money than you can give, help him explore ways to earn extra money. Allow him to negotiate with you to help with part of a large expense.

Keep a chart recording when allowance was paid.

Establish a list of jobs that your child can do to earn extra money. Take *time to teach* her and keep your expectations reasonable. Establish wages before a job begins. Do not underpay, yet do not overpay for a job poorly done. Use a notebook or a chart to keep track of work hours.

Do not rob your child of the opportunity to learn to wait or work for something he wants. *"Robby, show me how important it is to you by earning half, and I will pay the rest."*

Your child will make mistakes and poor decisions. Help her learn from them. Do not pity and rescue her. This is very hard. *"Ginny, you bought an expensive sweatshirt. Now you can't buy a shirt for school. What do you think you will do next time?"* Your child learns to manipulate when you give in to pleading requests for handouts.

Do not bribe, punish, or reward with allowance. *"You didn't clean your room, so no allowance for you this week, young lady!"* When your child is bribed with money for chores, she may demand more and more as she gets older. She will not learn to take responsibility for being part of the family. And she may say, *"I don't want the money,"* and refuse to do her chores.

Floating loans too big for your child to realistically pay back is discouraging. Do not nag or lecture with *"I told you so"* or *"If only you hadn't spent . . ."*

Negotiate raises in allowance at a *family meeting*. Birthdays or the beginning of the school year are good times to do this. This helps to eliminate daily hassles and teaches good negotiation skills. *"Mindy, convince me that you need a raise in allowance. We gave Peter a raise because he is buying his own lunches now. Tell me why you feel you need more money."*

## PREVENTIVE TIPS

- Comment on what your child does well with money. If she has saved even for a short time, comment on her efforts. *"Hilary, you are a good decision maker! That was very grown-up. It is hard to pass up something you can have right away when you are saving for something else."*
- Listen to her carefully and be aware of peer pressure. Often if you acknowledge her feelings she will work through her wants and needs more easily.
- Establish family values with discussion. Talk about wants and needs at bedtime. Your child won't save if you give him everything he asks for. Give him what he needs and help him plan to earn what he wants.
- Discuss reasonable money issues in front of your children. (Do not dwell on adult money issues that may worry or concern you.) Sharing a bill at a restaurant is healthy. One family had a "family fun kitty." Money was collected in the communal jar in various ways: sometimes loose pocket change, a quarter from anyone using bad manners, or a quarter added by the parent for every person using good manners at a meal. The money was used to take the family to dinner, and one of the children was elected to pay the bill with money from the kitty.

# MOODINESS

*"My child is very irritable and moody."*

### UNDERSTANDING THE SITUATION

All children are moody at times. Certain situations will set some children off, and most children go through stages of moodiness at certain ages. Some children tend to be moody or irritable because of a serious temperament. Whatever the case, bad moods are exasperating and very tiresome to live with. You will not be able to make your child change her mood. *"Wipe that scowl off your face and sweeten up"* doesn't work; it draws attention to unwanted behavior and encourages power struggles. Instead, decide what you will do. As hard as it may be for you, this is one parenting issue that will take a bundle of energy, patience, and a positive attitude.

### WHAT TO SAY AND DO

Keep your sense of humor and do not let your child's mood affect yours. With a young child try a lighthearted approach and do the unexpected to distract her. Sing a funny song. Try *"There was an old woman who swallowed a fly . . ."* or ask, *"Samantha, would you like to hear a silly story about an old man who went to town in a bathtub?"* Be prepared with others. This takes creativity.

Very young children are often predictable. If you know your child will be grouchy for an hour after her nap, plan for it. Take the time to hold her and comfort her through it.

When she is in a stubborn, irritable mood, give her space. Do not bug her and try to coax her out of it. If she is affecting others, ask her to take *time out* someplace by herself. *"Marnie, you are very irritable. Your actions affect us all. Please take some time out in your room to feel better."* Later, discuss her feelings and talk about why she felt as she did.

Help her get in touch with her feelings and understand her needs so that she will become aware of and responsible for her actions. *"Hilary, you seem irritable. You are very tired from the slumber party. Take a rest in your room. If you want to continue to go to those events you will need to learn how to handle the next day."* A logical consequence, if this is a repeated problem, is to say, *"No sleep-overs until you handle your moodiness the next day. Skip this one, and we will try again next time."*

Do not label your more serious child "the grouch." Keep your comments positive. *"Ryan, you often seem serious. You are very thoughtful today."* Or *"You are an analytical person."*

## PREVENTIVE TIPS

• Keep a log of your child's behavior for a couple of weeks. Observe when she tends to become moody and plan with her ways to help her successfully avoid these situations. Some children become very irritable after naptime when they are in a transition trying to give up naps. You may observe this behavior when she is around too many children, or maybe when she is alone and bored. Some children become out of sorts before they show any other signs of illness. Some are more irritable when they are working at achieving a new level of capability or understanding. While it's difficult to live with, this is constructive crabbiness!

• Try to take a walk, exercise, or take a little break from your child if you feel you are getting sucked into her bad mood.

• During comfortable times read children's books to initiate discussions about feelings. Try *Alexander and the Terrible, Horrible, Not Good Very Bad Day* by Judith Viorst (New York: Macmillan, 1972), *Feelings* by Aliki Brandenberg (New York: Morrow, 1984), or *Grandpa's Face* by Eloise Greenfield (New York: Putnam, 1988).

# MORNING HASSLES

*"Mornings are such a rush, with lots of yelling, tears, and chaos!"*

## Ages 2½–5

### UNDERSTANDING THE SITUATION

When morning hits, the hassles begin. All children seem to know when parents are in a hurry and have less time for giving attention, and this is when they act out the most. Nagging and coaxing leads to bribing and threatening. If you fall into these patterns you are not alone. Many parents begin a workday exhausted, feeling angry and sometimes guilty. Many children are dropped off at day care or school feeling resentful and unhappy—never a good way to begin their day. Morning hassles will never disappear entirely, though you can plan for a successful morning by designing a routine and providing *time to teach* personal responsibilities. Let go of perfectionism and set reasonable expectations for your child's age and stage of development. You are a wise parent to establish a morning routine in the early years. Always try to leave your child for the day on a positive note. Even if your morning has been frustrating, stop and take time to give him a hug and a kiss and an *"I love you."*

### WHAT TO SAY AND DO

Begin the night before. Your young child can select her clothes for the next day and set them out. Discuss the morning routine with her before she goes to sleep. Even though you may be tired, show your enthusiasm and use humor. This often sets the stage for morning.

Take *time to teach* one thing at a time. If your child can do it, you should not be doing it for him. Show him how to wake up to his own alarm, use the bathroom, and get dressed. Training charts are helpful tools. *"Here is a new chart. Put a star on it when you finish morning bathroom and dressing. You are a very capable four-year-old!"* If you feel he needs a reward for finishing the chart well, do not use toys or candy. Inspire instead with an outing of his choice or a project you can work on together.

Take time to greet him with a good-morning cuddle. Spend five minutes. This takes personal organization on your part so that you have time and patience for him. It may help you to get up a bit earlier and allow yourself more time.

When he starts to hassle, help him assess his feelings. Then tell him what you will do, not what you will make him do. *"Jimmy, I know you would like my attention. My hands are in soapy water. Please put on your shoes and I'll dry my hands and read a story with you."* Try to ignore any protests. Use a *poker face* and leave the room if he acts out. Or do the unexpected. Use humor, hugging him with soapy hands and a big smile. *"Okay, you have my undivided attention."*

If he refuses to dress, do not nag. Use *action with few words.* Put his clothes and shoes in the car. He can choose to dress at pre-school or in the car. Use this method once or twice, and you will win cooperation. *"Johnny, we need to leave now. I have your clothes. You may dress at pre-school or in the car."* Remain *poker faced.*

Give your child something to look forward to. Let her know that when she gets ready she can do something special. *"Heather, as soon as you dress, come in for breakfast. You can pop the waffles into the toaster. If you're quick I'll have time to tell you a troll story."*

## PREVENTIVE TIPS

- At a *family meeting* have "Morning" on the agenda. List all family tasks that need doing and get agreements from each individual to help (age three is not too young). List each child's personal tasks for getting up, dressed, and to the breakfast table.
- Stay on task in the morning. If you get sidetracked by the telephone or other interruptions, so will your child.
- If you have a rough morning (and you will occasionally), make peace with your child before leaving him for the day. Separate the morning incidents from your love for him. *"Jason, we had*

*a bad start this morning. I'm sorry I yelled. What can you do differently tomorrow? I love you, and I need a hug and a kiss before you go to school."*

## Ages 6-10

### UNDERSTANDING THE SITUATION

Please read the above, for ages 2½–5. Morning hassles are more complicated with the school-age child. There is often more to organize and remember: musical instruments, homework, permission slips, written excuses, daily schedules, lunches, etc. This added to waking, breakfast, and getting out the door on time can be awesome. Your child is old enough to assume more responsibility. Nagging and coaxing are not helpful. Yelling and screaming is a frantic parenting style that leads to attention seeking and power struggles. The best morning routine is one that is planned together with your child, and the plan needs to be consistently followed. Teaching a morning routine is a process. Consider these years *time for teaching.* You are teaching your child a lifestyle with communication and understanding.

### WHAT TO SAY AND DO

The night before, talk about what is expected in the morning. Have your child lay her clothes out for the morning and organize what she needs to take to school.

Buy her an alarm. *"Molly, here is your very own alarm so you can get yourself up."* Even though she wakes up on her own, offer your time for a good-morning hug and kiss. Often five minutes of undivided attention makes the morning.

Establish a morning routine. Making a training chart listing all tasks needing to be done. This is an opportunity to teach your child organizational skills and how to be responsible for himself and to the family:

• Wake up and get up
• Use the bathroom

- Get dressed
- Make the bed
- Eat breakfast
- Feed the dog
- Organize lunch, schoolwork, instrument, and sports clothes.

*Encourage* by catching your child following the chart. Look for all her improvement and effort and comment on it.

Use logical consequences. *"Hilary, if you are not ready when I need to go I will assume you have chosen to walk to school."* Be sure you follow through with what you say. Do not rescue her; she may walk. If you find her leaving her lunch, reports, musical instruments, etc. at home consistently, do not rush to give them to her. This is the ultimate in rescuing and will not build responsibility.

**PREVENTIVE TIPS**

- See Preventive Tips for ages 2½–5.

*See also: Brushing hair; Chores; Clothing, choosing; School, won't go*

# MOVING

*"My child is upset about our moving."*

## Ages 2½–5

**UNDERSTANDING THE SITUATION**

Moving from a familiar community of home, friends, and activities will be stressful for you and your child. Your younger child may begin clinging, acting out, or slipping into younger behavior (crying, whining, wetting, etc.). These behaviors are tiring and frustrating and certainly complicate an already difficult situation, yet they are a signal that your child feels the stress of the move. Do not yell and scold him when you grow tired and lose patience. Your positive attitude is a must. Your child will reflect your actions. Your worry, guilt, and anxiety need to be replaced with optimism. *"Change is healthy, and the challenge will be exciting."* Give your support and ideas. Leaving friends, relatives, school, and a secure bedroom with familiar furnishings is hard, but there are ways to make the move exciting rather than terrifying. Take time for yourself. Your energy and well-being are musts. Be patient, and keep the faith in your child. His behavior will normalize in time.

## WHAT TO SAY AND DO

Keep your child's routine as regular as possible. She will be happier if you allow her to remain in her day care routine or with a familiar sitter than if you take her to look at houses.

Let your child know what to expect each day. She has no concept of time and will do better knowing her daily schedule and where you are. *"Lily, you will be with Auntie Mo this morning. Mommy will be looking at houses. I will pick you up at lunchtime."* If you must leave town, give her a calendar so she can put a sticker on each day until you return. It may help to call her while you are away.

Take time to stop what you are doing and talk about feelings. Hold her and play with her. Rock and hum. Say, *"Hannah, moving is hard. Mommy gets tired and cranky. I love you, and soon we will be settled!"*

Distract her with humor and the unexpected. Try a silly game: *"Who is coming to our new house? Mommy, Daddy, Kitty, dandelions—oh, not dandelions? I bet our new house has dandelions!"*

Offer her choices and show enthusiasm! *"Morgan, this will be your room. Do you want your bed here or over there? Good choice! The sun shines right through that window, and you will see the moon!"*

Transfer as many of her belongings as possible. Have her help choose the bedding, special toys, furniture, and clothing you can bring to your new home. Have her help pack. *"Molly, you are great at moving. What a help you have been."*

PREVENTIVE TIPS

• Take her to visit your new home and neighborhood so she is familiar with it before the move.
• Take time for yourself. Keep up your rest and exercise. You will need plenty of energy for her and the move. You may have to give up some outside activity until this is over.
• Take regular *special time* with your child—walking, reading, or playing games. Giving ten minutes of undivided time two or three times a day will give you more time alone in the long run.
• Keep your child's schedule as normal as possible. Late nights, hurried meals, or lots of company will add stress.
• Read *I'm Not Moving, Mama!* by Nancy White Carlstrom (New York: Macmillan, 1990).

## Ages 6-10

UNDERSTANDING THE SITUATION

Please read the previous section, for ages 2½–5. Your school-age child may have noticeable behavior changes, as with a younger child. One boy, when told his family was moving, shut down. He refused to cooperate at home, and his schoolwork suffered. His comments were harsh and hurting. *"You are ruining my life."* Some individuals, no matter what age, find change very difficult. Parents often feel their children are unappreciative, and a first reaction is to feel defensive. *"He doesn't realize what sacrifices we make for him. This is no piece of cake for me either!"* You may find the circumstances of the move hard for you and the added complaining and poor behavior tedious and maddening. Be patient and stay out of arguments and defensive postures. Work on listening and understanding. Keep the faith. This will pass.

## WHAT TO SAY AND DO

Identify your child's feelings and show empathy. Be sad with him over leaving his home and friends. It is important that he experience the feelings in order to understand them better. Do not try to "fix" or deny his sadness. Share how you feel as well.

Offer support. Help him put together an album of the past, throw a good-bye party, have his friends sign a t-shirt or an autograph animal. Give him a new photo album for pictures of his new home and friends.

Be optimistic and enthusiastic. Moving provides a wonderful experience in flexibility, risk taking, and handling change, all necessary skills. Give your child a new diary. Say, *"Anne, I am so excited for you! You will learn so much about yourself as you make new friends and face new experiences. Keep track of each day and your new experiences."*

Let your child know what to expect by providing information. Say, *"Ryan, Dad and I are going to Chicago to look at schools and houses. I'll take pictures of everything we see. We will share as much as we know with you."*

Involve your child. Say, *"Mindy, we are having a garage sale. Let's look at what you want to sell. You keep any money you make."* Involve her in packing.

Climb into your child's world. Learn about his new school, the activities it offers, and the neighborhood. Say, *"Tren, I visited the school you will be attending. They have sports every day after school! I videotaped some tennis and some baseball. You will have many choices."*

It is important that he feel some control over his life. Give choices when possible. Sometimes it is even possible to visit several schools and offer your child a choice of where he feels most comfortable.

## PREVENTIVE TIPS

• Take time to communicate your feelings. He may assume he is the cause of your stress.
• Offer extra *special time* for him. Though this is a busy time,

take an extra ten minutes to listen to his feelings and show support.

- If you must leave your child to look at your new location, choose an understanding and patient person to look after him while you are gone.
- Keep your child's daily routine as consistent and normal as possible.
- Together read *I'm Not Moving, Mama!* by Nancy White Carlstrom (New York: Macmillan, 1990) and ask a children's librarian for other book ideas on moving.

# NAIL-BITING

*"My child bites and picks her nails."*

### UNDERSTANDING THE SITUATION

Nail-biting is a common habit, often starting when thumb-sucking ends. You may feel annoyed at the behavior and try coaxing, scolding, or rewarding. Nail-biting is often a tension reducer. Your child may not even be aware she is doing it at the time. You are raising a child who is learning to think for herself and make good decisions. If you nag and disapprove, you take away her power to decide what to do. This behavior may be very hard for you to ignore, because it annoys you; however, with too much pushing you may create an attention-getting situation or even a power struggle. Point out once what she is doing, give support, turn the responsibility over to her, and then try to ignore the habit. Do not ignore her. Your trust and confidence in her ability to stop is very important. Be patient. Waiting for a habit to stop is never easy. It will take time. Do not give up!

### WHAT TO SAY AND DO

Make your child aware of his nail-biting, show understanding, show confidence, and offer support. *"Andy, I've noticed that your nails are red from biting, and they look sore. I bit my nails when I was your age when I was excited or nervous. I stopped because they would hurt and bleed. I was embarrassed to show my hands to my piano teacher. I know you can stop too, and you will when you are ready. Let me know if I can help you."* Then ignore the nail-biting unless he asks for help from you.

If your child is willing, help her find a solution. *"Andrea, you have asked for help in stopping your nail-biting. Let's brainstorm all the ideas you might find helpful. Then you can choose which idea you'd like to try."* Brainstorming ideas might be: Mom gently touching Andrea's shoulder when she is biting nails, keeping hands busy by doing a puzzle while watching TV, keeping hands in pockets as much as possible, painting bad-tasting liquid on nails, sitting on hands in the car, tying Popsicle sticks to fingers.

Give your child a nail kit and show him how to care for his nails. Nail kits are designed for both boys and girls. One mother took her daughter for a professional manicure.

Keep a chart and have your child add a sticker each day that she abstains. Do not give expensive rewards, toys, or candy. Comment on her efforts and celebrate her success by giving her a *choice* of something she would like do with you or with a friend.

### PREVENTIVE TIPS

- Exercise reduces stress. Consider a noncompetitive activity for your child such as yoga or Tai Chi lessons. These build concentration, relaxation, and self-confidence. Teach her to relax with music, massage, or reading.
- Develop awareness of why your child might be biting his nails. Keep a log for two weeks when you notice him doing so. Try to observe what stresses may be causing the biting. Discuss this with him and ask him to think of what may be causing him to feel stress.
- Consider music lessons, which keep the hands busy and provide opportunities to relax and feel good about accomplishments.

*See also: Nose picking*

# NAKEDNESS

*"How should I handle questions and other issues about nudity?" "Should my child see me naked?"*

## Ages 2½–5

### UNDERSTANDING THE SITUATION

Nudity is natural between very young children and parents in the home. As long as the atmosphere is relaxed about nakedness and discussions about the body are respectful and candid, children develop a healthy feeling about their sexuality, important to self-esteem. Important questions will come up often during showers, dressing, or other private times; they provide opportunities for sharing feelings, attitudes, values, and accurate information about sexuality that will be so important in later growing-up years. If you make it clear that you can freely discuss naked bodies now, you will have an easier time discussing serious issues such as birth control later. Your child will learn to use good judgment and make good choices about his body if your attitudes and values are clear from the beginning and supported by accurate factual information.

### WHAT TO SAY AND DO

If you are uncomfortable with nudity and your child's curiosity, be honest and let him know how you feel. You want him to understand that you are uncomfortable with nakedness but that he didn't do anything wrong to make you feel that way. Don't be afraid to explain, *"We didn't see our mom and dad naked in our family, and I feel uncomfortable undressing in front of you."*

Take *time to teach* your child manners abut nudity. He may understand other people's negative reactions to mean *"I'm a bad person."*

1. Bring up the difference between private and public sharing.

*"When you are home and we have no company, it is okay to run around naked. We do not go naked in public."*

2. Let your child know what to expect about how other people may feel about nudity. *"Megan, Granny and Papa do not run around their home naked. It would make them feel all funny if you ran around naked when they visited."*

3. How you behave in your family home will be different from how you conduct yourself in other places. *"When you are at Mary's you do not run around naked. When you are visiting at other people's homes you wear your clothes. I do too."*

Showering or dressing together provides relaxed time to answer personal questions. This is also a good time to talk about appropriate and inappropriate touching. Young children love to poke and touch. Be loving and kind if you need to set some limits. Your body language is as important as what you say. Use correct terminology. *"Heidi, that is my breast, and I don't mind if you feel it. I don't like when you poke it. You are the boss of your private parts. You don't let anyone touch you where you do not want to be touched. Mommy doesn't either."*

Treat adult nakedness with respect. Children have boundaries just as adults do. An adult naked body parading through the house may be overwhelming to a young child.

If you should at any time want your privacy, set a standard routine: Close your door, have your child knock if he needs you, and be consistent. Should your child walk in on you and your spouse when your door is closed, tell him firmly and kindly to leave. *"Matthew, this is private time for Daddy and me. Close the door, and I'll be out in a moment."* Immediately dress and go to talk to him. Sit next to him and say, *"You walked in on Dad and me when we were having a loving, quiet time together. When we close our door we want to be private. If you really need us you can knock. When you close your bedroom door I will knock too. We do love you!!!"* And hug, hug, hug! Later check his understanding of your discussion. *"Matthew, when our door is closed what do you need to do first if you want us?"*

PREVENTIVE TIPS

See Preventive Tips for ages 6–10.

# Ages 6–10

UNDERSTANDING THE SITUATION

Please read Understanding the Situation for ages 2½–5. Your goal for your school-age child is to continue to help him understand his sexuality, feel comfortable with his body, and feel free to ask you important questions. Around age six your child will indicate when he becomes modest and wants his privacy. Honor his need to have you be more private as well. Be aware about what might embarrass him, close doors behind you, and be discreet about your own nudity. Some parents wish to continue to shower, soak in the hot tub, etc. naked as a family. Remember the principle of mutual respect. Your feeling of what privacy should be is not the same as your child's. Let him find his. He may become very modest during puberty and then later relax.

WHAT TO SAY AND DO

As your child shows modesty, tell her you see her growing up. Verbalize that you understand she is ready for more privacy and that she shouldn't feel she is bad or hiding. You want her to feel privacy is deserved and respected; it is okay. *"Jill, I notice that you shut the door when you dress lately. You deserve your privacy. You are growing up!"*

The transition between the younger years and school age is subtle. Discuss the change openly. *"Scott, there was a time when you were little and we all shared the family tub. It is normal to outgrow that."*

PREVENTIVE TIPS

• Have children's books about the body available to read aloud together to provide good communication and closeness. Children are naturally curious and should hear the facts. See a children's librarian or knowledgeable bookstore clerk for book suggestions. One excellent book is *The Bare Naked Book* by Kathy Stinson (Ontario: Annick Press/Firefly Books, 1986).

- Look at photo albums often and talk about how your child is growing and changing.
- Take parenting classes, and work on being relaxed and open to discussion about sexuality with your child. Fathers are every bit as important to these discussions as mothers. Read *Rasing a Child Conservatively in a Sexually Permissive World* by Sol Gordon and Judith Gordon (New York: Simon and Schuster, 1989).

*See also: Sexuality, questions about*

# NAPS

*"My child refuses her nap though she still needs it."*

### UNDERSTANDING THE SITUATION

Age 2½ is the typical age a child begins refusing her naps. Prepare yourself. For some parents, this is a very difficult and tiring stage. When her sleep patterns change everything may get out of whack—her disposition, her eating, her bedtime, etc. She may go without naps and then one day sleep three hours and not want to go to bed that night. Children's needs for sleep vary tremendously. For a parent at home with a preschooler, at least an hour break for resting is needed for both. You cannot force your child to sleep, so do not get into a power struggle over whether she sleeps or not. Take care of yourself and get what you need to have the energy for her. Hang in there. This is often a transition stage. It will pass, but it may take time—maybe months.

## WHAT TO SAY AND DO

Usually establishing a naptime routine is helpful. Be very consistent (be home at the same time) while you are working your child back to a schedule. *"Nick, I will read with you and tell you one story. Then you need an hour to yourself to rest. You do need to be quiet on your bed."* Be flexible. You cannot make him sleep, but you can teach him to have quite time for an hour. If he follows you out of his room, walk him back with a *poker face*. Use this *action with few words* as many times as it takes to train him to stay in his room.

Lie down initially with your child. She may be worried she will miss doing something with you if she sleeps. Let her know what you will be doing while she is napping. *"Laura, while you nap I will rest too. We both need our rest time."* If you are lucky enough to be able to do this with her, lie down on your bed with her and sleep too. A half hour will do you good.

Try hiring a baby-sitter to handle naptime once a week. Many children nap better at day care or with a baby-sitter than they do with a parent.

If she refuses her own bed, gave her a *choice*. *"Jessie, you need a nap. You may be in your sleeping bag on your pad or in your own bed."*

Offer something to look forward to after her nap. *"Auntie Mo will come see us with the new puppy after your nap."*

Never base your love on whether she naps or not. Do not say, *"Mommy loves you so much, especially when you take your naps."* Your love is unconditional. She needs to know that you will love her regardless, though you may be frustrated with her actions. *"Mary, I love you to pieces, though I do get very tired and cranky when you do not nap."*

## PREVENTIVE TIPS

• Tire your child out with more activity in the morning such as swimming, playing at the park, taking long walks and tricycle rides. Calm her down with reading. Do not watch television before the nap; for some children it is too stimulating.

- Discuss how she feels when she is tired. Take *time for teaching* and discuss listening to your body and finding out what it needs. When she does have a good nap, ask her how she feels.
- Read together children's books about naptime, such as *No Nap for Benjamin Badger* by Nancy White Carlstrom (New York: Macmillan, 1991). Children's librarians and knowledgeable boostore clerks will have other suggestions.

## NEW BABY

*"Our child feels our new baby is definitely a disruption."*

### UNDERSTANDING THE SITUATION

After the excitement of the new baby wears off, the reality is *"Mom, I liked it better before. Take it back now. We don't want it any-more."* Your young child may not verbalize this, but he may act out by aggressively hugging the baby much too hard, hitting, or dropping toys onto the baby. He may revert to younger behavior with wetting pants, wanting a bottle, and refusing to cooperate. Your school-age child may also feel slighted over the time you must spend with the baby. Though these reactions are common, they make any parent feel terribly weary, concerned, and perhaps guilty for even having another baby. Behind your child's actions lies a fear that you are replacing him and that you will love the new baby more. Imagine how you would feel if your spouse decided to bring another partner home. Jealous? Resentful? Fearful? Do not shame your child with *"You should love this baby."* Scolding or punishing will only cause more resentment and lowered self-esteem. Instead, give him all the *encouragement* you can muster up. He needs your reassurance that you love him as much as before and confidence that you will continue to count on his love and help, and that he is needed. You will need energy, patience, and a loving sense of humor. Cultivating loving relationships is a lifelong process. The dust will settle, and with consistency and good communication, the new baby will soon be better accepted.

## WHAT TO SAY AND DO

Maintain your first child's routine as much as possible. Continue taking him to his activities rather than having a sitter do this for you. The sitter can stay with the baby.

Express to your first child that your love grows. Do not assume that he understands that you won't love him any less. *"Andrew, my love is like a huge flame that grows and grows and grows. I love Daddy, you, and now the baby too, and I always will."* You will want to reaffirm this often.

Though you want to give your child opportunities to feel needed, do not give her too much responsibility. First take *time for teaching.* Teach her about what her new brother needs. This is a wonderful opportunity for a lesson in child development; she will learn about herself as well. Tell her how helpful it is when she models behavior the baby needs to learn. Make a chart with words or pictures, and call it "What Helps Andrew To Be Happy." Show your confidence under select circumstances, leaving her to baby-sit for two minutes while you disappear around the corner. Your chart might include:

Talking softly or singing          Happy voices
Keeping him clean and dry          Quiet time for sleep
Feeding him on schedule            Modeling: eating from a
Small, soft toys                   spoon, sipping from a cup,
Nothing too close to his face      sitting at the table.

When your child shows jealousy, show understanding with a kind and calm response.

1. Reflect her feelings. "You feel ____ when ____ because ____ . Let's ____ ." *"Josie, you feel jealous when I feed Nick because you want my attention. Let's think of what you could do instead of hitting him."* Share ideas. *"Cuddle up with us and bring a book for me to read to you, get your doll and feed her next to us,*

*tell me a story, sing to us, or listen to your tapes until I finish, and then I will put Nick down and play with you."*

2. Recognize her feelings. Use "You wish." *"Josie, you feel jealous when I feed Nick. You wish he weren't here."* Or *"You wish I could give you all my time."* Pause and wait to listen for her response. Feelings can't be fixed, they just are. An understanding hug may be needed.

3. Empower her to act more responsibly and compassionately. *"Holly, you hit Hunter. Hitting hurts and is not okay. What is it you really want?"* She may need *time out* to *cool off.* Then explore positive ways she can get your attention. *"What other ways can you think of to get what you want?"*

Catch her being good. Comment enthusiastically when she helps and occasionally celebrate. *"Amy, you helped when I needed it this morning. I got all my work done. We will leave Andrew home this afternoon with a sitter and go to the zoo or park. You choose."* Be sure to use *special time* daily, even if only for fifteen minutes.

Look for opportunities to delight your child with the joy he brings the baby. *"Look, Adam, your brother is wiggling all over because you smiled at him."* Or *"Joey, Jeffy wants to show you he can wiggle his arms and legs just like you. You are very gentle and a good teacher."* Or *"Andy cried when you left for school. He missed you."* One mother told her preschooler that when the baby held her finger, that meant he loved her.

If your young child reverts to wetting pants, rather than pulling diapers out again, give him the extra attention the baby gets. Dress him on the changing table, singing and even using a little powder. Give him attention when he is being good as well, and the younger behavior will stop. If he demands a bottle, try giving him all that he drinks in a bottle. If you use a *poker face* and seem unimpressed, he will tire of it. Be patient; this may take time.

Your child may refer to "the baby." Do not correct him, but do use "new brother" or call him by his given name. *"Andrew, your new brother loves to have you sit near."* Or *"Andrew, Jason smiles when you sit near."*

Do not compare children. Do not say, *"Derek learned to crawl so much faster than Jody."* Instead, say, *"Derek is learning to crawl early."* Do not put your children in categories. *"Derek will be our athlete because he crawled so early"* may be interpreted by your older child to mean that the athletic position in this family is occupied, or that he will have to try very hard to outdo his brother to be a good athlete.

## PREVENTIVE TIPS

• Involve your child in the baby's coming. Hospitals have sibling classes. Take her to your pregnancy appointments to hear the heartbeat of the new baby. Ask for her help decorating her new brother's room, etc.
• Give your son or daughter the present of a new baby doll when you arrive home from the hospital with the new baby.
• Reduce outside activities and identify your priorities. Find time for yourself. You will need a good sense of humor to give time for family fun as well as family responsibility.
• Do not expect perfection. Keep your expectations reasonable for your child's age.
• It may help your first child to enroll him in nursery school, enrichment lessons, or after-school activities. Do this well before the baby is born or wait until six weeks after the baby comes home so that he doesn't feel you are shoving him out.
• Read children's stories together. Try *Daniel's Dog* by Ellen Bogart (New York: Scholastic, 1990), *Anna in Charge* by Yoriko Tsutsui (New York: Viking, 1989), *Julius, the Baby of the World* by Kevin Henkes (New York: Greenwillow/Morrow, 1990), *I Love My Baby Sister (Most of the Time)* by Elaine Edelman (New York: Puffin Books, 1985), *Will There Be a Lap for Me?* by Dorothy Corey (Morton Grove, Ill.: Whitman, 1992), *The New Baby* by Fred Rogers (New York: Putnam Sons, 1986), or *A Baby Sister for Frances* by Russell Hoban (New York: HarperCollins, 1964).

*See also: Fighting, between siblings; Pregnancy*

# NIGHT WANDERING

*"My child gets up in the night and wanders through the house."*

### UNDERSTANDING THE SITUATION

Night wandering is most common around the age of three. It is not uncommon to hear from parents that their child deliberately gets up during the night and wanders through the house, eats out of the refrigerator, uses the bathroom, gets a drink, sits in the dark, turns on lights or the television, and possibly even wanders outside. Night wandering is not the same as sleepwalking. Generally night wandering is intentional. Sleepwalking is unintentional; the child wanders throughout the house or yard while still asleep. Both of these behaviors are matters of concern, and you need to be an alert parent at possibly the hardest time for your tired body. Night wandering can be quite an adventure. It is a powerful feeling to your young child to have the house to himself. Do not panic or overreact, or you'll likely exacerbate the problem. For both sleepwalking and night wandering you need to stay calm and design a plan of action. As tiring as it may be, you need to wake up and consistently return your child to his bed.

### WHAT TO SAY AND DO

When your child is up, you need to be up. Find ways to wake up when he is up. Tie bells on his bedroom door and on other doors he may open so that you will hear him. Turn up your baby monitor when you go to bed. If you are a heavy sleeper you may have to install an alarm system. Make the house unappealing to your night wanderer. Cut off the breaker switch so that the lights will not go on. (Be sure to keep a flashlight near your bed.)

Before you panic, watch what routine your night wanderer establishes. Do not let him see you. He may keep it short, get a drink, check out the test pattern on the TV screen, get bored, and go back to bed. With no interference from you, he may return to his bed quite safely. He may repeat this benign procedure several nights, then lose interest and stay in bed. If he follows this procedure, he will have learned some self-control. However, you need to intervene when it becomes a problem for you or him.

When directing a child back to bed, remain calm and with a *poker face* walk him back to bed. Do not feed him or engage in any conversation. Your sleepwalker may not wake up. The night wanderer should receive no social benefit for this activity. Walk him back to his bed as many times as it takes. Be consistent and do not give up.

Eliminate potential excuses to get up. Keep a glass of water near his bed, a cup of dry Cheerios, a light with a dimmer switch, a small tape recorder with calming music. Establish a rule: *"Get up only to go to the bathroom."*

## PREVENTIVE TIPS

- Keep your child's eating and sleeping routine consistent. Children with immature sleep patterns need help training the body. Even if he is up late into the night, wake him at a regular morning hour. Try waking him from his naps earlier so he will sleep at night.
- Take *time to teach* him relaxation exercises that will help him fall asleep. When he wakes up it may help him to know he can close his eyes and think calming thoughts—running on a beach, playing in the sand, etc. Some children do well to have calming music near their bed to play.
- Cut out evening TV, which may stimulate a vivid imagination. Your child needs calm.
- Celebrate bedtime with a quiet routine and time together. Allow no roughhousing, wrestling, or other stimulating activity. Tuck your child in with the understanding that you will see him in the morning after you both have a good night's sleep.

• Discuss night wandering the next morning. Comment when he does better and make sure he gets recognition for staying in his bed.

*See also: Bedtime, staying in bed*

# NIGHTMARES

*"My child often has nightmares and wakes up frightened."*

### UNDERSTANDING THE SITUATION

Children have nightmares at different ages and stages of growing up. An occasional nightmare is normal. It is not a sign of bad parenting. If your child is having nightmares very often, she may be feeling abnormal stress or anxiety. You may not ever know what is causing a nightmare. Your positive comfort and support are necessary to reassure your child she is safe, and your *encouragement* is necessary to assure her she can handle the situation. Nightmares are different from night terrors, which are not dreams at all but are thought to result from an immature sleep pattern. An occasional night terror is frightening to the parent, as the child sometimes screams or yells but doesn't respond. The child experiences no bad dream and usually won't recall the episode, and the parent can only wait it out. If your child experiences excessive night terror or nightmares, you should consult your family pediatrician for support.

### WHAT TO SAY AND DO

When your child has a night terror, hold her and be with her as she wakes up wondering what is happening. A cool washcloth may help soothe her. Stay calm and quiet. She probably will not remember the incident in the morning.

When she has a nightmare, offer calming support. You may have to wake her up. Hold her and remain calm and kind. *"Carli, you had a bad dream. You are safe."* Do not "rescue" her with *"Mommy is here. I will protect you."* You want her to feel she is capable of handling the situation.

Suggest to your child that he can change his dreams. *"You are the boss of your own dreams. You can change the scary guy into your friend or use your magic to make him disappear."*

Suggest that he use the bathroom. Sometimes the urge to go to the bathroom creates dreaming. Do not get involved in talking or making this too enjoyable. Get him back to bed quickly with a hug and kiss.

Your child may have a hard time getting the image of the dream out of her mind. Take *time to teach* her what to do when she needs to comfort herself.

1. Briefly discuss the dream and offer a new ending, a successful and happy one. *"Laurie, sometimes I have bad dreams and I make up new endings. I always win."*
2. It may help to put more light in her room. A lamp with a dimmer switch works well.
3. Offer to stay fifteen minutes with her while she calms down. Your closeness is comforting.
4. Some children want to crawl into bed with Mom or Dad after a nightmare. If you don't sleep well with her in your bed, put a sleeping bag on the floor next to your bed. When she wants to be near, she can be—without disturbing you.

**PREVENTIVE TIPS**

- Keep your child on a regular bedtime schedule and see that she gets needed rest.
- Monitor her television viewing. She may do better not watching television in the evening. Instead read interesting and calming stories, listen to soothing music, or play a quiet game before bed.
- Discuss the bad dream during the day with her. This will help you understand any fears or stress she has so that you can reassure her.

- *Encourage. "Wow, you handled that dream really well!"*
- Be sure you let your child know what to expect during the day. Limit her stress by letting her know what the schedule is, where she will be. Keep her routine calm and regular.
- Keep your expectations reasonable for her age and let go of your perfectionism. Children are expected today to live a very hurried life. For many children the pace is too fast and much too stressful.
- Read together with your child. Try *There's Something in My Attic* by Mercer Meyer (New York: Dial Books, 1988), and ask a children's librarian or knowledgeable bookstore clerk for other ideas.

*See also: Dark, fear of; Night wandering; Sleeping with parent*

---

# NO!

*"My child is saying no to everything!"*

### UNDERSTANDING THE SITUATION

Your young child may say no to just about everything, including even things she wants. It is exasperating and very time consuming, yet this is your youngster's job. The behavior is normal and actually very healthy for your child. The "terrific twos" have the reputation for no-saying, and some threes, fours, and fives practice it as well. No-saying is one of the first opportunities your child has to begin separating from you and practice self-assertion, so very important to self-confidence. Be patient, stay calm and positive, but set your limits. Say what you mean and do what you say you'll do, and be very consistent. Though it is very hard, do not overcontrol or get sucked into a power struggle. Give lots of love and *encouragement* throughout this stage. Your child needs to know you will love her and not abandon her even if she says no. She needs to know she is safe when she is independent from you.

## WHAT TO SAY AND DO

Give "yes" responses and tell your child what to do rather than saying *"No!"* or *"Don't!"* to her. *Rather than "No! Don't get marker on the counter!"* say, *"Meg, please put this newspaper under your picture to protect the counter."* Rather than *"Don't squeeze the kitten!"* say, *"Ryan, please hold the kitten gently."* Save "no" for times when it really matters, like *"No! The burner is hot!"*

Set limits. If your child's choice is definitely no but is unrealistic to the needs of the situation, stand firm and remember to use *action with few words*. Do not nag or coax. Say it, mean it, and do it. *"Nick, you need to wear your pj's. Either I put them on you or you do it."* If you need to do it, use a *poker face*.

Make your requests assertive and clear. Do not end your requests with a lilt in your voice or a question. *"Carolyn, it's time for pj's. Okay?"* This leaves room for her stubborn no. *"Carolyn, bedtime. Please, you need to put on your pj's."*

Her stubbornness reflects a new stage of thinking. When she says no, try to encourage her to think about cause and effect. *"Brit, I know you want to play with the stove. What do you think will happen to you if you touch this hot burner?"*

Take *time for teaching*. Take time to show how she may be hurt if she refuses to do what you ask. You could have her touch a warm (but not very hot) burner to learn the concept of a stove getting too hot to touch. To teach the danger of the street, have her stand with another adult and watch as you run over a toy truck or grapefruit with your car.

Offer *choices* whenever possible. *"Nick, it's time for your pajamas. Do you want me to snap them in back, or do you want to snap them in front?"* Encourage his good thinking and decision making. *"Alright! I love snapping these pj's! Good decision!"*

Use a sense of humor. Try distracting your child when he is negative. Sing, "Row, Row, Row Your Boat" as you brush teeth. Play animal walks as he makes his way to bed. Count or play counting games as you dress him.

Do not put negative labels on your child. *"She's going through the terrible twos at age three"* is negative. Say positive things to other people in front of her. *"Mary is a terrific three. She is very assertive. She really sticks to things that are important to her."*

### PREVENTIVE TIPS

- Give your young child plenty of warning and let him know what to expect. If he needs to stop playing with his friend, let him know five minutes in advance. Tell him every two hours what will happen next. *"Alex, we will go to the bank and then the pet store."* Often a child who will say no to the unwelcome or unexpected has an easier time accepting transitions if he is prepared in advance.
- Plan for the time it takes to raise a "no sayer" and avoid power struggles. When he knows you are rushed and in a hurry, he may use *"No, I'll do it myself"* more.
- Keep your expectations reasonable for your child's age. Set realistic limits.
- Make opportunities to explore feelings. Read children's books together, such as *Where the Wild Things Are* by Maurice Sendak (New York: HarperCollins, 1963), *Feelings* by Aliki Brandenberg (New York: Morrow, 1984), and *Sometimes I Get Angry* by Jane Werner Watson, Robert E. Switzer, and J. Cutter Hirshberg (New York: Crown, 1986). Ask a children's librarian or knowledgeable bookstore clerk for other ideas.

*See also: Stubbornness*

# NOSE PICKING

*"My child picks her nose all the time."*

## UNDERSTANDING THE SITUATION

Nose picking is an age-old habit among children, most likely because it is soothing and pleasantly efficient. You probably find it annoying, unattractive, and socially embarrassing. Best that you remain calm and appear unimpressed. When you cannot ignore the behavior, act but don't overreact. Address what your child is doing and offer alternatives.

## WHAT TO SAY AND DO

With a *poker face, action with few words,* and a tissue, kindly and firmly take her hand and hold it. This works at home or in public.

Keep tissues available. Hand one to your child when she is picking her nose. Suggest, *"Margie, use the tissue so that you won't hurt your nose."*

Give a logical consequences. *"Bill, you have been picking your nose. I'd like to hold your hand after you wash."* Or, with a knowing glance, say, *"I have a great story to read to you as soon as you wash your hands."*

Use the mirror as an educational tool. Do not use sarcasm or ridicule. *"Julie, stand in front of the mirror and watch yourself pick your nose. Do you find that pleasant to look at? I don't like watching you pick your nose. I love seeing your whole beautiful face instead!"*

Brainstorm all that your child might do instead of picking. Encourage him to keep his hands in his pockets, sit on his hands, color, hold a toy, etc. Keep tissues readily available.

*Encourage* with comments when your child is not picking her nose. Catch her often making an effort.

## PREVENTIVE TIPS

• Take *time to teach* your child how to blow her nose instead of picking it. Blowing is a hard concept for some children. Start by having her blow air out of her mouth with bubbles or a straw. Next show her how a light tissue moves when she blows air through her nose.
• Be a good observer. Watch and record when your child is picking his nose most often. He may be bored, or perhaps he picks when he is nervous in front of others or under stress. Say, *"Michael, I notice you often pick your nose when you are tired and watching TV, and you aren't aware of it. I am going to touch you on the shoulder so that you are aware. What can you do instead?"*
• Arrange a visit with your family physician or the physician's nurse and learn together about the body and proper care— particularly, but not only, the nose.

*See also: Nail-biting*

# OUTINGS

*See: Zoo (and other outings)*

# OVERACTIVITY

*"My child is so active he needs constant supervision. He's an accident ready to happen!"*

## Ages 2½–5

### UNDERSTANDING THE SITUATION

Some children seem to be born with their legs running and by preschool age are considered overactive and difficult. Parenting a very active young child is exhausting and frustrating. The active child is often wild, disruptive, demanding, and into everything at home, never still and overly demonstrative in public places. Your friends may avoid inviting her to play, and relatives may be directive and critical and may not welcome her either. Hang in there; keep your faith in her. Her persistent, high-energy temperament is part of her makeup, and when nurtured and managed well, her strong personality will be an asset to both her and the world! Her disruptive behavior may become one major way she feels noticed and gets what she wants. The overactive child is too often labeled "hard to handle" very early in life and may come to believe that she is troublesome and bad. This belief can carry on into her school years. You and she are both fortunate that you can begin at this young age to stop noticing what she does wrong and notice her improvements. Set your limits and be very consistent with follow-through. Your goal is to have your child develop self-control, which is necessary to her healthy self-esteem. This is a process that develops slowly, over years. It will be very hard at times, so be patient and consistent.

## WHAT TO SAY AND DO

Greet your child in the morning with a smile and a hug and give him your attention. Five minutes of your time first thing is calming and reassuring, and he won't have to dart around to find ways to get you to notice him.

Tell him the structure of the day. Let him know what to expect in the morning, the afternoon, and the evening. *"Joey, we have four stops to make. We are going to the bank, the store, and the cleaner's, and then we are meeting Aunti Mo at Friday's for lunch."* After completing a stop, *encourage. "Now just two more stops before lunch. You are terrific!"*

Structure his environment with clear limits but allow for his energy level. Give him a warning, then act immediately. If he climbs and jumps on furniture in the living room, say, *"Scott, not in the living room."* If he continues, redirect him with kindness, using *action with few words,* to someplace where he can jump, such as on an old mattress. *"This is a good place to jump."* Or, if he is bugging someone, say, *"Sam, Laurie doesn't want to play that game. The dog will play with you. She would love to have you throw her the ball."* He can either quit bugging and do something positive or take *time out.* It is his choice.

Before you go into a store or a public place:

1. Check with him. *"Ronnie, we are going to the video store. What do you remember about how you act in the store?"*
2. Offer a choice of consequences before entering the store. *"If you can use good in-store behavior you may pick out a video for yourself and Julie. If not, we will not get you a video this time, and I will take you home."*
3. Give him an active job, such as holding the video or choosing one for himself. If he misbehaves take his hand and with a *poker face* go outside. Give a second opportunity. *"You climbed on the stands. Do you wish to try again or go home?"* If he repeats

the misbehavior, go home. *"Ronnie, it seems you have chosen to go home."*

Anticipate how long your child will last at an activity and redirect her before she melts down. Her attention span is not as long as yours. Too many *time outs* can be eliminated by changing activities, both quiet and vigorous ones. Offer the change, but do not force it. *"Jill, you are having such fun with the paints. Would you like a break? Let's have juice. I need to weed the roses. You might like to dig in the dirt or go back to painting."*

Refuse to put negative labels on your child. If an acquaintance says, *"My, he is a little terror today,"* respond in a positive way. *"Kyle is very energetic and very curious."* If you think positively and use positive adjectives, he will live up to what you feel and say about him.

Make specific, positive comments when he does well. *"Nick, you did very well in the movie. You moved around some, but you were very quiet. We can do that again. You are terrific!"*

## PREVENTIVE TIPS

- Talk with grandparents, other relatives, and friends and ask for their support. *"Mom, Jessie is very energetic. We are disciplining her the way we think is best for her. Please let us handle her the way we feel best. It is not easy, and we need your support, not your criticism."* If this does not work, limit the time they spend with your child.
- Give your child quiet times throughout his day. Rub his back, play music, play with water, or blow bubbles to teach him to relax.
- A "happy box" will entertain an active, fidgety child through a lengthy church service, a restaurant meal, etc. Supply it with crayons, paper, clay, stencils and some new items from time to time.
- Keep him on a consistent schedule with regular mealtimes, bedtime, etc.
- Keep your child's environment calm, stick with small groups and avoid too much stimulation.

- Take *time for teaching* her to feel her body's signals and to act responsibly. For example, some children need more space. *"Marti, you need your space. Too many children make you feel crowded and nervous and you begin to push and shove. When you feel you need space, tell someone or move to another area."* Many active children need to physically move more often. *"Heidi, when you feel you are getting restless, like you might hit someone, ask to go outside and climb or run."* Let caregivers know this is what you are working on.
- Take regular breaks from your child and get your needed sleep to build your energy level. For you to have the patience and creativity it takes to be a Positive Parent, your energy level must be a priority. Hire an older, school-age child to take your child walking or to play with him actively and regularly. This is a perfect solution to the five o'clock arsenic hour! Find good, patient, mature caregivers to help relieve you for longer periods of time. It may cost some money, but you'll feel it is well spent.
- Talk with teachers, day care help, sitters, and family members who interact with your child about using the same positive approach that you are using.
- If you are a working parent you will need to limit your outside activities and obligations. If you are a single parent it will be important for you to find a good, mature family member or babysitter to spell you.

## Ages 6-10

### UNDERSTANDING THE SITUATION

Read the preceding section, for ages 2½–5. Overactive children often are noticed so many times a day for their negative behavior that they seek attention both at home and at school in very disruptive, demanding ways. You and your child's teacher may begin wondering if medication may be necessary for your child. If this is a concern of yours, seek advice from your pediatrician. No medication should be prescribed without a complete professional

evaluation. More than ever, your child needs to feel your unconditional love and acceptance. Obnoxious behavior is a sign of his
discouragement. You may be greatly frustrated with his actions, yet
if you give up on him, he will likely give up on himself. This may
be a very trying situation for you. Gather support for yourself and
your child in order to continue working on the positive skills that
will help him develop an inner sense of self-control, an awareness
of others' feelings and needs, and a sense of healthy self-esteem.

## WHAT TO SAY AND DO

Have a pediatrician give your child a thorough exam. Call the
physician to share your concerns before your visit. Have specifics
logged from both home and school to share with the doctor.

Work together with your child's teacher. Meet regularly to
make sure that you are both using positive approaches. Overactive children are often kinesthetic, visual, hands-on learners and
have a hard time sitting for long periods listening to lectures.
Your child needs a very clear structure at home and school, limited choices, and consistent follow-through.

She needs to feel your love, especially at moments of mistakes
and error. Use this time to teach responsibility and good thinking. Follow these steps:

1. Separate what she has done from her. *"Susie, I am very angry
   about the broken window."*
2. Do not blame her, but help her be accountable. Be firm and
   kind and involve her in finding a responsible solution to remedy the problem. *"Susie, I'll need your help to sweep up the glass.
   Your allowance will help to pay for the new glass. I think you and
   I can put the window back together."*
3. Follow through by checking her understanding of what happened and what she learned from the mistake. *"Susie, what
   happened to break the window? What might you do differently next
   time to prevent such an accident from happening?"*

Encourage your child to take more responsibility for his activity
level. He can begin to sense what he is feeling before he acts

out, and possibly take *time out* before he disrupts others. Use questions to stimulate his thinking. Catch him before he melts down. Kindly and firmly put your hands on his shoulders, make eye contact, and say, *"Ryan, you are very energetic. What happens to you, or how do you feel before you want to explode?"* Next, ask, *"What is a good way for you to release that energy?"*

If he is nearing disruption, give him a job to do. *"Ryan, you are very energetic. Here's the vacuum. Please run it through the family room."*

When he acts up, do the unexpected. Be creative. *"Mark, I'll set the timer. See how many times you can run around the outside of the house before the timer rings."* Or *"I have fifteen minutes. Let's shoot baskets."*

Find a good time to *problem solve* together. You may not get any farther than exploring his feelings. This is a sophisticated technique. Work on it, build on the process, and soon it will feel natural. *"Ned, you were angry today at Cub Scouts when you got into trouble. It was hard for you to sit still. Am I right? I remember when I was eight I hated having to go to choir after school. I wanted to be home climbing trees. This is becoming a problem, as you are disturbing the leader and the other children. Let's think of what we might do about this situation."* Then choose one idea. In a week, talk about how it is working.

## PREVENTIVE TIPS

- Help your child succeed. Cub Scouts after a full day of school may be too inactive, asking for trouble. Sign him up for a sport instead. Be sure to find a coach who understands all kinds of kids, a coach who does not encourage competition and winning as much as having fun and learning good skills. If your child goes to after-school care, work with caregivers to develop a working plan that includes physical activity and good supervision.

- Listen to him, discuss feelings often, and spend quality *special time* with him regularly. Your very active child may get a lot of negative comments during the day. Provide time to listen and explore and do not lecture or moralize at this time.

- Taking care of yourself is a number-one priority. Get plenty of rest and exercise. You may need to give up some activities in order to take care of yourself and be home with your child as much as possible.
- See your pediatrician for any continuing concerns.

# PEER PRESSURE

*"My child worries about wearing the proper clothing, using the right expressions, and his popularity."*

### UNDERSTANDING THE SITUATION

You will know peer pressure has hit your home when your child needs a green stripe in his hair, his lunch must be in a sack, his tennis shoes are tied from the top down or are without laces completely, and the family car is just not good enough. The need to belong is powerful, and most children are afraid to be left out—that is, to not be accepted. This can be very frustrating for you, and your entire household may be disrupted as he focuses on peers rather than on cooperating with family. The parent trap is to become involved in the pressures along with your child. We all want our children to be well liked. Be supportive and listen, but be careful not to rescue. Teach him to be assertive and to think for himself. He'll need the courage to say no when his peer group wants him to go against his better judgment. Help him lead with his uniqueness rather than follow others. As a teen your child will have more critical choices than you ever did. Use these years when friendships are more flexible to teach him to use good wisdom and judgment.

### WHAT TO SAY AND DO

Show understanding about your child's feelings; they are real. Never laugh or ridicule. Identify the feeling, use *you* messages, and reflect what she says and feels. *"Mindy, you feel left out. You are afraid that you won't have friends."* Notice the happy times as well as the sad ones. *"Mary, you are very happy. You were invited to the birthday party."*

Be an available listener. Children open up on their own

time—sometimes after school, sometimes at bedtime. However, learn the difference between empathy and overattention. Do not get sucked into resolving the same emotional issue over and over. Address it and redirect your child's attention. *"Amy, we have talked about the girls at lunchtime for three evenings now. I want to let you handle it alone for a while. Let's spend our time together working on this new sewing project."*

Do not advise or be judgmental, because that stifles thinking. Empathize: *"No wonder you feel bad. I would feel awful if that happened."* Don't get involved with peer politics. Sometimes there isn't any way to fix a feeling; it just has to be.

Teach *problem solving* and include your child in decision making. Look at what might be in his control to change, both in attitude and situation. Questions stimulate thinking. *"André, you did not like the way Billy treated you. What do you want from Billy? What could you do next time if that happens again? What will you do differently tomorrow?"*

When he wants expensive clothing to be like the others, do not be too quick to say no. *"Jeffrey, I will pay for new jeans. If you want the expensive brand, you earn the extra money that it will cost."*

## PREVENTIVE TIPS

- Be an aware parent. Keep communication open between home and school. Be sure your child's schoolwork is satisfactory and on grade level. If it is not, consider tutoring. Be involved, drive car pools, volunteer at school.
- Encourage outside interests and activities beyond your child's peer group.
- Get to know your child's friends. Talk to the parents before letting her go to their home. Take her there and meet them. Develop a relationship with them; your children are your common interest.
- Give your love randomly for no particular reason. Comment on your child's talents and uniqueness rather than on how she looks or what she wears. *"Hillary, I just love you so much. I watch you using your free time drawing. You have very special interests. You are unique."*

- Organize activities with other families. Help your child build relationships with other mature, encouraging adults. Studies have shown that kids prefer to befriend more mature people who are accepting and noncritical.
- Talk with a children's librarian or knowledgeable bookstore clerk about books on peer pressure. Some read-aloud books may seem young but are fun and stimulate good discussion about peer pressure. *Camper of the Week* by Amy Schwartz (New York: Orchard Books, 1991), is a children's book with a theme that some older kids like.
- Television advertising reinforces commercialism and the "I wants" of peer groups. Limiting TV and allotting more time for family activities are advantageous.
- Keep your home atmosphere nonjudgmental and uncritical. Let go of perfectionism. Mistakes provide opportunities to learn.

# PET CARE

*"My child asked for a cat, and now I take care of it."*

### UNDERSTANDING THE SITUATION

Pets can be a wonderful addition to family life, but for some they may cause disaster. When your child asks for a pet, gets it, and doesn't help with the care, it is frustrating. As the romance of the new pet quickly wears off, all kinds of yelling, scolding, and threatening may happen. With your understanding and proper planning, this can be avoided. Pets are a plus for your child when you are prepared and willing to commit the support your child will need from you. This will take a great deal of your time. Your child does not need your blaming and scolding at any age; instead he needs your support and consistent follow-through to make sure agreements are kept and that the animal gets proper care. Consider the amount of time you have to give to both your child and the pet. It is not fair to expect that this will be your child's total responsibility.

## WHAT TO SAY AND DO

Establish a routine for pet care. Increase the responsibility for the pet's feeding and care in small steps. At two and a half years your child can help you put food and water out and by seven he can be counted on to feed the pet himself. Do not let your pet suffer because you are teaching your child a lesson.

Alternate the care for the family pet between parents and siblings. The pet will receive more respect and love if the care is a team effort. It is not realistic that one child should take all the responsibility unless the pet is to be just that child's. In that case, the pet stays only as long as the child cares for it.

Take *time for teaching.* Make sure your child understands how to feed and care for the pet. Review with the vet or pet expert what the pet needs. Set up a training chart that your child can mark when she feeds the animal, trains it, or plays with it. The animal comes first before free time. Do not make a habit of rescuing your child and feeding the pet yourself. This may be more expedient, but you will grow resentful, and she will not learn to be responsible.

Do not threaten ("If you do not care for Rufus we will give him away.") unless you plan to carry through with the threat. Mean what you say and be prepared to do what you say you'll do. If necessary use logical consequences. *"Alex, as soon as Woody is fed you can have dinner."*

Use your family pet to teach your child an understanding of animal behavior. *"Mary, when you tease Hobbes or treat him roughly he will be mean to people. He will want to be nice to you and be with you if you take good care of him." "If you chase him he will run from you." "He loves to play with you when he feels good. He needs food and rest just like you."*

Do not tolerate any abusive treatment of the pet. Should your child be too rough, use *action with few words.* Depending on what works for your child, separate the two, give *time out,* or give a logical consequence. *"Leah, we will keep the cat in the laundry room today. You can try to play nicely with her again tomorrow."* Or *"Roger, you need to stay home today. You and I will take Smiley for a walk and play with him to help you remember how we treat him."*

Introduce feelings through your pet. *"Jason, how would you like it if I forgot to feed you for a day? How would you feel if I kicked you?"* If a pet runs away or dies, do not blame anyone and be sure your child attaches no blame to herself or others. *"Rufus ran away. Cats do run away sometimes. It was nothing you did. It is not because he did not like you. He was a born wanderer."*

Plan a funeral for a dead pet to help with closure. Do not belittle the situation. (*"He was only a dog. Don't carry on so."*) Offer comfort. *"Michael, I know you are sad that Brutus died. I feel bad too. How can I help you? Perhaps we could plan a funeral together."* Read together *When a Pet Dies* by Fred Rogers (New York: Putnam Sons, 1986) and *The Tenth Good Thing about Barney* by Judith Viorst (New York: Macmillan, 1971).

## PREVENTIVE TIPS

• Take time to choose the proper pet for your life style. If it is to be your child's, start small. A goldfish or a hamster is a small step before a puppy. A family pet must be suited to your family for it to fit in and be loved and cared for properly. Visit a vet or pet store and discuss the options best suited to your family. If you choose a pet and discover that it is incompatible, learn from that experience and return it or find it a new home.
• Getting a pet is a topic for a *family meeting*. Before bringing a pet home, have a realistic agreement about how the pet will be cared for. List what the pet requires on a chore chart. Decide what will happen to the pet if the agreement is broken.
• Plan for a successful beginning. Have your home well prepared to receive the pet.

# POSSESSIONS

*"My child has little appreciation for her possessions."*

### UNDERSTANDING THE SITUATION

It is extremely irritating when your child breaks toys apart, leaves a brand-new coat at school, leaves a new bike in the rain, or forgets her sister's baseball glove at the public field. Nagging, lecturing, scolding, moralizing, and punishing are neverending. *("How could you be so . . . Why can't you ever remember . . . So many children have so much less . . . See if you ever get another . . .")* and yet do no good. The value of caring for possessions is a challenge to teach children in today's modern society where many people feel it is easier or cheaper to buy something new rather than fix the old items. Children see many ads on TV advertising the new and better rendition of an expensive toy they got last year. The value of quality versus quantity is challenged by the familiar bumper sticker that reads *"He who dies with the most toys wins."* Today the stores display many dolls, and a child may have so many that one is shoved aside for a fancier, new one. In Grandmother's day one doll was coveted and the doll clothes were handmade. Your child will learn to be responsible over time as you share your values and establish rules about possessions. Take *time for teaching* what you expect, and work with consequences. Age two and a half is not too early to begin. Forgetfulness and carelessness will appear time and again as she grows. That is part of the learning process. Mistakes are for learning. Be sure that you model what you are trying to teach.

**WHAT TO SAY AND DO**

Store toys, clothes, and other possessions in clearly marked spaces and containers to establish a sense of order and help your child learn what belongs where.

Rotate your younger child's toys. Have a few out at a time. As a reward for putting toys away and treating them with respect, bring a new one down from the shelf or out of the toy chest. Ask her to put one up she may be tired of. *"Toby, nice job! You have really treated your toys nicely this week. Choose one more off the shelf that you would like to play with. Which toy would you like to put back to save for later?"*

Work together to establish rules for property. *"Now you have a big bike with training wheels. Each night be sure it is in the garage."* Set consequences and follow through with consistency. *"Andy, when you leave your bike in the driveway I will tell you once to put it away. If you do not, I will put it up for one week."*

Do not concentrate on blame (*"If you hadn't forgotten your coat you wouldn't have to be looking for it."*) but on solutions to a problem. Allow consequences to work. Teach your child that some problems are his to handle. Sincerely, say, *"I cannot afford to buy you a new coat now. I understand you have a problem."* Take the *time for teaching* problem solving. Make a plan together. *"Mark, you forgot your coat yesterday. What can you do at school to find it? Let's make a plan."* (Put signs up at school, put a notice in the school bulletin, ask a custodian, check lost and found.) Support him with follow-through. *"Mark, what did you learn about your coat? It seems it is lost. What do you think we should do about finding a coat for you for the winter?"* (Use his own money for a used jacket at Goodwill, wear a hand-me-down, etc.)

Rather than lecturing and reminding, try checking with your child before she leaves home. *"Sally, what are you taking to school? What three things will you have when you come home?"*

Celebrate when she cares for her possessions responsibly. *"Kelly, you have really taken good care of your bike this week. Let's celebrate and go ride on the bike trail at the lake!"* Or *"Jen, you have worked hard to earn your new bike, and you are showing a lot of effort taking care of your things, especially caring for your rabbit. I'd like to help you by buying you a lock for your bike."*

### PREVENTIVE TIPS

• Do not buy buckets and buckets of toys. Cultivate caring and respect for property by buying one special truck (instead of seven). Choose a doll that you and your child can sew for or buy clothes for over the long-term. One nice wooden train set that you and your child can add parts to and build things for develops pride in ownership.
• Before buying more toys, check out a charity that needs the used ones. Have your child select some toys for the needy each year before birthday or holiday presents are received.
• Do not rush out to buy a new toy or item of clothing to replace a broken or lost one. Help your child decide how he can replace it.
• Teach that privileges come with responsibility and that natural or logical consequences happen. Keep your expectations reasonable. Children will be children and will forget. Demanding absolute perfection never leads to improvement.

*See also: Carelessness; Morning hassles; Toys, picking up*

# PREGNANCY

*"How involved should my child be in my pregnancy?"*

### UNDERSTANDING THE SITUATION

When you learn of your pregnancy you may experience guilt and anxiety and wonder if having another child will disrupt a good situation. Your first child is obviously the center of your world. How to introduce the topic of pregnancy may be a concern. The older the child, the more easily the concept will be understood. Your positive attitude and that of significant others will determine a lot of your child's reaction.

## WHAT TO SAY AND DO

When you tell your child, be enthusiastic and confident and follow these guidelines:

1. You and your spouse are the ones to tell your child you are pregnant. She needs to hear about it from you, not the neighbor. She can be the one to tell the neighbor.
2. Indicate that the baby will take a long time to grow before it is born. Don't tell very young children until you are halfway; nine months is too long for them to wait. *"Jessie, we are going to have a baby."* Show her a calendar. Give her a landmark date she can identify with. *"I will be pregnant a long time. I will have the baby after Halloween."*
3. Give her time to ask questions. Give her a well-illustrated book about pregnancy. Answer her questions with honest, anatomically correct information. If you are not sure what to say, tell her, *"Leslie, I need some time to think about your question so I can explain it right."* Be sure you follow up with an answer for her.
4. Reaffirm your love. *"Cory, I love you this much now"*—hold arms far, far apart—*"and I will love you just as much when the baby comes."*

Let her feel the baby's movements. Arrange for her to visit the doctor with you to hear the heartbeat.

If your child is very young, do not make big changes or try to teach new skills right before the baby comes. If she is moving into a bed and giving up the crib to the baby, make the move several months before the birth. Do not demand potty training. If she is to begin preschool, day care, or any new play group, do this well before your due date or wait until after the baby arrives and the adjustment is well under way. Do not make her give up her bottle at this time.

Help your child feel included and useful. A three or four-year-old will be encouraged by attending baby showers and helping to prepare the layette and nursery.

Prepare for the delivery:

1. Let your child know what to expect. Before you deliver, visit the hospital with her. Many hospitals have classes for siblings.
2. Share your plan with your child. *"Marnie, you will stay with Auntie Mo when I deliver the baby."*
3. Call her from the hospital. Have her visit you as soon as possible after you've delivered.
4. Arrange for significant people to be with her and to spend quality time with her while you are away.

## PREVENTIVE TIPS

- Though the baby is a big event for you, nine months is a long time to wait in the eyes of your child. After you've mentioned that the baby's coming, continue with life as usual. The baby should not be the major topic with your child for the next nine months.
- See a children's librarian or knowledgeable bookstore clerk for good books for you and your child. Try *She Come Bringing Me That Little Baby Girl* by Eloise Greenfield (New York: HarperCollins, 1993), *A Baby Sister for Frances* by Russell Hoban (New York: HarperCollins, 1964), and *Will There Be a Lap for Me?* by Dorothy Corey (Morton Grove, Ill.: Whitman, 1992).

*See also: Nakedness; New baby; Sexuality, questions about*

# PRETEND FRIEND

*See: Fantasy*

---

# PRIVACY

*"My child refuses to let me into her room."*

### UNDERSTANDING THE SITUATION

It is surprising to see a KEEP OUT sign on your child's door for the first time. You may feel a bit suspicious *("What could she be doing in there?")* and possibly a bit insulted by being shut out by a sign with a skull and crossbones. A brother or sister is sure to challenge the sign, and suddenly you have a frustrating new sibling issue to deal with. Many children begin to ask for their privacy by age five or six. Some start with closing the door when using the bathroom or dressing, and by age eight most children enjoy playing with a friend privately in their room. This privacy issue can upset you, yet to your child it is an important part of growing up and asserting her individuality. Privacy is earned by showing responsibility. Over the next few years she will need more space to feel she can make her own decisions and be responsible for the consequences. You have shown your faith and confidence in her since she was very young, so do not stop now. With effort and a sense of humor you can keep the lines of good communication open. You will be glad you made the effort as she becomes a responsible, confident teen who has a working relationship with you and uses good judgment even when you are not there.

## WHAT TO SAY AND DO

Provide many opportunities for your child to feel your respect. Do not go into his room and poke through his things. Ask his permission to look at his schoolwork, do not open his mail, leave his room if he requests it, and knock before you enter. Respect him, and he will in turn learn to do the same for others.

Talk about each issue of privacy. Do not assume you both perceive it the same way. *"Heidi, Mom and I notice the sign on your door. What does the sign mean to you?"* Show understanding. *"I think I understand how you feel. I had my own fort at your age. We will knock before entering."* Your open communication and trust give her permission to be private and not feel sneaky or bad about it. She will cooperate better with you when you show this respect.

Make sure she understands the family rules about her bedroom. One family's rules were:

1. No food or drinks.
2. Room cleaning is Saturday morning before soccer.
3. Change sheets.
4. Put away clothes and other belongings.
5. Dust and vacuum.
6. Family members will knock when door is closed.

When your child shows a lack of responsibility, she is making a bad choice. For example, if you find her playing with matches with a friend in her room, take the matches, send the friend home, and *cool off*. Then discuss a logical consequence: *"Rosie, you have chosen to lose the privilege of playing with a playmate alone in your room with the door shut. You will need to leave your bedroom door open when you have friends for the next month."* Let her know she can try again at a later date.

Be an active parent and stay in touch. Give your child time alone for his privacy, but also ask for time together. *"Billy, you have spent a great deal of time in your room today. I'd like to spend some time with you. How about some ball in the park?"* Too much isolation is not healthy.

**PREVENTIVE TIPS**

- Every family has different standards for privacy. Take *time to teach* your child those that are important to you. Do not assume she knows them and then get mad when she makes a mistake. For example, if you want her to knock when your door is shut, tell her beforehand rather than yelling at her when she unintentionally does the wrong thing.
- Cultivate her willingness to be open, to cooperate and to work with you. Do not assume she understands what you are thinking. Ask for her perceptions. Avoid being too directive, judgmental, and critical. Ask questions to encourage her to think. This promotes working together as a family.
- Watch for what she does right. Comment on it and celebrate it. *Encourage* her.
- Spend quality time together. This does not mean going on expensive outings. Have fun together, take a bike ride, invite her to shoot baskets, and have talks about feelings openly and often.

*See also: Nakedness*

# RESTAURANTS

*"My child will not behave in restaurants."*

### UNDERSTANDING THE SITUATION

Young children are very often noisy and disturbing in restaurants. Older children can sabotage the event as well with disruptive behavior, slouching, lying down, pouring salt in pepper, blowing straw wrappers across the room, etc. If your child will not behave it may be because she is too tired or very hungry; the waiting may be too long, or she may sense she has an arena in which to grab your attention or to control. Whatever the reason, her behavior is embarrassing and very frustrating. However, it is doing your child a disservice to give up. Be patient with your young child and sensitive to her age and temperament. Never put your child in a situation she is too immature for and expect perfect behavior. Your child will grow up; do take the time to improve her behavior if you enjoy eating out. Families that enjoy eating out together have a whole world of wonderful experiences to share.

### WHAT TO SAY AND DO

Today many restaurants are fun and child-oriented. Some have crayons and paper on the table, some have trains on the ceiling. Many have special chairs for youngsters. Make an effort to go to a fun restaurant where children are welcome and everyone has a good time.

Take *time for teaching*. Begin with small steps by starting in small, fast-food restaurants. Never try to teach your child during an event that is important to you; if acting out occurs, you need to be free to follow through with the consequence of leaving.

This is not the time to dictate table manners. One caring comment if necessary to correct poor manners is enough.

Be clear about the kind of evening you want. If you want a relaxed, three or four-course dinner, leave your child home. If you take her, keep your expectations reasonable for the length of time she can sit. Before going in give her something to look forward to and ask her how she will behave inside. *"Heidi, we are going into the restaurant. This restaurant has a big water fountain, and they serve yummy fruit plates. How do we act in the restaurant? Do you stand up and stare at people next to us? Do you lie down on the seat?"* Or *"Jeremy, this is TacoTime. I need you to stand next to me in line to order our food and then stay with me to help find a table. What do I need?"*

Be prepared. If acting out occurs, know what you will do rather than what you will make your child do. One of these approaches may work:

1. Try taking her outside and sitting together on a curb. *"Molly, we'll sit here until you are ready to go in and use nice manners. All these people going in may take our table."*
2. Put her in the car in her car seat and wait until she is ready to go in. If she screams, stand outside the car. With a *poker face* say, *"Molly, I'll stand right here where you can see me. When you want to go in like a big girl you let me know."*
3. Rather than an order, give a *choice* once. *"Molly you need to sit in your seat or we will have to leave and go home."* She won't want to go, especially if others at the table are staying. However, never give a choice without intending to follow through. If your choice is to sit or go home, be prepared to go home without fuming. Stay cool. *"Heidi, I'm disappointed we can't stay. We will try again."*

Comment on good behavior very specifically. Reward with another meal out of your child's choice. *"David, we can come again! I enjoy eating out with you as much as a good friend. You are really growing up!"*

**PREVENTIVE TIPS**

- Role-play eating out at home. Have fun. Set up a play scene, serve food, have all the players.
- Bring a "happy box" into the restaurant with a variety of activities, crayons, pens, paper, pipe cleaners, etc.
- Don't ignore your child. Engage him in conversation and have a good time together. Keep the conversation fun and interesting to your child. Treat him as if he were a friend dining out with you.
- Choose fun restaurants that are age appropriate. If your child is used to going out and having fun, he won't mind an occasional boring, sophisticated, adult restaurant once in a while.

*See also: Mealtime, manners*

# ROUGHHOUSING

*"Our home is treated like a gymnasium!"*

Roughhousing is common and becomes an annoying issue for most families. When they roughhouse, your children may be feeling bored and energetic, or they may be seeking your attention. Typically the problem begins small with a tussle, and you half ignore it and half remind your children to stop. This builds into a crescendo of flying pillows, tipping tables, and overturned lamps. Worse yet, someone gets hurt. Maybe then you take action, yell, scold, blame, spank, and/or isolate them unreasonably. *"How many times have I told you to stop? You just don't think! Now you have really done it. Go to your room for the rest of the weekend!"* The situation can be different. With effort and consistency you can provide a more positive end result for you and your children.

## WHAT TO SAY AND DO

Do not nag or yell. Children become "parent deaf" when you nag four times and yell the fifth. They will learn you mean it on the fifth time and push you to your limit. Say it once and mean it, and do what you say you will do.

Apply the most logical consequence by redirecting. With a *poker face*, say, *"Jeffrey and Mikey, you are jumping all over this living room. You are very active and energetic. Please head outside to the yard or down to the playroom."*

Let them know what to expect. Tell them when they can have your attention before they ask for it in a negative way. *"Jason and Laura, we will go shoot some baskets after I do these dishes."* Do not spank and punish. If something is broken, give *time out*; you both need it to *cool down*. Then discuss the responsibility. Younger children need to help clean up a mess they made. Older children can do more. *"Susan and Derek, you will need to clean the glass up and pay for the repair with your allowance."*

If someone is hurt, do not blame any one person. Treat both children involved equally. Take time to cool off. Calmly say, *"Brian needs stitches. This could have happened to either one of you."* Ask each child, *"How do you feel about what happened?"* Listen and reflect. *"It sounds as though you feel . . ."* Ask each child, *"What one important thing did you learn from this?"*

## PREVENTIVE TIPS

- Plan active *special time* with your child. Some dads love to wrestle roughly. Controlled roughhousing can delight a child. Ride bikes, shoot some hoops, kick a soccer ball through traffic cones set up in the yard. Children won't act out for attention if it is promised already.
- Stop a problem before it begins. Observe your children's play and before it breaks apart into chaos, interrupt to change the activity. Offer a snack, pull out some art project, suggest going to the park.
- Read up on things to do with kids. *Child's Play: 200 Instant Crafts and Activities for Preschoolers* by Leslie Hamilton (New

York: Crown, 1989) and *Kids Create! Art and Craft Experiences for 3 to 9-Year-Olds* by Laurie Carlson (Charlotte, Vt.: Williams Publishing, 1990) will give you lots of ideas.

- Keep a log of when roughhousing occurs. If you spot an over-active time of day, plan for it. Sometimes a bath is a good way to calm down the end of the day.
- At a *family meeting*, suggest places for physical activity. Old mattresses are good for jumping on, unfinished basements are great for trikes and ball playing, etc.

# SADNESS

*"My child often seems very sad."*

## UNDERSTANDING THE SITUATION

Sadness can be caused by the death of a pet or a loved one, lone-liness, divorce, a friend moving, or someone mean at day care or school. Some children have very sensitive temperaments, tend to be more serious and analytical, and may appear sad more often. Your child may cry, refuse to cooperate, be very angry, or emo-tionally withdraw. This can be a very frustrating situation for you if you believe your job is to make it all better. You definitely cannot demand that he feel better. You cannot fix his bad feel-ings, and you cannot make him not feel sad. You may help your child learn to label his feelings and with empathy help him to understand them and deal with them. With your help, he will learn to allow himself to feel sad as well as to let go of sadness. He will learn to find ways to overcome it and not let it control him. This will take your time and patience and—most im-portant—your loving sense of humor. It is hard work. Hang in there and do not give up on him.

## WHAT TO SAY AND DO

Do not label your child as sad or depressed. Use words that are positive. Think about her as serious, thoughtful, sensitive. Your child will believe what you reflect about her. *"Shelly, you seem very thoughtful today. What is it you are thinking about?"* Wait for her response and use your active listening. Reflect what she says or feels. Do not jump in with your direction, judgment, or words of wisdom.

Take *time to teach* your child what to do with bad feelings.

Teach him to feel the sadness and then to do something to make himself feel better. He needs to learn that he does have control over his emotions. *"Chris, when I feel sad I decide how much time I need to feel that way. Our dog Woody is wonderful to cry on. I allow myself the time to be sad, and then I find something to make me feel better. Sometimes I take long walks. I know running helps some people. I like to go to lunch with a best friend. I like to take you to the park and play."*

Sad behavior can become attention-getting behavior. If you begin feeling annoyed with your child pursuing you with it again and again, say, *"Mike, we talked about this yesterday. I know you can handle it now."* This may be very difficult for you. You are not ignoring him, just the behavior. Give him positive attention at other times.

Pull out puppets, stuffed animals, or dress-up clothes and play with your young child. Ask him to create a pretend situation. Often you will get some insight as to what is bothering him through play. Your school-age child will enjoy hearing stories about your youth when you experienced similar feelings.

## PREVENTIVE TIPS

- Develop a good understanding of your own feelings and take care of them. Model emotional self-control, and in time your child will mimic you.
- Give quantities of quality time. Take time during the day and especially at bedtime to talk about your child's day. Listen carefully. Read children's books together about feelings, such as *Feelings* by Aliki Brandenberg (New York: Morrow, 1984), *Grandpa's Face* by Eloise Greenfield (New York: Putnam, 1988), and *I Am Not a Crybaby* by Norma Simon (Morton Grove, Ill.: Whitman, 1989).
- Model taking care of yourself. Set limits and priorities and take time for exercise and your health. When your cup is full you are a happy person. This is necessary to your child's happiness.
- Loneliness, feelings of inadequacy, anger, or depression all may require the help of a counselor. If your child's sleep is disturbed, his eating patterns change, or he is saying that he has

no friends and is unhappy with himself, see your pediatrician and discuss referrals.

*See also: Feelings*

# SAFETY

*"My child is fearless."*

### UNDERSTANDING THE SITUATION

You will be challenged more than once in your life by your child's confrontation with danger. She is likely to run into the street, balance on the edge of a swimming pool, light a pack of matches, climb onto a rooftop, etc. Most parents panic and react with screaming, spanking, blaming, lecturing, and punishing. Unfortunately, when you act from fear, the message she gets is not of love but of anger. This will not teach your child why you panic at the danger. What she knows at this point is that *"Mom really flipped out."* Your child may think it quite a game. *"Look at Mom chase after me."* Yet after you punish her, she may think, *"I'm a bad person."* This is not going to build her self-confidence. She is young and ready to take her chance at the world with zest. With a Positive Parenting approach you begin an important process in giving her reasoning skills, understanding of cause and effect, and responsibility for her actions. You will continue to supervise, yet perhaps when you are not there, she will be safe because she will think before she acts.

### WHAT TO SAY AND DO

When you find your child suddenly in a dangerous situation, do not overreact. Stop his action, hold him, and count to ten to let your adrenaline slow down. Your adrenaline rush makes it impossible for you to think. If your young child runs into the street, go after him. With a *poker face* remove him. Do not say, *"You worried me."* He will then worry or feel guilty that he worried you. Say, *"Tony, you ran into the street. That was a very dangerous action."* If you are in a parking lot, put him in the car. If at home, put him in the house or in a fenced area.

Give yourself time to *cool down*, then follow through. He will become "parent deaf" when you lecture. Instead ask questions to make him think. *"Alex, what would happen if that match lit up in a flame in your hand?"* Or *"What would happen to you if you were in the street and the truck came?"* Do not get scary and gory with detail.

Take *time for teaching*. Your energetic young child needs to learn about the danger of the deep water, or the speeding cars in the street, or the hot flames of matches. He will understand the danger of these situations with safe demonstration. Be creative and teach about trouble spots before trouble happens. Here are a few:

1. Children have no concept of the power of a moving vehicle.
   a. With another adult demonstrate a car running over a grapefruit or a toy. One adult drives, the other stands with the child. *"Willy, what happened to the truck? What do you think would happen to you if you ran into the street and a car was coming?"*
   b. *"Joey, I want you to see what it feels like to be a driver in a car. You sit in the car, and I will sit on your trike in front of the car."* Put him in the driver's seat. He probably won't even see above the bottom of the steering wheel. You sit on the trike outside. Talk to him. *"Joey, can you see me? I'm in front of the car. Do you see me?"* Follow through with a discussion about how children are usually too hard to see by a driver.
2. Children are curious about the magic of matches. When denied, they become more intriguing.
   a. Take time to sit with your child and demonstrate how matches work. Light one, let him hold one with your help. If he gets aggressive and wants to be unsafe, a quick touch of the flame will sting and leave a lasting impression. Light some

paper. *"Zack, what would happen if the flame touched the couch? What would happen if the match fell on your hand or on your clothing?"*

b. Provide opportunities for him to be useful. When you light a fire, have him help you. Even a three-year-old can light matches with you holding his hand. This will show him the danger of fire and is better than a tantalizing warning, *"Don't touch!"*

3. Water is intriguing. Satisfy your child's curiosity.

a. Give an opportunity to wade in water, safely float in a life jacket.

b. When you are worried about her understanding of water safety, stand with her next to the shallow end of a pool. If she tests you and leans over too far, let her gently fall in and go under. Lift her out and hold her but do not coddle her. Stay calm and kind. *"Elizabeth, you went for a swim without me. You went under the water. Wow!"* When she calms down, talk about being safe. *"When you go too close to the edge, what happens? Did you know you would fall in?"*

c. Give her swim lessons with a competent instructor who works well with children.

After each training episode make a plan for dealing with dangerous situations. Your child will honor the agreement because of his hands-on learning. *"Michael, now that you have learned about matches we need to have an agreement. If you want to use matches, either Dad or I must be with you. Tell me what I just said about matches."*

If you do blow it and react to a dangerous situation with words and actions you regret, have the courage to apologize. We all make mistakes. When you calm down, tell your child you're sorry about what you did. Make sure he hears you love him. Calmly and sincerely say, *"Mark, I yelled and spanked you. I'm sorry. I yelled at you because I was scared to see you run in the parking lot. I do love you."* Ask for his help in finding a solution. *"When you are in a parking lot and you do not hold my hand you are unsafe. I do not want that to happen again. Let's make a plan and stick to it."* Be very consistent and follow through.

PREVENTIVE TIPS

• Ask a children's librarian or knowledgeable bookstore clerk for read-aloud children's stories that might satisfy curiosity and stimulate conversation. *Playing It Smart* by Tova Navarra (New York: Barrons, 1989) and *What Would You Do?* by Linda Schwartz (Santa Barbara: Learning Works, 1990) are guides that teach school-age children about safety and good thinking in difficult situations. *Madeline's Rescue* by Ludwig Bemelman (London: Puffin, 1953) is fun to read aloud.
• Keep your expectations reasonable. Keep poisons, matches, and other dangerous materials out of sight and mind. Young children do not comprehend cause and effect as adults do. Do not assume anything; young children need supervision.
• When it is very quiet, often trouble is brewing. Check it out.
• At bedtime ask about the best time your child had that day and the worst. Tell him what yours were too. If he had a dangerous experience that day, this is a good time to review ideas about safety.

# SANTA CLAUS

*"Santa Claus is causing a major problem at our house."*

**Ages 2½–5**

UNDERSTANDING THE SITUATION

Most children are fascinated with the festive lights and windows full of toys during the holidays. The horse-drawn carriages, caroling, and friends gathered together are awesome. Santa Claus is usually a part of the holiday tradition, with a line of children waiting to sit upon his knee. It may be a great surprise to you when your child, who has been thrilled with it all, bursts into tears and clings tightly to your neck as you try to get him closer to Santa. What is wrong with this picture? You may have made great effort to dress your child up for one of his first Santa photos only to have him dissolve into a nightmare of fear and crying. One child would not go to bed on Christmas Eve fearing Santa's arrival in the dark of night. As wonderful as the tradition of Santa is to you, to your young child he may be a strange, fat, bearded, frightening man. As disappointing as it is, you need to respect your child's need to back off. Positive Parenting is based on mutual respect. *"I will not treat you any way I would not want someone to treat me."* Let go of the dreamed-of picture for the mantle collection for that year. Either that or find a clever way to win your child's cooperation to be in a picture.

## WHAT TO SAY AND DO

Do not tease, ridicule, or threaten. Do not force your child to sit on Santa's lap. Do not say, *"Santa won't bring you anything this year."* Or *"You baby. Everyone else sits on his lap."* Appreciate his caution. Identify his fear, reassure him, and be positive. He is not doing anything wrong. In fact, you want your child to be cautious of strangers. Give him time to think for himself. *"Nick, you are afraid of Santa. You are being cautious. You are very safe, and I would never force you. We'll just watch him from here."*

Do not tuck your fearful child into bed and make a big deal about Santa's visit in the night. You likely will have a child who will lie awake fearing the fat, bearded man creeping through his house, and he will not sleep Christmas Eve.

Try to find a small, quiet place to visit Santa. Make several visits to observe Santa from a distance. See if your child is ready to move closer. Accept that it may not happen until a year from now.

Your child may be willing to sit with an older sister or brother or close friend who is sitting on Santa's lap.

## PREVENTIVE TIPS

• Read picture books at home to become familiar with Santa.
• Have fun with the rest that the holiday has to offer. Do not get hung up on Santa this year. Let it go.

# Ages 6–10

## UNDERSTANDING THE SITUATION

When your child begins school she is likely to hear from some other child that there is no Santa. This often brings many tears and questions. You may feel angry that someone has ruined the fantasy or feel frustrated over how to answer the many broken-hearted questions. Do not lie to your child. You don't have to tell her more than she wants to know, but you do need to tell your child the truth if she asks a straight-out question. Santa is a fantasy. Fantasy is good and healthy. Do not overprotect, as if she were a victim, but empower her to choose whether to continue believing in the fun of Santa or not.

## WHAT TO SAY AND DO

Do not blame or pity. (*"Johnny shouldn't have told you there is no Santa. He ruined it for you."*) Show understanding and show your faith and confidence that your child can handle the situation.

Identify her feelings, listen and reflect what she says to you, and explore with questions to help her think. *"Jen, you are very upset that Peter told you there is no Santa."* Do not feel you need to "fix" the disappointment. Keep listening and reflecting what she says. This will help her work through it on her own.

Answer her questions honestly. (It helps to have considered the scenario before it happens.) Show understanding by telling her about the time you learned there was no Santa and what you felt like. Ask her, *"Maria, instead of Jimmy telling you there is no Santa, what would you rather have happened?"*

Often there is an underlying fear on your child's part that she won't receive presents if the Santa tradition stops. If this is your tradition, reassure her. *"Connie, the fantasy of Santa will always be in our home. He will always bring presents to all of us."* Use questions. *"Would you like to know what I believe?"*

This brings up the value of caring about others and whether it is fun to ruin someone else's fantasy. Later, at a good talking time, say, *"Mike, you did not like it when Gerry told you about Santa. What does that help you decide about your sister who still believes? Would you want to tell her like Mike told you?"*

### PREVENTIVE TIPS

- This is a great time to discuss the fact that all people are different and have very different beliefs. Read children's stories about different races and different traditions.
- Read books together about how the tradition of Santa began. The stories of St. Nicholas introduce children from all over the world.
- Tell stories of your childhood holidays as well as what you know of your parents' and grandparents'. Tradition is very important to your child.

---

# SCHOOL, WON'T GO

*"My child doesn't want to go to school."*

### UNDERSTANDING THE SITUATION

When your child is extremely upset and doesn't want to go to school, he may complain or cry. He may fabricate tummy aches and other physical ills, so he may truly worry himself into a stomachache or headache. This is one of the most stressful of parenting issues. It takes a great deal of time, understanding, and patience. It also takes good communication with teachers and professionals with whom you may feel uncomfortable talking. The root of the problem is often well hidden, not obvious even to your child. A small matter can induce insecurity—another child getting sick, a substitute teacher, a crowded lunchroom, friendship troubles, or the anger of a teacher or playground supervisor. You are your child's advocate. Support him, yet refrain from taking sides. This is not a win/lose proposition. Your approach with the teacher may make all the difference in the world as to whether you resolve this or not. Teachers today have a very stressful job, and few are in the teaching profession to make children feel miserable! Today classes are so large that making time for individual attention is difficult. Today more children, their emotional needs unmet at home, are coming to school in need of a hug before anything else. They often do not ask for the hug, and sometimes they hit and act mean for the attention. More time and attention goes into behavioral issues than into teaching in many classrooms. As difficult as his situation may be for you, spend the time and win the teacher's cooperation. Ironically, this may turn out to be a most positive experience, drawing you closer to a better understanding of your child and how to help him succeed at school. Keep the faith. Do not give up on your child.

## WHAT TO SAY AND DO

Begin logging your observations of your child's behavior daily. Check with your pediatrician to rule out any physical problems that could be causing stomachaches, headaches, etc. You do not need to elaborate on your concerns; the doctor will most likely initiate questions about school.

Whenever a school experience is new to a child of any age, you may expect discouraged behavior. Imagine beginning a new job with thirty strangers and a new boss. You might need extra comfort too!

Do not overprotect. Do not coddle your child and let him stay home. He needs your positive attitude and *encouragement* and to hear from you, *"I know you can handle it."*

Be direct. Tell him what you observe. *"Andrew, you have been home for two days. Your tummy is better during the day and seems to bother you at night or in the morning."* Do not label this "school phobia." Your child's perception of a label will make the situation worse.

Work on a plan together. Identify feelings and empathize. *"Michael, you seem afraid to go to school."* Pause, listen, and reflect his feeling. *"It sounds as though you feel . . ."* Show understanding. *"I remember a time when I was afraid to go to school. It happens to kids. I'm sorry, I'd like to help."* He needs to hear that you are on his side and will work with him. *"We will work on this together. Let's think of some ideas to help."*

If you can identify the fear, help encourage assertion. Take the time to teach. *"Do not be embarrassed to ask for help. When you do not understand or the teacher talks too fast, let her know. You can raise your hand or tell her after class."* Or *"You know you may use the bathroom whenever you want. The teacher has a card on the wall to turn over when you use the bathroom."*

See the teacher. Do not wait until conference time. School conference should be in addition to this.

1. Tell the teacher what the visit is about in order to allow the time needed. *"Ms. Morgan, I would like to make an appointment with you to discuss some concerns about our son, Matthew. He has not been wanting to go to school."*
2. Have a written record of your school-related concerns. If you have logged your child's behavior, bring the log along. You do not want to forget to mention any details.
3. Do not blame or accuse. *("You do not like him, you never call on him, you are always yelling at him.")* That will only make the teacher feel defensive, and rightly so. Before jumping into your business about your son, show the teacher empathy and appreciation. *"You have a lot of energy to handle this class size."* *"We have been impressed with the time you take to write and send your newsletters."* There is always something good to comment on, and the teacher will listen better to you after being appreciated.
4. Ask for help, using an *I* message: *"I am concerned that Greg is having tummy aches and complaining about school. He has always loved school. I need your help with what you observe happening at school. I'd like to determine what we can do together to help him."* Together, try to get a feeling for what has changed at home or at school to set the problem off.
5. Plan a meeting with you, your child, and the teacher to brainstorm helpful solutions to the problem.

6. Follow through with notes from home to school and vice versa or have another parent/child/teacher visit.

This is a very difficult time for your child. He is obviously discouraged. Look for all the good your child does and try to comment on what he is doing right.

If you have worked with the teacher, the school counselor, and the principal and the problem does not improve, consider that a different teacher may be the answer, not because the current teacher is a bad one, but because your child may work better with another person.

**PREVENTIVE TIPS**

- At bedtime or another good time, talk with your child about the school climate. Be specific. *"Michael, what did you like best at school today? What didn't you like? Is anything different from before?"*
- Take the time in the spring to observe the classroom teachers your child may be assigned to in the fall. You may be able to request a teacher that you feel is suited for your child. Write a note to the principal. This note needs to be very specific. *"Mark needs a teacher who gives very clear instructions."* Or *"Taylor is very active. He needs a teacher who uses learning centers."*
- Make every effort to volunteer in your child's classroom and help at the school. This will give you the opportunity to observe your child's interactions more and create good communication with school authorities.
- Hire a tutor to work with your child to boost his confidence in academic areas.
- Spend quality time with your child discussing feelings and daily experiences.
- Seek out outside activities to help your child make friends and be successful in an area he likes. Consider gymnastics, basketball, soccer, art, music, Scouts, etc.
- Supportive friends with children his age are a help. Organize family activities such as hiking, skiing, barbecues, and traditional events such as a 4th of July party.

- Find children's books on school-related subjects to read together. *Annabelle Swift, Kindergartner* by Amy Schwartz (New York: Orchard, 1988) is good reading for early grades. *There's a Boy in the Girl's Bathroom* by Louis Sachar (New York: Alfred A. Knopf, 1987) and *Romona the Pest* by Beverly Cleary (New York: Morrow, 1968) are good for your school-age child to read to herself or for you to read aloud. Louis Sachar has written other fun books for early readers. Ask a children's librarian or knowledgeable bookstore clerk for helpful suggestions.
- *Keeping a Head in School* by Dr. Mel Levine (Cambridge, Mass.: Educators Publishing Service, 1990) is adult reading about learning abilities and learning disorders.

*See also: Day care, dropping off*

# SCHOOL BUS

*"My child doesn't want to ride the school bus."*

### UNDERSTANDING THE SITUATION

When your child does not want to ride the school bus he may tell you outright or merely cry about it. He may also refuse to go to school without mentioning the bus. This is a worrisome issue, especially if you work and rely on the bus for his transportation. Finding the reason for the negative reaction to the bus may be like a treasure hunt. Perhaps the driver is scary and gruff when he disciplines. Other children on the bus may be very aggressive, and teasing and fighting may occur. Your child may be sensitive to noise; a busload of children is noisy. He may not like sitting for a twenty or thirty-minute ride. If he is just beginning kindergarten or first grade or is new to the school, he may fear leaving you and facing the huge new situation of school. (*"The bus is so big, and I feel so small."*) Bus anxiety is very normal. Be sensitive to your child's plea. Take the time to work through the problem and support him. With your patience and effort he will learn to cope. Show understanding and help him find a way to make the bus more enjoyable. With time and understanding, your child will adjust.

## WHAT TO SAY AND DO

You may need to take some time from work to help your child through this. Taking time initially will prevent prolonged hassles. Try putting her on the bus and following the bus to school. Be there when she climbs off. If she is afraid she'll miss her stop on the way home, be there to greet her several times so that she learns the stop. And so on. Your attitude when greeting her is important. *"Wow! How do you feel? Terrific job!"*

Identify her feeling. *"Michelle, you dislike the school bus."* Show understanding and help her identify the problem. *"When I was your age I hated the bus because it took so long to get home. It was very big and noisy. It sounds as though you feel . . ."* Listen. Do not coddle and overprotect. Take *time to teach*; there is a solution to every problem. *"You need to cope with the ride on the bus. Let's talk about ways to help with this problem."* If the ride is too long, send her with pens and paper. Provide a snack to eat after school before she gets on the bus.

Make your resources work for you. Tell the school principal and classroom teacher about the problem. Each of them cares about your child's school adjustments and can help at school. If the driver is abusive or disrespectful, seek assistance from the principal.

Talk to the driver with your child. Many drivers pride themselves on caring about the children. Other children may be picking on her. He will want to know that. He will learn her name and may temporarily provide a special seat up front for her, until she feels more comfortable.

**PREVENTIVE TIPS**

- Before the first ride, take your child to look at the school bus in the bus yard.
- Meet the driver so he can get to know your child on a first-name basis.
- Ask the teacher or the school principal for the names of other children at your stop or on your route who could be friends for your child to ride with on the bus.
- Give support in small steps. The first day your child rides the bus, be at the school to greet her when she gets there. Send a note to her teacher to be sure she is assisted onto the bus in the afternoon. Be at your stop to make sure she gets off after school.
- Greet the driver and have conversations. He will love to hear a thank-you and an appreciation.
- Use books as a springboard for discussing feelings or fears about the bus. Ask a children's librarian or a knowledgeable bookstore clerk to suggest books about school issues, friendships, and self-esteem. You may even find one specifically about riding the school bus.

---

# SECURITY BLANKET

*"My child won't give up his blanket."*

**UNDERSTANDING THE SITUATION**

We encourage toddlers to hold security objects to help them to be independent, and then we struggle with worry and frustration over how to get them to let go of them when they are older. You nag and try to remove it, and your child cries. You constantly remind him that he is old enough to not use his "blankie," then madly search for it when it is lost and rant after it is found. Your reaction invites demanding behavior. Getting your child to give up the blankie will be a very difficult process if you allow your guilt and anxiety to control you. Take on a positive attitude. You are raising your child to be a self-confident individual, and with the right timing, teaching, and *encouragement* he will learn he can do without the blanket. You need to show him you have faith in him and are confident he will quit when he is ready. Develop a plan and start with small steps. Few students enter high school carrying security blankets, though ironically, some high school teachers are encouraging students to bring teddy bears for test taking. Grade school and high school teachers have been known to have teddy bears in their rooms for when students need hugs.

## WHAT TO SAY AND DO

Don't compare your child to other children. It may take more time for him to feel independent. He will do it. Having two identical blankies may ease the struggle of always looking for it and thus keep you less involved. One can be in the wash or left at the sitter's and there won't be a major meltdown.

Give your child the responsibility for keeping track of his blanket. *"Joey, I know you love your blanket. It belongs in your bed. You are in charge of knowing where it is."* If the blanket is lost, do not panic. Ask *what, when,* and *where* questions to encourage him to think and take responsibility. Calmly, ask, *"When did you have it last? Where does it usually stay?"* Then help him look. When found, ask, *"What are you going to do next time so that you know where it is?"*

*Set limits* regarding specific areas where he may use his blanket. *"Cory, your blanket stays in your bed. You may use it there anytime you need to."* Be consistent and do not waver. When you make too many exceptions to the rule, he will begin testing.

Try distracting by giving *choices* of different objects. *"Mark, Pooh Bear would love to have a turn with you tonight, or would you rather give your troll a chance to sleep with you? Lucky toys to have you to take care of them!"* This encourages flexibility.

When you feel he is ready to do without it, take a trip and

forget to bring the blankie. Be sincere, firm, and caring. *"Roger, blankie did not get in the car. Pooh Bear came. He would love to sleep with you. Next time we come you can remember blankie. I know you can handle sleeping without him."* There may be tears, but he will learn he can do without.

If you are working on giving up the blankie, use a *training chart* and have your child record successful nights and days without it. *"Casey, you will give up your blankie when you are ready. I can't do it for you. Here is a chart that will help you get started."* Congratulate her efforts and reward with a "grown-up" event. One six-year-old-girl had her ears pierced for giving up her blanket and thumb-sucking, and going without them for over six weeks.

### PREVENTIVE TIPS

- Timing is critical to successfully breaking the habit. Don't start if your child's world is in turmoil due to disruptions within the family, e.g., moving, a new baby, illness, death, or divorce.
- Should the security object become frayed and torn, do not rush out to replace it with a new one. As the blanket wears out, so may the habit.
- Spend quantities of quality time with your child on a daily basis. Children today experience great stress and pressure. Do your best to slow your pace. Have fun together, take long walks, read together, listen closely to his feelings with acceptance rather than judgment.
- Begin increasing your child's personal and family responsibilities. He can now dress himself, feed the dog or cat, help make meals, empty trash, etc., and feel he is growing and capable.

# SELFISHNESS

See: Sharing

# SEPARATING, FEAR OF

*"My child is afraid to have me leave."*

## Ages 2 ½–5

### UNDERSTANDING THE SITUATION

Some children will dive easily into new situations such as play groups, birthday parties, lessons, sleepovers, camp, etc. Others cling, want more time to observe, and are reluctant to leave the parent or try new situations. Your reluctant child may be sincerely fearful of new experiences with or without you. He also may be trying to control you, even if subconsciously. You understandably may be terribly frustrated and concerned with his lack of maturity, especially if you compare him to children who have no trouble leaving their parents. Forcing him will not build his self-confidence. It seems to be a law of nature that the harder you push your child away, the tighter he will cling to you. Take the time to read and understand about stages of development. Certain ages and stages are known to be more difficult. Some children have temperaments more resistant to change. Be patient. This is a maturing process that for some children takes a long time. Take time to provide small, gentle steps leading to his self-confidence and independence. Do not give up on him. He needs to know you have confidence in him.

## WHAT TO SAY AND DO

Separation anxiety is normal for different ages and stages of development. This can be exacerbated by a crisis such as a divorce, a death in the family, a move, a parent's loss of work, etc. Seek professional counsel if you feel unsure of how you should deal with this problem. Your pediatrician, day care professional, or school counselor can be of great help.

When your child is timid, leave her with familiar people, leave less frequently, and be absent only for short periods. Some absences are unavoidable, such as going to work or taking a necessary trip to visit a sick relative. This stage will pass. Stay close and be patient.

Let your child know what to expect. Do not assume he cannot handle your leaving. Tell him in advance in a positive, matter-of-fact manner what will happen. If he cries, comfort him, but be aware that coddling for extended amounts of time may send a message that he needs your protection.

Sneaking away will not help your child handle separation. Do not be afraid of his reaction. Tell your child when you are leaving and explain when you will be back. An enthusiastic hug and a smile from you will encourage him to feel he is safe. Say, *"Mike, I'll be back with all the other parents when the birthday party is over."* Do not prolong your exit.

Be your child's advocate. Ask the sitter how long your child cries when you leave, and what happens after you exit. Your child may be trying to tell you something about the baby-sitter and be truly distressed. Sometimes the child is right to worry!

Celebrate each progressive step your child makes toward independence. Say, *"Alright, Zack, you cried only two minutes when I left today. You had a great morning swimming! Let's celebrate with a picnic at the park!"* He may regress the next day and cry longer. *Encourage.* *"You had a harder time today. We'll try again tomorrow."*

**PREVENTIVE TIPS**

- Examine your own fears or anxieties regarding your leaving. Your child will pick up any guilt or concern you show and feel less secure. As he becomes more independent you may feel a loss of parental control and be surprised at your mixed feelings. These are normal. Find someone to share your feelings with and try not convey your ambivalence to your child.
- At a good listening time, ask your child how he felt when you left him and show understanding. Brainstorm ways he could feel better.
- Read *Will You Come Back for Me?* by Ann Tompert (Morton Grove, Ill.: Whitman, 1988) and *Waiting for Mom* by Linda Wagner Tyler (New York: Puffin, 1989) with your child. Ask a children's librarian or knowledgeable bookstore clerk to suggest other books appropriate to read with your child regarding separation.

## Ages 6-10

**UNDERSTANDING THE SITUATION**

Read the preceding section, for ages 2½–5.

Some children who have shown no fear in their younger years over separating begin feeling anxious about circumstances such as going to school, playing at friends' houses, going on sleepovers, or trying new activities. There is no magical age when the timidness begins or ends. This is quite frustrating as your child grows older. You may not be able to know what causes his anxiety, but you can work with him to overcome it. Be careful not to let others' opinions influence you. Welcome support but not criticism. Do not compare children. Your child is unique, with his own temperament and experiences. Be patient, do not force, and keep the faith. This will pass.

**WHAT TO SAY AND DO**

Give your child time to assess his feelings. *"Ryan, you seem afraid to sleep over at Mike's."* Don't lecture or jump in to offer your advice. Reflect his feelings. *"You really want to go, but you seem afraid."* Often a child will work through a situation when he begins to understand his feelings.

Reassure him he is normal for feeling as he does. *"Ryan, many children feel homesick when away from home. Some adults do too."* Or give your own childhood memory of a similar experience. *"I remember when I was eight and had to take swim lessons. I had to be pushed by my dad. I was scared."*

Give helpful suggestions. *"Plan to take a favorite picture with you or something that smells like home. Your pillow or Teddy would surely be comforting."*

Give suggestions for a way out so your child feels she has some control over what happens to her. *"Heidi, I will be home. You can always call me. Do not be embarrassed."* Be there for her. You may help her by suggesting she takes small steps toward a bigger goal. For example, if she is afraid to go to camp, suggest, *"Stay one night, and if you are unhappy call me and I will willingly come get you."* Or if she doesn't want to go to an activity say, *"You need an activity. We signed up for three classes. Go to those, and if you still do not like it you may quit and we will find another activity you like better."*

Let your child know what to expect. Children who fear separating need time to adjust, work through it, and discuss it.

**PREVENTIVE TIPS**

• Read together *What Would You Do?* by Linda Schwartz (Santa Barbara: The Learning Works, 1990) and *Playing It Smart* by Tova Navarra (New York: Barron's, 1989). These books present different situations teaching children what to do if . . . Teaching ahead of time and discussing any difficult situations always help with handling fear.

• Every time your child is successful with a challenge it will be easier to face a new one. Give many opportunities and chances for him to try new and different things and do not give up on him.

• Take family outings together and join other families in their activities. Your child's confidence will grow with exposure.

*See also: Day care, dropping off; Sleeping, away from home*

# SEXUAL PLAY

*"I found my son naked with the little girl next door!"*

### UNDERSTANDING THE SITUATION

You may discover your child exploring private parts with another child—or worse, you may hear from the indignant mother of the other child. You will most likely be shocked and unsure about what to do. Sexual play is normal at around the age of four. Children are curious and attempt to learn from comparing and exploring. Most parents feel inadequate to handle the situation. Stop the behavior kindly but firmly, avoiding giving undue attention or causing embarrassment. Do not scold, lecture, or send the playmate home the first time. This will only create guilt. Your child is indicating he is curious. This is a cue to you to provide more information, address his curiosity, and find time to discuss appropriate touching and private, personal parts of the body. This is an opportunity for you to express your values and feelings and to give accurate information that will help him learn to use good judgment and make good choices about his body.

Note: Excessive sexual play at any age may be a sign of an underlying problem. It is important that you discuss any concern with your pediatrician or a school counselor rather than ignoring the matter. Do not take for granted that this behavior will disappear on its own.

**WHAT TO SAY AND DO**

Address the issue of touching. This may be your child's first lesson on appropriate and inappropriate touch. Children need to learn what is right and wrong; they also need to be taught to be respectful of others and assertive to protect themselves. Often one child is being told to play and doesn't know how to say no. Be direct in front of both children. *"Jenny, your body is yours and you are the boss! If you don't want someone to touch you, say so! If you do not like the way it feels, say so! Even if it is a big person!"*

Curiosity may be the motive for your young child's sexual play. Explain that injury is a reason for not touching other people's private parts. *"You are curious about private parts. You might hurt your friend by poking or cause an infection by getting dirt in her vagina."*

Discuss the situation with the parent of the other child. Each of you needs to discuss your own values and rules with your child individually. If the other child plays often with yours, ask the other parent's consent to read well-illustrated and well-written books together with both children to help satisfy their curiosity. This is a good alternative to scolding when you find the children together in an uncomfortable situation. *"Here is a book that shows all the parts of your bodies that you are curious about. When you are curious, tell me and we will read together."*

Children will sometimes repeat the same act if they play together often. Announce the consequences should it happen again and be sure to follow through. Deal with them together. *"Peter and Anna, I am upset to find you with your pants off after you were told it was not okay. You both have made a bad choice. Peter will have to go home. You may try again to play next week."* It is very positive for the children to know they will have another opportunity to do better. They should not be together unsupervised if they repeat the activity consistently.

**PREVENTIVE TIPS**

• Sexual play sometimes comes with boredom. Intervene by offering new and fun activities. Do not be fooled when your child and a friend are playing quietly and are "out of your hair." Redirect their play to something different when you find them involved in sexual play.

- Spend *special time*. You need to make opportunities for listening and talking *with* your child (not *at* her). Make opportunities to share feelings and answer questions when she has them, not just when you want to talk about them.
- Maintain the ever-so-important sense of humor that raising children requires.
- Alert your child's teacher or sitter if you are aware that this is a time of special interest in private parts. The same Positive Parenting approach should be consistently used at home, school, and day care.
- Read children's books with your child. Try *See How You Grow* by Dr. Patricia Pierce (New York: Barron's, 1988) or *The Bare Naked Book* by Kathy Stinson (Ontario; Annick Press/Firefly Books, 1986). An educational kit, *The TLC Kit* (Harvard Community Health Plan Foundation, 27 Mica Lane, Wellesley, Mass. 02181) includes the pamphlets "Touch Talk" and "Talking with Your Child about Sex." *Straight Talk, Sexuality Education for Parents and Kids Ages 4–8*, by Marily Bratner and Susan Chamlin (New York: Penguin, 1985) is another book you might want to read.
- A knowledge of stages of sexual development will help you understand the normalcy of sexual play. Suggested adult reading: *Raising a Child Conservatively in a Sexually Permissive World* by Sol Gordon and Judith Gordon (New York: Simon and Schuster, 1989).

*See also: Masturbation; Nakedness*

# SEXUALITY, QUESTIONS ABOUT

*"My child asks questions about sex that make me uncomfortable."*

### UNDERSTANDING THE SITUATION

Your young child may ask, *"Why is the grass green?" "Where is the moon?" "What is a penis for?"* all with the same curious tone. Can you answer all these questions with the same matter-of-fact attitude? Sexual questions may make you feel terribly uncomfortable and embarrassed. That is normal. Be honest and let your child know if the subject is difficult for you to discuss. Don't be afraid to say, *"I need some time to think about that one!"* Children are born sexual. Sometimes we forget that while they are learning to walk and talk they are also learning what's going on with themselves sexually. What we know about healthy self-esteem today is that children need to feel good about their sexuality, to feel good about being a boy or a girl, to have a good body image, to know that sexual feelings are normal, and to not feel guilty about being curious. Don't limit yourself to thinking about sex education as only the facts about intercourse or lovemaking. At all ages your child will need accurate information using correct anatomical terms. Be a loving and approachable parent so that questions will be asked. Maintain a sense of humor. Your child will see plenty of sex on TV and in other media and will be exposed to slanted values and information of dubious worth. Your responsibility is to provide her lovingly with proper information which will establish healthy patterns for later growing-up years.

## WHAT TO SAY AND DO

If your child asks a complex question, answer her with a question. *"Golly, that's a good one. What do you think?"* This will help you determine what she is really asking.

Listen carefully to your child's question and do not feel you need to answer a simple query with a lengthy explanation. For example, if her question is *"Where did I come from?"* clarify what she is really asking. The answer she wants may be *"You were born in a hospital in Los Angeles, California,"* or she may want *"You came from a special place inside Mommy called the uterus."*

Use books to get you out of embarrassing situations and to insure that you are giving accurate information. *"Jeremy, that is a good question. Let's see if the answer might be in this book."*

If you're in public and your child asks an embarrassing question, answer her very matter-of-factly with a *poker face* and refrain from acting embarrassed or drawing attention to the matter. If you feel that she is trying to embarrass or annoy you, give a touch with a knowing smile and whisper the answer in the same matter-of-fact manner. Later, say, *"Jenny, some questions are for private times with Mommy or Daddy. It's hard for me to talk about your private parts in the grocery store. Next time you bring it up in public I'll just say, 'Later, Jenny.'"*

Take opportunities to address your child's curiosity. Your little girl may sit naked in front of a mirror looking at herself. Take a flashlight and show her the clitoris, vagina, and anus. The urethra is not visible though that is the correct word for where the urine comes.

Find out what she thinks. Be careful if you answer your young child's questions by using analogies. (For example, seed planting may leave the strange impression that Mommy will grow a tree in her uterus.) Lectures often stop thoughts, while questions stimulate thinking. *"Julie, what do you think your belly button is for?"*

If your older child is not asking questions or showing curiosity, it may mean he is going to outside sources for his information. His peers will not provide accurate factual information and cannot give him your feelings and values. Introduce the subject with a book. *"Jake, I found a great book today about sexuality. I would like to look at it with you."* If he says no, leave the book for him to look at alone. *"I'll leave the book for you. If you have questions, I would like to talk about them with you. I do love you, and I want you to have accurate information."*

### PREVENTIVE TIPS

• Be ready for the same questions year after year. What a four-year-old child is ready to understand is quite different from what a seven-year-old needs to know.

• Touch and hug respectfully and often. When it is necessary to touch private parts, such as to clean a sore penis or properly apply medication for chapped skin in the vaginal area, let your child do as much as possible. If you need to help, explain what you are doing.

• Do not get caught up in what others think. The neighbor or relative may not agree with your straightforward approach. Your responsibility is to inform your child properly.

• Use the family photo album and notice together how your child has changed physically as she has grown up, how different she looks, and what she can do at different ages.

• Read children's books together, such as *See How You Grow* by Dr. Patricia Pierce (New York: Barron's, 1988). For preteens (ages 9–12), try *What's Happening to Me?* by Pete Mayle (New York: Carol Publishing, 1975) or *How You Were Born* by Joanna Cole (New York: Morrow, 1993).

• To inform yourself, read books written for adults, such as *Raising a Child Conservatively in a Sexually Permissive World* by Sol Gordon and Judith Gordon (New York: Simon and Schuster, 1989).

# SHARING

*"My child will not share."*

### UNDERSTANDING THE SITUATION

Very young children struggle with the difference between "mine" and "yours." They think differently from how an adult thinks. *"What's mine is mine, and what's yours should be mine too."* One expert likened a preschooler's feeling about sharing his toy to giving up one of his arms. Many school-age children have strong feelings of ownership, a difficult time parting with their possessions, and a more competitive attitude which makes giving and taking turns a struggle. You may feel embarrassed when your child fusses or complains about sharing, and it is certainly frustrating to watch a temper tantrum over selfishness. It will help you to keep these points in mind:

1. *Learning to share is developmental.* There is no magical age when a child should be able to share. A young child initially plays alone or alongside others and in time interacts with others. Learning to share is a process that develops with the child's maturity. It takes time, and it requires a parent's *time to teach* the child to give as well as to take turns.

2. *Learning to share is influenced by environment.* Children need an atmosphere in which adults give and take, in which cooperation rather than destructive competition is encouraged.

3. *A child's temperament affects his learning to share.* Some children are very intense. Change is difficult for them, and they need more time to consider a new idea.

Keep your positive attitude, and keep faith in your child. With your patience, your modeling, your teaching, and your consistency with follow-through, he will become an assertive yet caring and sharing person.

## WHAT TO SAY AND DO

Never shame or embarrass your child by saying something like *"You are so selfish. You'll have no friends if you keep that up."*

Teach your child some strategy. Let her know what to expect. Invite her to put away things she does not want other children to play with and to display (or bring along) toys she does not mind sharing. *"Joanie, before Colin comes to play, show me what toys you do not want him to play with and we will put them away. Pick some toys that you do not mind if he plays with. He is very excited about coming to play with you."*

Establish a system defining ownership at home. Sharing comes easier when a child feels she has things she can claim as her own. Label personal toys or clothes. Define the ones to be shared by the whole family. Teach how to share with sisters and brothers. (At gift-giving time, give a present to the whole family: a game, a teddy bear, etc.)

Use *"You have a choice."* The consequence of your child's not sharing works well when it is his choice. Be very consistent and follow through.

1. *"Mark, either take turns with the scissors or I will put them away."*
2. *"Vickie, you can stay as long as you can share the toys. If you do not share, we will go home. It's your choice."*
3. *"Russ, you need to share with your brother or go to your room for time out."*

Look for opportunities at home to teach sharing. Do not assume because you discussed the matter one time your child has learned. The process takes years. *"Audrey, if you want your turn on the swing, use your words to ask. Do not push and hit."*

*"Here is one pair of scissors and one pack of crayons. You two share."*

*"Ginny, when you want to wear Marcie's sweater, ask her first. Try using that magic word, 'Please.' "*

*"Mikey, if you are not willing to share with him, tell him why. Let*

*him know the glove is still too new and special to share just yet. He will then know you like him but do not want him to use your new glove. You also could offer him your old glove."*

Share with your child and tell her what you are doing. Cooperation needs to be taught as sharing rather than as obeying your orders. *"Kelly, here is part of my milk shake. I am sharing with you because it makes me feel good to see you enjoy something so much. I hope you will share with me too." "If you will help stir the cookie dough I will share the cookies with you. That's cooperation."*

Look for the little things she does well and compliment her. *"Wow! Good sharing. Ginny really likes riding your bike. You made her day!" "Audrey, nice sharing. She asked for her turn and you gave it willingly. You are terrific!" "Denise, I liked the way you used your words to tell her you wanted your doll back."*

If sharing has been hard for your child, invite a child to play for short periods. Supervise the play. *"Mindy, you ride on the swing while Kyle is on the glider. Nice cooperating." "I have some cookies and milk to share with you. Mindy, you can pour the milk for Kyle."*

## PREVENTIVE TIPS

- At bedtime discuss feelings related to sharing. Sharing isn't easy for all children. Listen and assess your child's feelings without judgment. Show understanding. *"You were upset with Jeremy today. Sharing is hard."* Or *"You had a morning of fun. I saw a lot of sharing."*
- Spend *special time* together regularly. Quality, fun time with your listening and understanding will give your child energy to cooperate with others.
- Read children's stories together about sharing and friendship, such as *A Bargain for Frances* by Russell Hoban (New York, HarperCollins, 1970). A librarian or a knowledgeable clerk in a children's bookstore will help you with the latest for all ages.

*See also: Bullied child; Bullying*

# SHOPLIFTING

*See: Stealing*

# SHOPPING

*"I dread taking my child shopping."*

### UNDERSTANDING THE SITUATION

Shopping with a young child or an uncooperative older child can be a hair-raising experience. When she asks for this and that, whines, and throws a screaming temper tantrum, you may wonder why you tried. Shopping with your child does not have to be a catastrophic experience; it can actually be a pleasant one. It may be more efficient to leave your child home, but if you never shop with her you are denying her an opportunity to learn self-control and responsibility for her actions. Needless to say, you will have many hurried trips to a store with your child in tow when you feel rushed and tired. That is reality. Let your child know what you are feeling openly and honestly so she will not have to guess why you are out of sorts or assume you are upset with her before she has done anything to provoke you. Successful shopping trips occur when you have more energy, when you have a plan, and when you are willing to take the time to follow through with a consequence if needed. *"Be prepared."* Your positive attitude and faith in her ability to hold together are musts.

## WHAT TO SAY AND DO

Let your child know what to expect. Before you enter the store, tell her where you are going and what you intend to buy. Show your enthusiasm. She will do better when she sincerely feels wanted and needed. *"Maggie, we are going into the store to buy food for the week. This will be fun with your help. I love having you with me."* Talk to her and include her in your thoughts and ideas as you move through the store.

Check her understanding of how she should behave in the store. Set your agreement before entering. Use very specific questions instead of directing and lecturing. *"Who will you stay with in the store? What can you touch?"* Offer choices. *"Will you ride in the cart or walk next to me?"* If she agrees beforehand to be good, she will likely follow through.

Give her a job. *"Carli, I brought the calculator. You add up the numbers as I put the food in the cart."* Or *"Help me decide on the cereal we want this week."*

Give her something to look forward to. *"As soon as we have all our groceries you may choose a coloring book on our way out."* *"If we have a fast trip we can go to the park on our way home."*

Have a creative plan if he acts out. Do not threaten or nag; stay cool and act:

1. Act unimpressed with his bad actions. Use a *poker face* and finish shopping quickly. Later, when you cool down, discuss the incident and plan for success the next time. *"Morgan, you wanted my attention in the store today. We had to leave early, I felt embarrassed, and you missed Julie's birthday party. What will you do differently next time?"*
2. Use a *poker face* and *action with few words*. Take your child out of the store, put her in the car, and wait outside the car for her to calm down.
3. Agree to consequences before going into the store if behavior has been bad in the past. *"Sophie, the last time we shopped you threw a tantrum for gum. Today if you misbehave we will go talk to the store manager. He will keep our groceries and I will take you*

*home to Auntie Mo."* Be sure you do what you say you will do; she may test you one time.

Comment on the good trips. *"Wow! Trent, you were a huge help today buying school clothes. Let's celebrate with the time we have left and go for a burger."*

### PREVENTIVE TIPS

- Keep expectations reasonable. Know how long your active three-year-old can be expected to last. Do not try to "shop 'til you drop." Do not get sidetracked with lengthy conversations with friends.
- Plan for a successful trip. A tired, hungry child will not be much fun in the grocery store. Try to shop when he is rested and fed.
- Keep an "emergency kit" of healthful snacks in the car for those unexpected stops when he is hungry and tired. A small bag of trail mix often helps a child get through a shopping trip.

---

# SHOWING OFF

*"My child is an annoying show-off."*

## Ages 2½–5

### UNDERSTANDING THE SITUATION

When your very young child shows off, family members may laugh at him and actually encourage his antics. Often the new baby brother or sister can trigger showing off in an attempt to draw attention away from the baby. It is cute when your child is little, but as he grows older the behavior will seem obnoxious, and if he is used to being laughed at, he may try harder to keep the attention he is used to. Some four and five-year-olds show off to feel important. It may be a signal that your child needs more *encouragement*. Give him your positive attention when he is not showing off and keep your sense of humor while teaching him to interact appropriately with others. Express your unconditional love. *"I always love you, yet I do not always like the way you act."* Set limits and be consistent in following through. Make it clear what is acceptable and not acceptable behavior. Be patient. The showing off will pass.

**WHAT TO SAY AND DO**

Identify your child's feelings, then tell him what you need. *"Michael, you want Uncle Page's attention. You are probably tired of the baby getting noticed all the time. Finish coloring, then Uncle Page will put the baby down and play with you."*

Inform him when guests are coming and let him know what to expect. Let him know if he can participate and when you need private adult time. *"Nick, Auntie Mo will be coming over with Uncle Page. They will want to see you. You can show them your new slide and tree swing. We are going to have adult time while you paint or color."* Clue the guests in that he needs some time from them.

*Set limits.* Do not embarrass him in front of others. Take him to another room. Identify his feeling and give him a choice. *"Morgan, you want my attention. I will be able to spend time with you later. You may stay and be polite or go to your room until you feel like being nice with the others."* Follow through. If you are in public, take him outside or to the car.

You may stimulate his showing off by bragging about his cute new sayings or behavior and having him demonstrate to friends. If he wishes to put on a play or display a new talent, help him ask politely and be sure the audience is interested. *"Ian, I know you want to show your new somersault to Morgan. Ask Morgan if he'd like to see you do it. Maybe he has one to show you too."*

**PREVENTIVE TIPS**

- Provide an area in your home where your child can color, cut and paste, etc. and be near you and your guests while doing age-appropriate activities.
- Find time to listen to and discuss feelings. Find children's books to read together about children and their important feelings, such as *Because of Lozo Brown* by Larry King (New York: Viking, 1988) and *Feelings* by Aliki Brandenberg (New York: Morrow, 1984).
- Give your child opportunities to be heard and help her know when she needs to listen. Teach her to "wait and listen" with a gentle hand signal, a kind glance, or a simple phrase: *"Laurie, it will be your turn in a minute. Hang on to your thought."* Do not make her wait too long. She will forget what she wanted to tell you. If she forgets, never say, *"Well, it must not have been important."*
- Provide playtime with other children. Your child's friends may tell him they don't like his showing off.
- Take *time to teach* him what he can do to get your attention when guests are at your home. Talk about appropriate behavior with guests. Tell him that some guests will say hello but won't give him much attention.

## Ages 6–10

### UNDERSTANDING THE SITUATION

Your school-age child may show off in front of his peers doing things he knows he is not allowed to do. He hopes you won't scold him in front of friends. Be clear about your limits and plan consequences together. Show understanding. He most likely is feeling inadequate. Find time to spend with him on a regular basis; listen to him and try to learn more about how he feels about himself. He needs to gain your attention with appropriate behavior and to learn to win others' approval in positive ways.

## WHAT TO SAY AND DO

Read the above section, for ages 2½–5.

Use an *I* message to let your child know how you feel, and discuss possible consequences if she shows off when she has friends present. This lets her know what to expect before it happens and may prevent the behavior. *"Erica, I feel embarrassed for you when you act that way, and I get angry when you are careless. I don't want to embarrass you in front of your friends. If you act the way you did today again, I will warn you once and then have you take time out. Your friends will have to go home if this behavior continues."* Do as you say you will do.

When showing off occurs, give your child one warning, kindly and firmly. If he continues, with a *poker face* remove him. Do not embarrass him. Take him into another room for *time out* or to discuss the situation. *"Ian, come out when you are ready to act nicely."*

Discuss ways to make friends. He may be feeling that showing off or being funny is what makes kids like him. Give him affirmation. Use questions to make him think. *"Ken, you are a fun person to be with. What are some things to do when you have friends over? Kids like it when you ask them what they want to play. What choices can you give a friend?"*

Arrange for significant people in your child's world to spend *special time* with her. She needs attention that she can count on from those who love her. Comment when you notice her efforts to behave well.


## PREVENTIVE TIPS

• At a good listening time, identify how your child feels when showing off. *"Zack, today you were showing off in the kitchen when Morgan was here. Could it be you wanted him to think you were really funny so he would like you better?"* Listen without lecture or judgment. You may learn what he is feeling. Show understanding. *"I remember a time when I broke a vase trying to show off to a friend. I got in trouble, and my friend didn't think I was so great!"*

- Discuss the difference between showing off and performing for fun.
- Find opportunities to build your child's self-image with challenges—through sports, social groups, and academics. This should decrease his attention-seeking behavior.

Note: If this behavior is excessive and you begin to see friend-lessness, lowered grades, or irritability, talk with his teacher or contact a school counselor.

*See also: Interrupting*

# SHYNESS

*"My child is too shy to join in with others."*

## UNDERSTANDING THE SITUATION

Forty years ago shyness was regarded as a positive trait. As children were to be seen and not heard, the parent of the shy child was happy to hear, *"She's so wonderful, sweet, and shy."* Children today need to be assertive. "Sweet and shy" is no longer a plus. We all want our children to be creative and resourceful and to flourish in any learning situation. Your shy child may seem to stand back and miss out when others join in. This is worrisome and at times very frustrating for a parent. Your tendency is to push, to try to force her out of her shell. This generally doesn't work with a child of this temperament. She needs your *encouragement* and support to build her self-confidence. Accept her temperament with a positive attitude and do not force her to be the hearty, impulsive type. Allow time. With your patience and positive affirmations, she will become a strong, self-confident adult.

## WHAT TO SAY AND DO

Do not refer to her as *"my shy child."* She is *thoughtful, cautious, quiet, contemplative,* and *very observant.* When someone says, *"My, she is so shy,"* respond, *"She is not shy. Sometimes she is quiet at first because she is cautious and observing the situation."* She will flourish from all the positive things that she hears you saying and believing about her.

Make positive observations to help her understand and accept her own temperament. *"Caitlin, you are a good thinker. You take your time and consider what you will do."* Or *"You are a good observer. You will have good friendships because you are cautious about choosing your playmates. You do not like roughness, but you do like to run and climb when you feel safe."*

Do not push her into situations she refuses. Allow her more time to observe and trust a situation. Provide opportunities for her to build up confidence in small, supportive steps. If she refuses swimming lessons, offer to go watch on the side at first.

Give her permission to stand back and observe. *"Katie, you can stand with me and watch the children. When you are ready, join in."*

Identify her feelings and empathize. *"Julie, you are afraid to tell the man what you want. I remember feeling the way you do when I was your age. It is scary, but I know you will speak up when you are ready."*

Do not rescue and overprotect. We grow the most and learn the most about ourselves when we have to do something we feel we cannot do. When you know your child is safe, allow a struggle. *"Josie, I know you feel afraid to go to Cathy's for two nights. I know you will be safe and have a fun time. You can handle it."* Or, *"Elizabeth, the boy in the fifth grade took your money. You need to go to his teacher and tell her what happened."* When she succeeds, celebrate with a cheer. *"I knew you could do it! How does it feel?"*

## PREVENTIVE TIPS

• Observe your child's behavior for a couple of weeks and keep a log. This will help you understand her temperament.
• Organize play at your home. Invite schoolmates over. If she

balks, have them come for just a short time. She will see that she can handle it and begin to warm up.

- Sign her up for individual physical activities. Swimming, gymnastics, dance, karate, etc. all build self-confidence.
- Read children's books together. Many good ones are written about feelings and self-esteem. *Shy Charles* by Rosemary Wells (New York: Dial, 1988) is a fun book about a boy who is painfully shy but shows that he can take command of a situation if he has to and still remain true to his retiring nature.

*See also: Friends, lack of*

---

# SLEEP, AWAY FROM HOME

*"My child will not spend the night away from home."*

### UNDERSTANDING THE SITUATION

Children in today's world are often expected to handle sleeping away from home. Situations arise for busy parents that require children go to a friend's or a relative's home for the night. Overnights with friends seem to start at very young ages, and many children are encouraged to go away to camp for weeks at a time. Some adjust very well to being away from home at night, but many do not. Some are unpredictable. Your child may have loved the experience at one time and now for some unknown reason has developed a fear. You may become impatient and frustrated with her behavior, as it can be inconvenient and sometimes inefficient when a child will not sleep away. Do not nag, force, or ridicule but instead offer your nurturing support and build her courage with small steps. This takes time, patience, and for some a lot of parental energy. Do not give up on her. With your reassurance she will in time become a confident person who will not be controlled by her fears.

## WHAT TO SAY AND DO

Do not ridicule, demean, or compare your child to others with comments such as *"Come on, don't be a baby. Look at Sarah, she is not afraid to be away."* Encourage with comments such as *"Marie, you do not feel ready to stay away from home now. It takes some time." "Sleeping away from home may be a little scary for you, but it is a lot of fun. You will like it when you are ready for it."*

Listen to her, help her identify her feelings, and show understanding. *"Josie, you seem afraid to stay with your cousin overnight. I used to be afraid at night away from home when I was six years old too. I was afraid I would wake up and be in the dark. Auntie Mo was afraid she would wet her bed. When you understand your fear you can help yourself. I carried a flashlight with me."*

Tell her the plan in advance. Do not coddle her; that says to her that she has something to fear. Show understanding, and help her to feel that she is in control and can handle it. Give *choices* when possible. *"Mary, tonight I need to work and you will stay the night with Grandma. I understand you do not want to stay away from home, though that is not a choice tonight. Choose what you would like to take with you to help you feel comfortable. Grandma says you can choose where you want to sleep."*

Share ideas that might help her. *"Michelle, you miss home in the night. Let's think about what you could take with you to help you feel better."* Before giving your ideas (her teddy bear, hot-water bottle, blankie), listen to her ideas first, then add yours. *"Affirmations help me. Say to yourself, 'I am safe, I am brave, I am in control.'"*

Practice in small steps. Have children over to your house for the night. Begin overnights with understanding relatives or close family friends when she chooses and build up to her school friends or others you may not be as close to. Take her to stay at a friend's house until 8:00 P.M., and work up to later. Tell her you will come when she needs to go. Be available to talk to her on the phone if she calls. Take her back for breakfast to show her the fun of completing a stay.

If you are eager for her to experience camp, begin with day camp experiences, build into one overnight, and then more.

**PREVENTIVE TIPS**

- Read children's stories about overcoming fear. Ask a children's librarian or knowledgeable bookstore clerk which books are best.
- Try overnights when your child feels good and is well rested.
- Comment on every success away from home. Recognize your child's efforts with enthusiasm.

*See also: Separating, fear of*

# SLEEPING WITH PARENT

*"My child crawls in with me during the night."*

### UNDERSTANDING THE SITUATION

When your child snuggles in beside you for the first time in a long time, it may feel good as she seeks the comfort of being close to you during the night. If the situation persists night after night, you may feel the frustration and irritation of being disturbed from an ever-so-deserved good night's sleep. You may be one of those parents who do not wake up, in which case you're surprised to find her taking up most of your bed in the morning. If your child has been ill or had other stresses, she may regress from good, independent sleeping habits to waking and coming into your bed for comfort. There are many philosophies about the family bed. If you feel guilty or are undecided about whether she should sleep with you, she will pick up on that. Decide what you want and need. If you feel she needs to be in her own bed, help her develop the strength and confidence to feel secure there. This takes patience, a positive attitude, and consistency on your part. It may take a lot of time. Do not give up.

## WHAT TO SAY AND DO

The first or second time she joins you she may be allowed to cuddle and stay with you or to fall back to sleep and then be carried back to her own bed. If you awaken, say, *"Kate, tonight you may stay with us, but tomorrow night you will need to stay in your own bed."* The next night, since it is bound to happen again, pick her up and gently set her down in her bed. Say, even if she is crying, *"I love you, and you are safe in your own bed."*

Walk her back to her bed and crawl in with her for ten minutes. Say, *"I will lie down with you for ten minutes, and then I need to go back to my bed to sleep."*

Leave a sleeping bag for your child next to your bed. You may feel exhausted during the night. You may try her in your bed and resent the discomfort. You may try sleeping with her in her bed (even for fifteen minutes) and feel *"This is not working."* The sleeping bag is an alternative that has worked well for many families. The child feels close to Mom and Dad for a time and eventually longs for the comfort of her own bed. You may explain sincerely, *"I need my sleep so that I am not so grouchy. Here is your sleeping bag next to my bed. We love you. If you need to be near me or Daddy tonight, crawl into your bag quietly."*

Help her set a goal and develop a plan. Discuss with her ways to help her cope during the night. Perhaps a new night light or a cuddly stuffed animal would help. Work toward something special, such as a fun event or a late-night TV show. Have her log on a chart the nights she handles not sleeping with you. *"All right, Sam! You have gone four nights in a row! Tonight we'll go for five! Then we'll go see the Mets!"*

## PREVENTIVE TIPS

- If you allow your child to sleep with you now and later change your mind, she may feel resentful and unloved. Better to be consistent now with her sleeping alone in her own bed than to suddenly have to break her of the habit.
- Fears are reinforced by your overprotection. Be positive and

encourage your child's small, progressive steps toward independence. Notice and comment only on her growth. Believe this is only a passing phase in normal development and convey your faith and trust in her.

• Be very consistent with bedtime routine. Emphasize the time for discussing feelings. Listen to her and help her work through her fears. Ask a children's librarian or knowledgeable bookstore clerk for books to read together about nighttime fears.

*See also: Bedtime, getting to bed; Bedtime, staying in bed; Dark, fear of; Nightmares*

# SLEEPWALKING

*See: Night wandering*

# SLOWNESS

*"My child is slow to do everything."*

## Ages 2½–5

### UNDERSTANDING THE SITUATION

When your child is too slow, you probably begin coaxing and nagging, feeling annoyed. *"Hurry, hurry!"* Typically this leads to your anger and impatience; perhaps you yell and spank him to get him to *"Move!"* The words *hurry, hurry* only trigger a response to go more slowly, and if used a lot at this young age can set up a battleground for years to come. When your child hears those words with a special frustrated note in your voice, he slows down to get you to help him. He enjoys being waited on! If a new baby has arrived, your older child may dawdle so that you spend extra time with him. Do not coax or get involved with his slowness, and refrain from labeling him with names such as "Pokey" or "Not-so-fast." His independence and maturity will come in small stages and will take time. Be patient and encourage.

## WHAT TO SAY AND DO

When you give directions, get down to your child's level and hold his hands or put your hands gently on his shoulders to get his attention. Have him look at you before you give the direction. Give one direction initially. Then calmly say, *"Brett, what do I need you to do?"* Have him tell you. When he says it himself, he makes it his.

Limit the number of transitions your child has to make in a day. Some children adapt to change slowly. They aren't trying to manipulate you, they just need more time.

Give the reward of extra attention at times when your child cooperates. *"Jimmy, if you are dressed when the timer goes off, I will have time to read you a story."*

Give a warning about what to expect. *"Russell, I need to leave the house when the timer goes off. You have fifteen minutes to dress."* If he is not dressed and you need to leave, pack his clothes in a sack and have him dress in the car, at day care, or at school. Use a *poker face* and *action with few words*. Most likely he will be very upset! Be consistent. He should believe you next time.

Develop logical consequences. Tell your child what you will do. That gives her the responsibility. *"Megan, I will tell you five minutes before we go to put on your shoes. When I need to leave I will tell you. If you are not ready, you may stay home with Dad. You have a choice."*

Use a training chart on which all tasks are noted. Your child adds a sticker as he finishes each task. Celebrate his success by doing something fun together. *"Jeffrey, the chart is full this week! Let's celebrate with a picnic at the pool!"*

Be very specific about what you noticed that was right. *"Jimmy, today for the first time you were in the car with your shoes on, on time!"*

**PREVENTIVE TIPS**

- Take *time for teaching*. If you expect your child to be dressed, be sure she knows how. A two-year-old should dress herself, but she needs to be taught how. Encourage her to be in charge because she is growing up! She can feed herself, dress herself, wash herself, etc. Stop doing these things for her—overprotection is demeaning.
- *Encourage*. Occasionally love and cuddle your child like a baby. Hold him until he volunteers to climb down. Comment on what a big boy he is getting to be, and comment on the new privileges he gets because he is older. *"Joey, I love hugging you and cuddling. That will never change! I am noticing what a big boy you are getting to be. Now you can stay up later at night, you can dress yourself, and I think you are old enough to learn to use the computer!"*
- Read children's stories together. *Pig William* by Arlene Dubanevich (New York: Bradbury/Macmillan, 1985) is a story about a pig being late.

## Ages 6–10

When your school-age child is slow, most often the words *hurry, hurry* trigger him to move more slowly still. Yelling and lecturing is upsetting, and sending him off to school after that negative atmosphere at home is disturbing. He may mistakenly believe the way to gain attention or to control the situation is to slow down and be noticed. Consider his temperament. If he is a very perceptive child he may be very easily distracted, and changing from task to task may be difficult. Try to adjust his schedule to allow more time. Pushing and nagging will not help. If you can relax and seem uninvolved with his slowness, and use techniques to give him the responsibility for being on time rather than depending on you to remind him, the situation should improve. Have patience. For some children this is a long-term effort.

## WHAT TO SAY AND DO

Stop nagging. Use a timer to *set limits* and help your child be in charge of the problem. *"Martin, you find it hard to be on time. I don't think it helps you go faster to hear me yell and remind you. Here is a timer so that you can be in charge of being on time yourself."*

Set consequences with him before a problem occurs. *"Randy, when the timer goes off it is time to leave for the school bus. I cannot drive you to school today. You will have to walk if you miss the bus."*

He may be easily distracted. Use a training chart so that he stays on task. *"Roger, you have three things to do before you go with Eric. Put a sticker next to each one as you do them."*

Celebrate when he is on time.

## PREVENTIVE TIPS

- If your child's teacher reports slowness, ask if this is a sign he is not succeeding in school. If so, help him learn better through tutoring, raising his level of concentration, stimulating his interest, and improving his self-image in the classroom. The teacher should not be expecting all the children to work at the same speed.
- Hold him to promptness at home. Stay on routine and be on time with bedtime, chores, etc.

*See also: Listening; Morning hassles*

# SPEECH, DIFFICULT TO UNDERSTAND

*"I understand my child's talk, but sometimes others don't."*

### UNDERSTANDING THE SITUATION

It is normal for some children's speech to be more difficult to understand than others'. Some parents can understand their own child when others do not. Since some speech sounds are more difficult than others, many children will go through stages when sounds are incorrectly produced. Substitutions and omissions are normal. For example, *r* is a sound that comes later. Do not worry when your three-year-old says "wabbit." Chronic ear infections are another reason a child may have immature speech. If these patterns persist they may cause difficulty for your child. By age four, though his sounds may not be perfect, your child's language should be intelligible to others. He will be frustrated if he cannot make himself understood, and humiliated if he is teased. His transition to school may be affected. Your concerns may worry him; he needs your patience and loving support. Talk with your pediatrician or a speech and hearing specialist if you are at all concerned.

### WHAT TO SAY AND DO

Improper speech, often cute to grandparents and other family members, can be mistakenly encouraged. For example, when a two-and-a-half-year-old says *"shoit"* for shirt, *"bubu"* for brother, or *"posha"* for spider, it may seem adorable, but it is not in his best interest to laugh and encourage.

Never criticize, label, or imitate his speech. If you know what he is saying, model good communication and repeat it back in a positive tone and correct form. If he says, *"Where's my wed wagon?"* respond, *"Oh, you are looking for your red wagon."*

If you do not understand him, ask him to show you. *"Alex, can you show me what you want?"* Stay calm and do not indicate you are having problems understanding.

Do not be distracted. Communicate your intent to understand so that your child feels you care. Give him eye contact, get down to his level, and show you are listening through facial expression, tone of voice, and body language.

### PREVENTIVE TIPS

- Be a good role model. Talk intelligently to your child, sing songs together, tell stories.
- Find time to discuss feelings. At bedtime, ask, *"What was the happiest time of your day? What part was the saddest?"* Poor speech can lead to lowered self-esteem and frustration, and a wise parent listens for concern from his child.
- Read children's stories aloud regularly with your child. The more you model good language use, the better.

*See also: Speech, late development*

# SPEECH, LATE DEVELOPMENT

*"My child is not talking as much as other kids his age."*

### UNDERSTANDING THE SITUATION

Just as children do not all walk at the same age, neither do they learn to talk at the same age. Some children are very verbal, some not. Some are easy to understand, some less so. Developing adequate communication skills, however, is an important milestone. A significant delay is often a sign of potential language dif-

346 POSITIVE PARENTING FROM A TO Z

ficulty and is best addressed early. By age two your child should be saying single words and using some two-word combinations, and by two and a half, though she may not be clearly understood, she should be using short sentences. Often parents see remarkable positive behavioral changes when their child learns to talk clearly enough to be understood. Late talking may cause secondary issues, such as frustration and anger, leading to hitting or biting. For some children, language skills can be a significant factor in making the successful transition to school. Factors such as chronic ear infections, allergies, and premature birth may cause speech delay. It is important to consult with your pediatrician or a speech and hearing specialist if you have concerns. They may be helpful in providing suggestions for encouraging speech and language development in positive ways. Be very patient. Your compassion and positive attitude play a significant role in your child's development of speech and language skills.

**WHAT TO SAY AND DO**

Empower your child to talk or to show you what he needs. Get down to his eye level or bring him up to yours. Say, *"Eric, tell me what you want."* Do not say, *"I can't understand you."* Just say, *"Show me."*

Do not talk for him. It is so easy to discourage a late talker with statements like *"Joey won't eat that. He doesn't like bananas."* Discourage brothers and sisters from speaking for him as well. *Encourage* in every way you can to help him feel capable. Do not baby and overprotect him.

Look at picture books together. Point at a picture and wait for your child to identify it. If he doesn't respond, supply the word. Do not point and say, *"What's that, what's that?"*

Prompt responses by suggesting choices, engaging but not demanding. *"Jes, which do you want to drink, milk or juice? Is it hot or cold?"* Use questions to help your child identify and express emotions. *"Are you happy about Larry coming to play? Are you mad you can't reach that?"*

PREVENTIVE TIPS

• Use a variety of words and expressions when you talk. Activities such as eating, using the bathroom, or going to the store are rich language experiences. Express feelings, describe actions, and name objects. *"The hat is on my head." "That is a big boat, and see the tall sail!" "The dog is on the green grass." "The dolly looks happy." "The puppy feels sad." "Rachael is running." "Lani, see the ball bounce!" "The truck is moving very fast." "The balloon is so big and very red!"*
• Have fun with communication and speak with enthusiasm and energy. Inflections are wonderful! Use expressions such as *"All gone!" "Uh-oh!" "No more!" "Pop!" "Boom!"* and other noise words.
• Play games that have words associated with them, such as *"Peekaboo!" "All gone!" "Mine . . . yours!"*
• Read often together. Let your child choose the book. She may want the same book read over and over, and though this may be boring for you, be patient; it will help her build a language base.

# SPITTING

*"My child spits on people."*

UNDERSTANDING THE SITUATION

Spitting is an annoying yet all too common childhood behavior. Your child may spit for attention or out of frustration. It is terribly embarrassing and shocking when she spits on other children, especially in front of their parents, and even more so in front of Grandma. As with other annoying behaviors, as disturbing as it is, act unemotional and unimpressed, but do act. It is never okay to spit at anybody. Getting your child to stop may take a few trials as she tests you. The problem may even get worse before it gets better. Stay calm, be consistent and positive, and keep the faith. It will pass.

## WHAT TO SAY AND DO

Do the unexpected. *"Lia, we do not spit on people. Here is a cup of water. Stand on the porch and spit until the water is all gone."* Direct her outside. Another option is to have her spit into the sink or toilet.

Before your child enters a play situation, discuss how to act. *"Amanda, you will be playing with Adam. What is our rule about spitting?"* Agree to a logical consequence if she forgets. *"If you spit, we will go home."*

Enforce the agreed-upon logical consequence, if necessary. *"Amanda, you have chosen to go home."* Calmly, with a *poker face*, put her coat on and leave. Do not give into wailing and pleading.

Use mature supervision. When you see her reach a point of frustration, intercede. *"Julie, Joey has the doll. Find him another toy and try trading, or play with another toy."*

Comment and celebrate when your child plays successfully without spitting. *"Hilary, you are terrific. You had a great day at pre-school. Let's celebrate and go for ice cream."*

## PREVENTIVE TIPS

- Keep play dates successful and short.
- Discuss feelings at bedtime. Talk about frustrations and proper ways to get attention from others.
- Be sure to give regular *special time* daily.

*See also: Hitting*

# STEALING

*"My child takes things that are not his."*

## Ages 2½–5

### UNDERSTANDING THE SITUATION

Your young child may seem to grab whatever he can get his hands on. You may be shocked and upset when you find loose change or a toy in his pocket that is not his. Do not mistake this for stealing; he is not a thief. In his mind he'd like everything to be his. His idea of right and wrong is not at the same level as yours. Downgrade the seriousness and refrain from using the label *stealing*. Your youngster does need to be talked with, and he should be given the task of returning the "goods." He may take things that are not his many times before understanding the difference between *mine* and *yours*, so use the opportunity to teach ownership. He made a mistake and will learn from it to make better choices. Be patient with his learning process and keep faith in him. Family or friends may offer well-meaning but unhelpful advice. Follow the Positive Parenting principles. Keep this matter between you and your child, and help him understand his limits with positive, firm, loving consistency.

### WHAT TO SAY AND DO

Do not scold with accusing questions, especially when you know the truth. *"Hilary, did you take this money from Grandma's purse?"* This causes fear leading to denial. Take *time for teaching* and say instead, *"This money is Grandma's, not yours. We need to return it to her and tell her you made a mistake."* Clue grandma in to the situation before returning the money. Her acceptance will help make this a good learning experience.

Be clear about *limits*, remain patient, and be consistent with your approach. Deal with the situation immediately, using *action with few words*. *"Kelly, we need to take the truck back to the store manager. The truck belongs to the store, not you."* By using a *we* statement you are taking some responsibility for the situation, providing a safer environment for your child's honesty.

Comment when he uses good judgment. *"Lanny, thank you for giving the book back to Josie. That is Josie's book, and this is your book. You are terrific!"*

This is a good time to teach how others feel. *"Jim, the ball belongs to Beth. She will feel sad if you take her ball. How would you feel if Beth took your red ball? Right, you wouldn't like it!"*

Help your child understand her feelings. Use *"You wish."* *"Molly, the doll is Heidi's. You wish you had one too."* Fantasizing is often a good substitute.

### PREVENTIVE TIPS

- Before a problem occurs, check with your child. *"Andy, what did we learn yesterday about Mary's toys? . . . Yes, when you play today you will leave her toys with her."* Or *"We are going into the store. Show me what you do with your hands in the store."*
- Take *time to teach* your child about the difference between *yours* and *mine*. Be creative. Identifying games are fun. *"My ear, your ear. . . . My shirt, your shirt."*
- Make sure your child has his own toys, even if he shares others with siblings.
- Read together children's books about values. *Airmail to the Moon* by Tom Birdseye (New York: Holiday House, 1988) and *Albert's Toothache* by Barbara Williams (New York: Dutton, 1974) are fun-to-read books about truthfulness.

## Ages 6-10

### UNDERSTANDING THE SITUATION

When you first learn that your child has intentionally shoplifted or has taken something from a friend's home or from school, you will likely feel shocked and hurt. You may worry, *"He's going to be a thief."* Though he knows this is wrong, his understanding of "wrong" is still not the same as yours. "Lifting" is common enough among children that some second-grade teachers check pockets routinely at the end of every day. Your child may take what he feels he deserves, or he may take what isn't his for the excitement of taking and not getting caught. Use the opportunity to have him be responsible for his actions and return the items. Do not lecture, spank, or punish. You are raising him to have self-control, to make good choices, and to use good judgment. Family or friends, critical of your approach, may suggest punishment. As hard as it is, be patient and keep faith in him. Check his understanding of why he stole something and be firm, loving, and consistent in assisting him to return it. With your follow-through, this behavior will most likely disappear.

Note: If the stealing becomes a recurring event, it may be more than a call for attention; it could be a cry for help, a signal that your child is hurting. He will need your Positive Parenting more than ever. If you have this concern, talk with his teacher and school counselor and/or ask your pediatrician for a counselor referral.

**WHAT TO SAY AND DO**

Do not scold or cross-examine your child, especially if you know the truth. *"Jeff, did you take these keys?"* or *"Where did you get that gum?"* will only create fear and will likely cause lying. *"Jeff, the gum was not paid for. It needs to go back to the store, now."*

Be clear about *limits* and your child's responsibility for his actions. He must return what he took. Encourage him to feel in control by offering limited *choices*. *"Andy, the model car needs to be returned. Do you want to return it by yourself, or do you want me to go with you?"* When returning the item, do not embarrass him. Give him the opportunity to talk, but if he doesn't, say, *"Michael took this today. We'd like to give it back. We are sorry, and it will not happen again."* Your taking some ownership of the problem may help him feel more secure and more capable.

Following through with a logical consequence works best

when it is decided on together ahead of time. Keep it reasonable and respectful. Say, *"Cheri, you took Julie's hair ribbons from her room today. You agreed to not take things from friends. It seems that you have made a choice to come home from school the rest of the week and not play with friends. You may play again beginning Monday."*

Try to determine what is causing the stealing. You need to continue listening to your child's feelings and helping her to understand the difference between truthfulness and dishonesty.

Help your child understand the reason for his stealing, and problem solve. *"Ryan, you wanted the knife because David has one. Sometimes you feel jealous."* Show understanding. *"I remember a time when I took a friend's bracelet that I wanted. She was angry with me and didn't want me to play with her for a long time. I understand how you feel."* Explore how others feel. *"I am upset that you took Mark's knife. He always considered you his friend. How do you think he feels? It is true that others may have things you don't. That can be frustrating."* Brainstorm with him and have him choose one solution. *"What could you do next time instead of taking things when you feel like you really want them?"* Suggestions: Make a wish list (discuss the fact that what we want is different from what we need), save up allowance or have a garage sale so the desired item can be purchased, etc. Your follow-up is very important. *Encourage and help him with the solution he chooses:* Help set up a savings plan, plan a garage sale with him, etc.

Give hugs often and tell your child you love him even when he does nothing to deserve it. Notice when he has refrained from taking things. *"Ryan, I appreciate your efforts. I know you want what other children have. I appreciate it when you talk to me about that."*

### PREVENTIVE TIPS

- Listen for reasons that may be causing your child's misbehavior. At bedtime ask what made her happy and what made her sad. Share your day with her as well. Work on identifying feelings.
- Even if the stealing recurs, assume tomorrow will be different.

Your child needs another opportunity. We use mistakes as learning tools.

- Schedule *special time*. Have fun together. Kick a ball around the yard, join in a game of hide and seek, play checkers or cards.
- Read together the books listed in Preventive Tips for ages 2½–5.
- Visit a local police station with a group (possibly a scout troop) and discuss the policeman's job. Meet with a department store manager to learn more about shoplifting policies.

# STRANGERS

*"My child trusts everybody. What do I tell her about strangers?"*

### UNDERSTANDING THE SITUATION

Some children are more at ease with people outside their immediate family than others are. Some children don't consider a person who is familiar a "stranger," while other children may be more wary. Not all hurtful acts committed against children are done by strangers. Whatever the case, your parental goal is to help develop your child's awareness of inappropriate behavior and her feeling of confidence and capability. Your calm attitude and confident tone of voice presenting common-sense guidelines are important to avoid senseless suspicion of all people. Rules about strangers should be as clear and matter-of-fact as the rules about any other safety issue. The rules should be clear to your child.

### WHAT TO SAY AND DO

The ideal is to never have your child in a precarious situation. Still, today's children need to be "street smart." Give *a few* clear family rules to create awareness and confidence; children feel safe with limits and want to feel they have some control over what happens to them. Rules should be reviewed often. When your child is very young, recite the rules (in front of her) to any care-giver you leave her with. Have your school-age child repeat the rules to you once a month. Your rules should fit the needs of the situation. Some ideas are:

1. Never accept a ride, food or candy, or an invitation to play without talking with mom or dad.
2. Do not talk to strangers. (Check your child's perception of what a stranger is. His "stranger" and yours may not be the same.)
4. If someone follows you, go to the nearest house and tell the Mom or Dad there (or anyone in charge) what happened.
5. Use the buddy system—walk with other children.
6. If Mom and Dad for some reason are not home, do not open the door.
7. If for any reason you are home without an adult and you get a phone call, say, *"Mom is busy. May I take a message?"*

Role-play what to do and say when a stranger approaches. *"Hilary, let's pretend what you would do if you were walking to school with Heidi and someone you did not know stopped you to talk. There is always a house to run up to. No need for talk."* This is not to give her a false impression that she can handle all difficult situations, but rather to let her know what she might do in a tight spot, which may promote confidence and awareness. That could help her avoid a bad situation.

Do not elaborate the gory details of bad situations. *("Don't get into a car with a stranger, because he might hurt you. He could have a weapon, take you far away, and I might never see you again.")* This only creates a world of fear.

### PREVENTIVE TIPS

• When possible, let your child be in charge of a controlled sit-uation in which he needs to deal with strangers. Even a six-year-old can run into a small store and buy milk while you wait outside in the car or on the sidewalk.

• Comment when your child uses good judgment. When you and she are together and she is confident and friendly with others, compliment her specifically. Compliment her when she is careful and follows rules. One mom had a friend call when she was not home to learn what her child would say. Her child followed the family rule and answered correctly, and Mom enthusiastically complimented her.

• Read together children's books showing a child using good thinking and good judgment. Talk to a children's librarian or a knowledgeable bookstore clerk about books that address dealing with strangers or difficult situations.

## STUBBORNNESS

*"My child digs his heels in and will not do what I ask."*

### UNDERSTANDING THE SITUATION

When your child treats your request with stubbornness and hostility, you most likely feel furious. The tendency is to demand his respect. All children act stubborn at times, and they should. Stubbornness is not always negative. Your child's stubborn behavior may be due to his thinking for himself and learning to assert himself. One important element of his self-esteem is a feeling of control over what happens to him. Your child will have different motives for stubborn behavior. Sometimes it may be because of a fear, sometimes it may be due to a dislike for transition or change, or he may be going through a brief stage of rebellion against authority. You may never understand the reason. Do not overreact with force and anger, because anger creates more anger. You have different options, depending on the situation. When safety or values are concerned, you must hold the power. With other situations you may compromise or negotiate. Or, you may let go entirely. Letting go is the hardest approach but often the most effective. When you stay calm and patient and are unimpressed with your child's stubborn attitude, there is no social reward for him, and the behavior will likely stop.

## WHAT TO SAY AND DO

If the situation is nonnegotiable, say what you need your child to do, give your reasons, and do not argue. Do not say, *"Because I said so."* Say what you mean and do what you say you will do.

Identify her feelings and seek a solution together. *"Jessie, you are afraid to go to swim class. Let's think of a plan to help you feel better. We could go early and tell the teacher you do not like getting your face wet. Any other ideas?"*

Try not to interrupt something very important. Your child will do better if you let her finish what she is doing before making a request. *"Kate, in five minutes we have to leave for the store. This television program will be over."* If you must interrupt her, apologize.

Let her know what to expect. Share the plan and give her a warning. Some children don't like to be surprised and will not cooperate if they are asked to respond suddenly.

When phrasing a request, be assertive. Do not end your phrase with a questioning lilt. *"Ben, you need to clean the family room. It needs to be done before soccer."* You cannot make him do anything. Instead, decide what you will do to show you mean what you say. *"I will be happy to take you to soccer when you have done what you agreed to do."*

Offer *choices*. *"Zack, you have a choice. You can come help the family clean the house or wait outside by yourself in the snow."* Be willing to allow either of the choices but follow through with his choice.

Have a creative plan. Attach to your request something your child will want to do. *"Shelby, the wood needs to be carried in before you go to Mary's."*

He may be "parent deaf." Use timers and clocks to direct him and get you off the hook. *"Jeff, when the timer goes off it will be time to mow the lawn."*

Compliment him when he cooperates and watch for the good he does.

## PREVENTIVE TIPS

- Plan for the extra time it may take to win your child's cooperation. When children sense our hurry, they know the button to push. Working together may require getting up earlier or starting sooner.
- Be flexible yourself. Save "no" for when it really matters. Use "yes" responses. Instead of *"No, not now!"* try *"Yes, you may have it after you eat dinner."* A good phrase to relieve you of pressure is *"I need some time to think about that."*
- Develop a routine to your day. Make charts for morning time, mealtime, bedtime, chores, etc. This is a way of letting your child know what to expect.
- Let him hear you talking to others positively about him and let him know you are on his side. Rather than *"Eric is such a handful and so stubborn,"* say, *"Eric is very assertive lately. When he is slow we do have trouble if I am in a big hurry. I try to give him warnings of what to expect."*
- Keep your expectations reasonable. He may feel he can't do what you are asking.

*See also: "No!"*

# STUTTERING

*"My child has started to stutter."*

### UNDERSTANDING THE SITUATION

If your child suddenly begins to stutter, you may be surprised, and if it continues or increases you may become quite concerned. Nonfluency (another term for stuttering) often occurs when children go through different stages of language development. It is normal for a child to be nonfluent, and it commonly occurs when he has more to say than his ability to organize words will allow. Until the appropriate skill level develops, it is important not to show your anxiety or draw attention to it. You will need to try to remain calm and patient, as hard as it may be. An accepting response is crucial.

### WHAT TO SAY AND DO

Relax and be willing to wait. Do not interrupt your child or finish sentences for him. In most cases the nonfluent speech will disappear.

Do not suggest that he slow down. Try a gentle touch, take his hand, or put your arm around him in a calm and caring way.

When he is talking to you, show relaxed body language. Stop what you are doing and listen to him "with your eyes." Lift your own eyebrows so you are not frowning and use a friendly tone of voice. Lift him up onto a counter so that he is at your eye level, or sit on the floor with him.

If he is trying to talk with you and you haven't time to listen right then, don't brush him off. Get down to his level and tell him you are rushed. *"Chris, I want to hear what you have to say, but right now I have to sign these papers with Grandma. As soon as she leaves with Sara, I will listen to you."*

## PREVENTIVE TIPS

- Spend one-on-one daily. He needs time with you with less stimulation.
- Read aloud together.
- Reduce stress as much as possible. Keep your child on a regular, consistent schedule.
- If your child is not bothered by his speech pattern, it's a good general rule to let it be. If the nonfluent speech continues for a prolonged period or increases significantly, or if your child stops talking, comments on his own speech, or shows exasperated looks, facial tics, knee slapping, etc., see a speech and hearing specialist.
- Talk with him and encourage his talk as if there were no problem. At times it may not be easy or efficient for you to listen, but it will be worth your effort.

*See also: Speech, difficult to understand*

# TALKING BACK

*"My child talks back with disrespect."*

### UNDERSTANDING THE SITUATION

All parents have experienced their child's sassy talk and hostile words. The disrespect most likely triggers intense anger in you, but yelling back, threatening, scolding, and punishing will only teach her to use anger. Talking back is normal; as your child goes through different stages of development she may test you with it. It may be due to a combination of her temperament and the pressure of daily stress, or she may feel discouraged by her environment. Think positively; talking back is an opportunity for her to practice assertion. You are a safe person for her to practice talking to this way because she knows you love her; however, a responsible parent believes *"I respect you and I respect myself."* Set *limits* as a parent and decide what you will do when she talks back. Remember to act, not emotionally react. Help her to practice good communication to get her needs met, and emotional self-control. Have patience. This stage may take some time to pass, and it may recur at a later time. Hug her a lot when she shows more mature behavior, and spend time with her to build a good relationship.

### WHAT TO SAY AND DO

Check with your child's caregivers or teachers. Try to find out what may be causing her discouragement; most likely it is subconscious. Is she learning to talk back from another child? What has changed in her world recently?

Do not push back with your anger. Remain calm. Decide what you will do, not what you will make her do.

Take ten deep breaths and repeat to yourself, *"I am the parent and she is the child."*

Lighten up! Use humor. Don't take her behavior personally or too seriously. *"Ouch, Jamie, that hurt!"*

Try heading for the bathroom. *"I'll be in the bathroom. Let me know when you can talk respectfully."* Leave with a *poker face* and come back when she is willing to show you respect.

Give *time out.* If you make a request and she flares up, identify her feelings and state your expectations. Calmly say, *"Jamie, you are very angry, but you may not use those words. Please take time out. Cool off and let me know when you are ready to be respectful."* When she cools down, repeat your request.

If in public, calmly remove yourself and your child. Go to the car, step outside, or go home. *Cool off* and calmly give a *choice.* *"Renée, you can go back in with me and be polite and respectful, or I will take you home."*

When she cools down, *problem solve.* *"Mary, when you talk to me lately you sound so angry."* Pause, listen to what she says and reflect her feeling. *"You sound as though you feel . . ."* Show understanding. *"I remember when I was your age I talked back to my dad. When you talk back to me I feel angry at the lack of respect. Let's discuss what you could do instead of talking back."* Follow up with her in a couple of days to evaluate how she is doing. She needs to hear from you that you either notice her efforts *or* that she isn't correcting the behavior.

**PREVENTIVE TIPS**

- Have courage to make mistakes yourself. No one is perfect. If you blow it and become angry, cool down and apologize! *"Jamie, I'm sorry. I blew it. I really got angry with you. When you say such disrespectful words I feel hurt and I get mad."* Ask for some responsibility from her. *"How can we work on preventing that from happening again?"*
- Model respect. Speak to her as you would want to be spoken to.

*See also: Anger, parent's; Dirty words; Meanness*

# TATTLING

*"My child is an annoying tattletale."*

## UNDERSTANDING THE SITUATION

Most tattletales are seeking attention. Your child feels quite powerful and important when he succeeds in getting you involved in his concern—that's why the baby of the family so often becomes the tattletale. A true tattletale may grow to be very annoying and will receive poor feedback from other people at play, sports, and school. It is best to take time to train him not to tattle so that he receives more positive feedback from others, which is necessary to healthy self-esteem. Take *time to teach* your child the rules about tattling and be very consistent with what you say and do each time he tattles.

## WHAT TO SAY AND DO

If tattling becomes an issue, create a rule about tattling with your family. This rule should be clear and understood by all family members. One well-used rule is: It is important to tell a parent, or the person in charge, if:

1. Someone is emotionally hurting someone with threats, bad words, or name calling.
2. Someone is being unsafe physically; that he may hurt himself or someone else.

Take time to teach the difference between tattling and reporting something important. Role-play a pretend situation. *"Molly, are you trying to get Greg into trouble or out of trouble?"*
Teach problem ownership. *"Cal, thank you for your concern. No*

*one is in danger or is unsafe. Mary will tell me if she needs to. This is her problem, not yours."*

When your child comes to you with genuine concern, do not belittle him or discount what he is saying. Decide if it is necessary for you to attend to the situation or not. *"Nate, thank you for the information. I am sure Molly can handle that one. It does not sound as if she is in danger."* Or, *"Thank you for letting me know that. Mary is liable to be hurt. I will go take care of it."*

If he is tattling, give the problem back to him. *"David, what would you like me to do about that?"* Or, *"I know you can handle the situation. What are some things you might do?"* If you need to intervene, do not rescue the child who told you of the problem. Empower him to handle the hurtful situation. *"Thank you for telling me. Those words that Bruce used are hurtful and not true. You can tell Bruce how you feel."* Talk to the child causing the hurtful problem privately.

## PREVENTIVE TIPS

- Role-play together what is important to "tell" and what is tattling.
- Make sure that you give plenty of attention to good behavior. Compliment your child on not tattling when he is making an effort not to.
- Together read children's stories that bring up the subjects of friendship, self-esteem, and perhaps tattling. See a children's librarian or knowledgeable bookstore clerk for ideas.

# TEACHER, FEAR OF

*See: School, won't go*

# TEASING

*"My older child teases my younger child and makes him cry."*

### UNDERSTANDING THE SITUATION

Both the teaser and the child being teased can create quite an irritating disruption to a pleasant environment. Teasing is such a common childhood issue that parents tend to accept that dealing with it just goes with the territory of parenting. Most parents tend to nag, nag, nag at their children to stop the attention-seeking problem. Then, when the situation reaches an intolerable level, the teaser is punished and the teased is rescued. Your teasing child does not have to tease, and your teased child can learn not to be a victim. Your reaction to the teasing will determine how much it occurs and how intense it is. Curbing the teasing will take time and effort on your part. Be very consistent. As trying as it is at times, keep the faith and maintain as positive an attitude as possible.

### WHAT TO SAY AND DO

Take *time to teach* about teasing. *"Mark, you enjoy teasing and sometimes Sarah likes it. When she has had enough, she will tell you and you must stop."* Practice this with role-playing.

Take *time to teach* the teased child to cope. *"Greg, when Gary teases you he wants to make you cry. If you want him to stop, you need to be strong. Go away and try to act unimpressed, not hurt. Walk away, ignore him, or calmly tell him to stop."* Teach him when he should ask for help. *"If you are being hurt with bad words or hitting, let me know. You can handle most of the teasing yourself."*

Give a logical consequence but address both the teaser and the teased together. Do not blame one and rescue the other. *"You two will have to come home after school every day this week and not have any friends over to play. I'd like you to learn to play together without the teasing."*

Let your child know what you will do when the teasing becomes a problem for you. Be creative in making it a problem for him too. *"When the teasing becomes a problem for me, I will stop the car and pull over and wait for it to stop. We may be late for swimming. You decide."*

Do the unexpected. *"Jason, use your creative abilities and energy in a positive way. Instead of teasing Jill with the rope, let's go build the rope swing you have all been wanting."* Stay light with a sense of humor.

**PREVENTIVE TIPS**

- Discuss the difference between good teasing and bad teasing. Your child will never be entirely protected from teasing. Take *time to teach* that bad teasing hurts people's feelings. Good teasing is being silly or funny and sometimes uses the imagination and should be encouraged. Word play and creative thinking build vocabulary.
- Explain that it is healthy not to take everything personally. Teasing is less rewarding when the teased child doesn't respond.
- Downgrade competition at home. Do not compare your children.
- Find challenging outside activities that the teaser can excel in. This may reduce his need to show his superiority.

*See also: Bullied child; Bullying; Tattling*

# TEETH GRINDING

*"My child grinds her teeth at night."*

## UNDERSTANDING THE SITUATION

Teeth grinding is a common behavior among children, yet for most parents it is a surprise and a concern. Dentists believe that it is commonly a symptom of the body adjusting to loose teeth; teeth losing support feel funny as new ones erupt. Generally, after baby teeth fall out and permanent teeth erupt, the grinding stops. It is also thought that some children grind their teeth to release tension. Often around the beginning of first grade parents notice the behavior. As the child matures and learns to relax, or as outside stress is reduced, the grinding stops. Some allergies have been found to induce teeth grinding. If you suspect this is the case with your child, you should consult your pediatrician. In most cases, if your child's teeth are aligned and she isn't complaining of other symptoms, such as headaches, you need to relax and wait for the grinding to pass. It is always important to limit the stress in your child's environment as well. Adult teeth grinding is a very different matter from childrens'; don't compare the two. You may hear horror stories from family or friends; don't be influenced. Jot down any concerning questions and talk to your dentist for a professional opinion about your specific situation.

## WHAT TO SAY AND DO

Do not ignore this behavior if you are concerned. Your worry will pass to your child, and you may also induce unnecessary attention getting. See your dentist. Have him explain the behavior to both you and your child and tell you if he sees signs of the teeth being injured from grinding. Dentists rarely prescribe any-thing to put in the mouth to protect baby teeth, though some older children are given plastic mouth guards to use at night in extreme cases.

Children are under stress today. Take *time to teach* your child relaxation exercises. No need to mention teeth grinding. *Yoga for Children* by Mary Stewart (New York: Simon and Schuster, 1993) has fun exercises that you can do together or she can do alone or with friends. *"Sally, I learned some stretching exercises that relax the body. These are fun and make us feel good too. They all have animal names. See if you can guess the animal I'm doing."* The "lion" is done sitting cross-legged, back straight, head tilted back, eyes looking at the sky; the mouth is moved in exaggerated open-and-closed and sideways movements. This is good for relaxing the face muscles.

Most advice is to ignore nighttime grinding. If your child is grinding her teeth during the day, give her a knowing glance, hold her face gently or put your hands on her shoulders, and say kindly, *"Julie, relax."* She most likely isn't aware she is grinding. Stay calm. Too much emphasis can make it worse.

**PREVENTIVE TIPS**

- Do your best to reduce the stress in your child's life. Watch for what she does right. How reasonable are your expectations? Stop yourself from constantly correcting her or commenting on what she needs to improve upon. No one flourishes with perfectionism. Spend more time together at home rather than racing around from activity to activity.
- Spend time talking with her and listening to her express her feelings about her day. Encourage her to talk about both the happy and the sad parts of her day. Perhaps you can get some clues as to whether she feels tension.
- Be sure she gets plenty of physical exercise.

# TELEVISION

*"I can't tear my child away from the television."*

### UNDERSTANDING THE SITUATION

Television is probably controversial in your home, whether your concern is *"How much TV is too much for my child?"* or *"What shows expose her to too much sex or violence?"* or just the basic issues like *"My child won't cooperate and leave the TV,"* or *"The TV causes fights among family members."* TV is here to stay. It is true that when it is off your child may fill her time quite differently with more creativity: reading, interacting with other children and adults, creating artwork, exploring music, etc. If a television is in your home and you never turn it on, you make your child want it more. Instead, make it work for you. Handle it as a resource and use it as a springboard to discuss values, good judgment, manners, and interesting information. Remember, your child will follow your example.

### WHAT TO SAY AND DO

Post a schedule in the TV room for the week's viewing. When you find your child watching at unscheduled times, use questions to check her understanding; do not lecture and direct. *"Mary, what is our agreement about the TV this week? Show me your schedule."*

Follow through with agreements established at family meetings. *"Jerry, it seems you have made a choice to lose TV privileges this week."*

Use *action with few words*. Do not lecture or remind. Remove the set or unplug it if TV privileges are being abused, and spend more time together at home rather than racing around from activity to activity.

Watch TV together and use it for discussions that stimulate thinking. Do not moralize or lecture. Ask questions. *"Rebecca, how did you feel when the little girl's dog died? What do you think you might have done if it were your dog that was stolen?"*

## PREVENTIVE TIPS

- At *family meetings*, plan together a family TV schedule for the week. Have your child select which shows he wishes to see; negotiate with him to determine the shows he may watch alone and those you'll watch together. Make up a family TV calendar and post it. This will help settle arguments between family members. When making up the calendar consider all the types of programming available and choose a balance.
- Use the TV listings to teach your child to think and select instead of simply turning on the TV and "channel surfing" through the stations.
- Though it is tempting, do not use the TV as a babysitter regularly. Help your child to be self-directed to books, music, art, etc.
- Celebrate when your child shows good TV-viewing judgment. *"Alright, Jan! You really followed the TV plan this week. You've earned a bonus. Do you want to go to a matinée Saturday or see the new play at the Children's Theater?"*

# TEMPER TANTRUMS

*"My child has temper tantrums!"*

## Ages 2½–5

### UNDERSTANDING THE SITUATION

Temper tantrums are explosions of rage or frustration and can happen at any age, though they are commonly worse among younger children. Young children often lose control when their communication is poor and they cannot make themselves understood. Molly, age two and a half, sometimes had nine tantrums a day until she learned to talk more clearly. Frustration builds up in children who feel they have no choices and are always being told what to do. Many children have learned to control others with temper tantrums *("Mom does what I want so I won't lose my temper,")* and this can continue into adulthood. Stomping, crying, pouting, and shouting are all forms of manipulation. Your child will someday have an understanding of his feelings and be able to control his temper rather than allowing it to control him. He will get his needs met with honest communication, not manipulation with tantrums. Mocking or punishing him with the intention of teaching him to control himself will only cause rebellion or lowered self-esteem. The most difficult task when dealing with an angry child is to keep your own anger controlled. You need to model self-control. This can be very tiring and difficult when a child has many tantrums. You may need to use all the *tools of the trade.* Learning to control his temper may take your child years, and when he is tired or stressed he may slip back to less-mature behavior. Be patient and keep your faith in him. The message of unconditional love is so important to a child who has just lost his temper. *"I will always love you. I may be very frustrated by what you do, but I will always love you."*

**WHAT TO SAY AND DO**

Do not spank your child to make him stop his tantrum. Hitting him only teaches him that when you are angry you hit. If you also grow angry, take *time out* when he does (in a separate space), vent your anger, and *cool down*.

Some young children with intense temperaments completely lose control when they are enraged. Stay near through the temper tantrum to keep your child from being frightened by her anger. Your child may calm down when you hold her tight. She may kick and scream initially. Rock gently back and forth. Use *action with few words*. Sometimes humming works. Your calmness will pass through to her.

Do not laugh at the uproar, as funny or off-the-wall as it may seem. Your child's anger or frustration is real to him, and laughing is disrespectful. Do not minimize it with *"Knock it off."* Identify his feeling. *"You are very frustrated."* Then:

1. Try distracting your child before she's totally lost it. *"Sylvia, you are tired of sitting in the cart. Hold my calculator and add numbers. I will be done very soon."*
2. Give a *choice* and *time out*. Get down on her level and put your hands gently on her shoulders. Calmly and firmly say, *"Marty, you are angry. Either use your words to tell me what is making you so angry or take time out to work through your anger and cool off."* If she continues the tantrum, say, *"I guess you have chosen to have time out."* Use *action with few words* and a *poker face* to direct her to a safe space to work through her rage. *"Come out when you are ready."*
3. Redirect your child's actions. Avoid embarrassing him when he has a tantrum in front of friends. Take him to a space where he can vent his anger. Firmly, kindly, and with a *poker face* say, *"Todd, you are very frustrated, but you may not throw toys. Here are balls you may throw against the wall instead. You may go back to play when you cool off."* Some children cannot handle venting their anger; they react better to calming activity. Your child might want to try stepping outside in the cool air, blowing bubbles, taking a walk, or playing music to cool off.

4. Do not give social reinforcement. After showing understanding, ignore the tantrum; try watering the lawn or vacuuming the living room. *"Andrew, when you calm yourself come tell me."* When he does, hug him. *"Wow. You worked through that well."* Then give your time. *"Would you like to help me cut flowers?"* Or *"Let's read a story."*

Take *time for teaching.* Before leaving for the grocery store, anticipate what could happen and tell her what you will do if she has a tantrum. If she does have one, use a *poker face* and calmly pick her up. Leave the cart where it is and go to the manager. *"We are having a hard time shopping. I will be back for the groceries in an hour. Please save them for me."* Leave and take her home to a sitter. *"Diana, I need to finish shopping. Auntie Cheri will come over and stay with you. We will try the store together sometime soon."* Be sure to leave her with the idea she may try again.

### PREVENTIVE TIPS

- Try to pinpoint what might be causing the tantrums. Are there changes at home such as a move, an illness, visitors, etc.? Is something new at day care or school, such as a change in teachers, or is your child possibly outgrowing her current situation? Does she need more challenge or more responsibility?
- Teach her to know when she is nearing meltdown. If you see frustration, intervene. Touch her gently and calmly and offer help. *"Ginny, you are working hard building the tower, and I can see you getting frustrated. You can ask for help."* Or intervene and use humor. *"Amy, you are a good dresser! Your shirt is upside down, though; that's silly and very hard to put on! Here, this is the way the firemen do it!"*
- Let your child *cool off* and then take *time to teach* him to recognize his feelings before he loses control. There are responsible ways to handle his anger and frustration. *"Ryan, you like space around you. When children sit very close to you, move to where you have more room. You can ask for help before you get angry."* Encourage him to express feelings and to grow in self-understanding.

*"How does that make you feel? What could you do when you feel too crowded?"*

- Take care of yourself: Get your needed rest, exercise, and breaks away from your child. You are the parent and must have energy to stay in charge.
- Read children's stories together at happy times. Try *Sometimes I Get Angry* by Jane Werner Watson, Robert E. Switzer, and J. Cotter Hirschberg (New York: Crown, 1986), *Feelings* by Aliki Brandenberg (New York: Morrow, 1984), *The Temper Tantrum Book* by Edna Preston and Rainey Bennett (New York: Puffin Books, 1976) or *Angry Arthur* by Hiawyn Oram (New York: E. P. Dutton, 1982).
- Spend *special time* daily.

Note: Chronic anger or depression may require the help of a counselor. If your child's sleep is disturbed, his eating patterns change, or he says he has no friends and is unhappy with himself, see your pediatrician and discuss counseling referrals.

## Ages 6-10

### UNDERSTANDING THE SITUATION

Please read the above section, for ages 2½–5.

Your child's anger is real, and he needs your acceptance when he is angry. You do not want him to fear his anger or deny it. Your goal is to help him assess his feelings, learn to vent his anger without hurting others, and put something else in its place. He will learn self-control. The skills you teach your child now will last him a lifetime. Schools today are teaching anger control as more children are in need of help and more children are exposed to other angry children. Your child will be ahead of others if you teach him at home to understand his feelings, the consequences of his actions, and alternative ways of dealing with anger. This will help him through his school years and in all stages of life.

**WHAT TO SAY AND DO**

Take *time to teach* him to vent his rage without hurting people or property. He can learn to control it. At a neutral time, say, *"Sam, when you get really mad, decide how long you want to be angry. Decide to be angry for ten minutes. Set the timer and hit your pillow very hard. When the bell rings, stop. Then go do something nice for yourself. Come get me and we will read or go to the park or walk."* Most children (and adults) who use this technique cannot be angry for the entire allotted time. Sometimes they end up laughing at trying to be that mad that long.

Identify your child's feeling, then calmly redirect him to a structured place for *time out* where he can work through his anger and *cool off*. Remain *poker faced* and use *action with few words*. *"Peter, you are very angry. Go to the room where you can punch pillows or jump on the bed."* Set the kitchen timer for five minutes. *"Here is the timer. Set more time to be angry if you feel you need it."* If the timer goes off and he is still ranting, go in and tell him to stop. Some very intense children need to be told to stop.

Ask for respect. With a *poker face*, say, *"Rob, you are very angry. I cannot stay in the room with you because your hitting hurts me. I will be in my room, and I will come back when you are ready. Let me know."*

If your child runs from you, do not chase him. The best intervention is for you to stay put. He will return. When he does return, calmly repeat what you need from him.

When your child calms down, use positive closure. Comment on something she did well. Say, *"Julie, you were very angry and yet you gained control. Tomorrow you can invite Ian to play again."*

**PREVENTIVE TIPS**

• Log observations of your child for two weeks. Record when she has tantrums and observe what stress may provoke it. For example, some children unconsciously have clear boundaries and are more sensitive when their territory is invaded. A tight, crowded group may cause a child to push or shove, or someone playing with her things may frustrate her. She may be an-

gry with you for having a new baby or working nights.
Hunger or lack of sleep will provoke temper in some children.
Discuss this with your child to help her understand what
brings on her temper. Discuss changes she can make.

- Teach your child ways to deal with his temper. It is okay to
be angry, and there are responsible ways to deal with it. *"Jeff,
would you like some ideas about what to do when you are so mad?"*
Suggest he run outside around the house, jump on an old mattress, hit a punching bag, or draw an angry picture.
- Take *time for teaching*. Temper can be due to stress from not understanding how to do what is expected. Are your expectations
reasonable for your child's age? Perfectionism often creates
frustration.
- Your child needs to feel that he contributes and is needed.
Expand his personal and family responsibilities, commenting
on how capable he is. Make sure he hears and feels how much
you love him.
- Anger can be due to a child's feeling a lack of control over
what happens to him. Offer him choices whenever possible.
Use questions—what, why, how, when, and where—instead of
lecturing and directing.

Note: Chronic anger or depression may require the help of a
counselor. If your child's sleep is disturbed, his eating patterns
change, or he says he has no friends and is unhappy with himself,
see your pediatrician and discuss counseling referrals.

*See also: Dirty words; Headbanging; Hitting; Meanness*

# THUMB-SUCKING

*"My child still sucks his thumb."*

## Ages 2½–5

### UNDERSTANDING THE SITUATION

You may worry when your child sucks his thumb. You may be concerned that he is too old for this habit, wonder whether he feels unloved or is poorly adjusted, or worry that he could hurt his tooth alignment. Many parents feel that thumb-sucking is a bad habit, but most experts agree that it is not negative behavior. Thumb-sucking is common and accepted at this age for self-comfort and coping. Many well-loved children suck their thumbs; some are born sucking. Coaxing, teasing, reminding, or removing your child's thumb from his mouth will probably only reinforce the behavior. Let it go and do not listen to friends' or relatives' negative, critical comments. As hard as it may be for you, remain patient. Do not nag or complain. He will stop when he is ready.

### WHAT TO SAY AND DO

Most modern professional advice is: Allow it! Ignore it! Don't worry! If this is too hard for you, talk with your family physician for your peace of mind.

See a dentist if you have concerns regarding whether thumb-sucking will affect your child's jaw or tooth structure.

### PREVENTIVE TIPS

• Spend *special time* with your child each day. We all want to feel we belong.
• Provide listening time for identifying and discussing feelings.

- Give your child the time he needs to learn to do tasks for himself. Avoid rushing and pushing your child to conform to your busy schedule. Less stress may translate into less thumbsucking.
- Remember *time for teaching*. Eliminate stress by making sure your child is prepared for what you are asking him to do.
- Keep a log observing when your child most often sucks his thumb. You may need to change his environment or provide confidence-building situations for him, such as smaller play groups or better-supervised play to teach him social interaction.

## Ages 6-10

### UNDERSTANDING THE SITUATION

Prolonged thumb-sucking may have you worried, especially if you compare your child to other children or are under pressure from family or friends to get your child to quit the habit. Most thumb-sucking will go away if ignored. Ignore it! If it becomes a dental concern see your dentist. If it is creating social or school-related problems, develop a plan with your child. Give him the responsibility for quitting and be supportive and patient. It will not disappear overnight, but it will disappear. He needs to hear from you that you have faith in him and that you know he will quit when he is ready. This may be his first opportunity to see that he has the self-control so very crucial to his self-esteem.

### WHAT TO SAY AND DO

Thumb-sucking can be used to get your attention. Appear unimpressed. Hug your child or hold his hand when he is not sucking his thumb and comment, *"Joey, I enjoy being with you!"*

Never make him guess why you ignore his thumb-sucking. He may misunderstand your indifference and think that you don't love him. *"Greg, I love you! When you suck your thumb, I ig-*

*nore it because I know you can quit, and you will. I never mean to ignore you!"*

Suggest a chart. *"Jake, would you like some help with stopping the thumb-sucking? Here's a chart, and here are some fancy stickers. Do what you need to to keep your thumb out of your mouth. Hold Teddy, put tape or bad-tasting stuff on your thumb, and each day you are successful put a sticker on the chart."* Try for three days at first, then increase. For this to work it must be his plan! Be an encourager. *"Thataboy! I know you can do it!"* When he reaches his goal, celebrate with something he has been waiting to be old enough to do. *"Wow! After a month of this you may get that new model you have been waiting for!"*

If thumb-sucking becomes a dental concern to you, see a dentist or an orthodontist who is good with children. Your child will feel proud and capable working with an expert who gives helpful suggestions and encouragement.

### PREVENTIVE TIPS

- Spend *special time* with your child daily. The stress and pressure on children today is enormous. Do your best to slow your pace. Taking long walks, reading together, and listening closely to his feelings with acceptance rather than judgment are all helpful. Listen to his concerns. Are they centered on social situations, school-related, or home-related?
- Find moments during the day to surprise him with a hug when he least expects it and isn't doing anything to deserve it. Leave little notes in his lunch box or on his pillow at night.
- Have *family meetings* weekly. Celebrate your child's growing up; she may be wanting to stay little for a while. Growing up means more responsibility and more privilege; give her new chores and new responsibilities along with a later bedtime and possibly permission to have a friend overnight on the weekend.

# TOILET TRAINING

*"My child isn't toilet trained like others her age."*

### UNDERSTANDING THE SITUATION

Children are not the same. Each will be toilet trained according to his own individual time clock. As much as eating and sleeping are inevitably up to the child, so is voiding. If you doubt this, just try to control your child. It won't work. Understanding about his body, his sexuality, and what makes which muscles work is a major job for this age. Coaxing and rewarding invite attention-getting behavior. *("If I stall, she'll get me some M and Ms and jump through hoops to get me to pee.")* Pressure invites power struggles. *("I've got her now. I'm in control.")* We discourage when we push a child to be trained for our reasons: the day care provider who will not take him in diapers, the trip to Grandma's, the desire to have him out of diapers before the baby comes. These issues are yours, not his. Children become responsible for their actions best with loving support and *encouragement* from parents who focus on what is going right, not on the mistakes. He may be trained or partially trained and then revert. This is normal, especially if a new baby arrives. Toilet training may take all the patience and energy you can muster up. For many it takes a long time. Keep the faith. He will be ready for kindergarten!

### WHAT TO SAY AND DO

Your message needs to be *"You will do this when your body is ready. I know you can. We love you, and you are in charge."* Let him hear you exclaim how well he is doing. *"Ryan is learning. He is doing a terrific job."*

Since control is often an issue, provide your child with a *choice*.

Have a potty chair next to the toilet. Also have a seat that fits on the toilet with a step up. *"Heather, you can sit on the potty seat or on your own potty chair to pee. Choose one."* Provide pants that are easy to pull on and off.

Take *time for teaching*. Children are mimics and learn best by observing. Relax and allow your child to be in the bathroom with you as well as with other family members. Show him the small steps: how to turn on the light, to sit or stand, to wipe, and to wash hands.

When she uses the toilet, *encourage* but do not bring out the balloons and candy. Ask her how she feels. *"Alright, Kate, I knew you could do it. How do you feel?"* When she has the inevitable accident, say, *"We all make mistakes. You'll get there. What will you do differently next time?"* Have her help clean it up. This gives her the responsibility. Mistakes are for learning. Avoid "good girl/bad girl" or "big girl/baby" statements. They say that when she makes a mistake she is bad, when she makes a mistake she's a baby. That may invite less-mature behavior.

When she is mostly trained and suddenly has an accident in front of you, do not yell or spank, though it is truly frustrating. Count to ten, stay calm, and with a *poker face* get a rag and have her wipe it up. If you are in a store, it is very effective to tell the manager you need a rag to wipe up an accident. Do not rush to get her into dry clothes. Have her wear her wet clothes a little while.

When you know she is urinating or moving her bowels in her diaper, do not say, *"Are you pooping?"* This encourages denying. Calmly and kindly say *"I see you are pooping. You can use the potty chair for peeing and pooping."* Guide her to the bathroom but do not push or force her. If she resists you when you change her diaper, say, *"Jen, I will not have to do this when you use the toilet."*

Design a plan before she wets. *"Meg, you wet your pants. When they are wet put them in the laundry and put on dry pants yourself. You can handle it."* Do not threaten her with *"You'll have to go back to diapers if you keep this up."* If you think she is not ready for training pants, buy the disposables that she can pull on herself. *"Meg, here are some diapers you can put on yourself. When you stay dry you can have the training pants. We will try again soon."*

**PREVENTIVE TIPS**

- Do not compare your child to other children who are trained. A child who is a very good family friend or a cousin of the same sex that is toilet trained may not mind your child watching when she uses the bathroom. Be sure you ask the parent and the child as well. Very young children are often proud to show what they have learned to do and modesty is not a big issue yet. *"Jenny, Julie is using the toilet. You will too someday when you are ready."* Don't say, *"Why can't you be as good as Julie and use the toilet? She learned faster than you."*
- There is no room for perfection in toilet training. Keep your expectations reasonable.
- Read *I Have to Go* by Robert Munsch (Ontario: Firefly Books, 1993), *Once Upon a Potty* by Alona Frankel (New York: Barron's Educational Series, 1980), *Going to the Potty*, by Fred Rogers (New York: Putnam Sons, 1986), and *Your New Potty* by Joanna Cole (New York: Mulberry Books, 1989). Ask a children's librarian or knowledgeable bookstore clerk about other children's books that are available.

*See also: Bed-wetting*

# TOOTH FAIRY

*"What do I tell my child about the tooth fairy without lying?"*

**UNDERSTANDING THE SITUATION**

It can be difficult to know what to say and do when your child asks about the tooth fairy. You may be concerned about starting the tradition because you want to be honest with your child and you worry about what to say later when she asks, *"Is there really a tooth fairy?"* This is one time a serious parent can relax. Losing teeth is to be celebrated. This is one of the first concrete experiences your child will likely remember about leaving babyhood. Every child is ecstatic over losing teeth. Celebrate with the fantasy! By the time your child learns there is no fairy, she likely will be old enough to handle the truth easily and continue playing the game. Play the game; you are not being dishonest. Use your sense of humor and have fun with your child. These light situations provide the opportunity to build good relationships so that you will win cooperation with more serious issues.

**WHAT TO SAY AND DO**

If you decide to play the tooth fairy game, do so without worry and concern. Be creative. Notes are fun and remembered for a long time after the truth is known. Jamie, age seven, has a note saved on her bulletin board written to her by the tooth fairy apologizing for coming a night late and disappointing her. Today, Jamie knows Dad wrote the note and yet feels special realizing that he took the time to play the game.

If your child asks you if there really is a tooth fairy, ask questions to make her think. *"Hilary, what do you think? What would you like to believe?"* Or ask with a smile, *"Do you want to know what I know?"*

Acknowledge your child's feelings but do not be afraid of her disappointment. She can handle situations like this if you are loving and matter-of-fact and show that you are willing to continue the game. *"Annie, I am the family tooth fairy. When I was a little girl my dad was my tooth fairy. I couldn't wait to have my own children and do the same. I love playing the game."*

Use humor. *"Yes, Jamie, I am the tooth fairy. When I am old and my teeth fall out, you can do the same for me."*

**PREVENTIVE TIPS**

• Young children don't need a lot of money from the tooth fairy. Be conservative. If you start too high you will set high expectations for the price of the rest of the teeth—and everyone knows molars are worth more! The fun should be in the surprise of the game, not how much money was received.

- Exaggerate the game and continue to be playful as your child grows doubtful or learns the truth. Leave her notes. *"Dear Lila, this tooth is the best ever! It will help to pave the streets of heaven. Love, your tooth fairy."*
- Have the older children in the family play the game for their younger siblings. Including them in the fun strengthens their feeling of importance.
- Read stories together based on fantasy. See a knowledgeable bookstore clerk or a children's librarian for good suggestions.

*See also: Fantasy; Santa Claus*

# TOYS

*"The toys my child wants are not the kind I want him to have."*

### UNDERSTANDING THE SITUATION

Your child will want to play with toys that you do not want him to have. Though you may dislike guns and military-type toys, these are exciting to an active child with a vivid imagination. You may detest toys that run on batteries, which never seem to work after the first week. Some toys are just not safe. Barbie dolls may drive you crazy. These issues can become quite emotional. You need to get in touch with your motivations. Consider whether your disliking a toy is based on a fear or a past belief that is invalid. Boys do play with dolls today, yet some fathers do not permit it. Experts agree that practice with fathering dolls is just as important for little boys as mothering is for little girls. Discuss these matters with experts you trust such as a teacher or pediatrician. Do not be too quick to say no. As hard as it is, stay flexible. If you decide against a toy, be sure you understand the reason. Never be afraid to say, *"Give me some time to think about that,"* if your child asks for a toy you're unsure about.

### WHAT TO SAY AND DO

If your child has a toy on his wish list that you do not want him to have, let him know ahead of time that it will be unlikely he'll get it from you.

1. Identify his feelings and show empathy. *"Brett, you loved playing with Robby's tank at his house. You would really like one."*
2. Give good reasons why he can't have a particular toy. *"Because I said so"* is no good. *"Brett, the military tank you want is very expensive to buy and to run. It takes six C-size batteries. Dad and I do not buy that type of toy."*
3. Leave him with a positive. *"Come up with other ideas for your list. We can go window-shopping if you would like."* Make sure you clarify which toys you will not consider having in the house and which toys he may earn and maintain if he wishes.

Remain flexible. A rule is a rule and is to be followed consistently. However, if you are visiting a friend and her child has a toy gun, your child is guaranteed to want it if you do not allow guns in your home. Take *time to teach* him how to hold it and play with it. *"Ryan, when you play with the gun you never point it at anyone. Point at a tree or a rock."* Relax, or you will have the problem of the "forbidden fruit."

Flexibility sometimes builds responsibility. *"Morgan, we will make a deal. You may have the battery-operated tank if you will follow the family guidelines. If you do not and we begin to have trouble about it, we will find another home for it."*

When your child plays with the toys or games you approve of and want him to enjoy, comment and show your enthusiasm. Join him. Play with him. Show him how to use the toys and have fun with him using them.

**PREVENTIVE TIPS**

- Discuss which toys you feel are permissible and which are not with your spouse and other significant adults in your family. Otherwise, Dad may bring home a gun not knowing how appalling it is to you. He may not understand how you could bring a doll home to his son. Grandma may give a new, expensive, battery-run doll after you have decided, *"No more newfangled dolls."* These situations are difficult for children. They become the center of a major problem.
- Take *time for teaching.* Walk through toy stores and discuss the different toys, explaining why you like some and dislike others. This is the way your child will learn to understand your values.

*See also: Possessions*

# TOYS, PICKING UP

*"My child will not pick up her toys."*

### UNDERSTANDING THE SITUATION

Your child (at any age) will no doubt challenge you about picking up her toys. That is a given. It is the most frustrating when she asks for your help and then watches you do it all. Feeling like a doormat (yes, even with a three-year-old), you may coax and bribe, then yell, scold, threaten, and punish with time out. Then you do it yourself, thinking that it is simply more efficient that way. Wrong! Parenting is not an efficient matter. In the long run it will behoove you to take the time to win your child's cooperation. First, take *time to teach* her how to pick up her things. Next, be very consistent with a regular routine. Inconsistency breeds hassle, hassle, hassle. Take a look at the number of toys you are buying and giving her. The bumper sticker "He Who

Dies with the Most Toys Wins" is a bad motto if picking up toys is out of control. This takes the patience of Job. Some children are more difficult than others to motivate. Do not give up.

## WHAT TO SAY AND DO

Do not give threats *("You have so many toys, I'm just going to throw them all away. I'm not buying you one more toy until you learn to pick up.")* unless you definitely plan to follow through. Threats set you up for power struggles and real control issues, and when you have no intention of following through, your child will quickly learn not to believe you. Say what you mean and do what you say you'll do. Introduce the "one-week box." *"Bill, when you do not pick up toys they will go into the box for one week. You will be without them for a week."*

Arrange a storage area so your child can reach her toys and put them away easily. Shelves or cubbies are easier than toy boxes. Show enthusiasm. *"Amanda, look at what a great set of shelves you have now. You certainly have a big-girl room. This will be fun to keep picked up."*

Try to develop one routine time of the day for your child to pick up toys. Let her know what to expect with some warning. *"Alison, we will pick up the toys after dinner."* Signal pick-up time with a song: *"Toys away, toys away, it's time to put the toys away."*

It's possible she will do better if you arrange toy pick-up daily before something she wants to do and use this as incentive. Give her something to look forward to. *"Amy, after the toys are put away we will have a bedtime story."*

You may have to help your very young child. Do not insist that she do it all. You have to teach her how. Make it a game. Keep your sense of humor. This will help you both when your child seems hopelessly stuck on not helping. *"I'm Hector Hector, the garbage collector"* is fun to sing, or use *"This is the way we pick up our toys, pick up our toys . . ."*

Do not get sucked into a power struggle. This should not be a win/lose situation. Make it a win/win. If you grow angry, walk away with a *poker face* if you must, *cool off*, come back, and be consistent. *"Misha, the toys are to be picked up."* If your child still resists:

1. Take her hand and do it with her.
2. Offer to help. Play a game. Throw the toys into a basket. Or play "your turn, my turn."
3. Give a choice. *"Do you want to pick up the toys with me or without me?"*

If your child gets sidetracked and starts playing with a toy, kindly and calmly say, *"Joe, this is pick-up time, not playtime. Put it right here. That toy will wait for you to finish."*

Rotate toys. Limit the number of toys in play at any given time. If your child is not interested in picking them up, maybe she does have too many. Put them away until she asks for them or every two weeks put some away and pull others out.

Comment on jobs well done. When you see her being helpful, comment on it. *"Marnie, you are making such an effort to help today."*

### PREVENTIVE TIPS

- Every six months, go through the toys to discard ones that are not played with or that have been outgrown. Save used toys for garage sales or to give to needy children.
- Do not buy, buy, buy. Tell grandparents that you are trying to instill values, emphasizing quality and not quantity.
- When your child is picking up, do not interrupt his train of thought with more instructions. *"When you have cleaned this mess up, you can do the TV area"* is sure to get him off track.

*See also: Possessions*

# TRADITIONS

*See: Holidays*

# TRAFFIC SAFETY

*See: Safety*

# TRIPS AND VACATIONS

*"My child is a trip on a trip."*

### UNDERSTANDING THE SITUATION

There are trips and there are vacations. Ask any parent and he or she will tell you the difference. Trips are usually with children. The better planned and the better prepared the parent, the better the trip. Usually it takes one or two trips to get everything right. After parents learn from their mistakes, the trips get better and better. If you love to travel and are lucky enough to have the opportunity, do not let taking children stop you. Plan ahead and keep your energy up. Be prepared when traveling with your young child and take this opportunity with your older child to let him help with planning. Offer him choices so that he will feel that he has some control over what happens to him. There may be complicated and uncomfortable moments traveling with children—long waits, suffering through heat, mixed-up reservations, illness, etc.—but the good will outweigh the bad. You will all grow closer, get to know each other better, and truly benefit from the rich experiences.

## WHAT TO SAY AND DO

Whenever possible, give your child *choices* about what you will do. A *family meeting* is a good time to plan a vacation and offer ideas. *"We have a choice of these three places. Let's decide where we will go."*

Traveling with young children takes planning and foresight. Safety-pin the security blanket to something obvious. Try not to be caught without the security object unless you plan to break your child's habit with a little suffering for all. Plan familiar foods and juices for snacking while traveling, and bring a small bag of activities.

Travel time should be as much fun as the destination. Interact with your child when traveling; do not ignore him. Younger children love surprises such as a box of new crayons and a pad of paper, puzzles, and little books. On a long trip, pull out something new each hour. Surprise! Your older child will love to be surprised as well. Teach her to follow your course on a map. Take along travel games that are available in educational toy stores.

When choices are not possible, let your child know that you are on her team. *"Marnie, we will be with Grandma on this trip. I'd like to see the zoo with you. We will try, but it may not be possible this time. I will do my best to try to make it happen."*

Discipline as consistently as you would at home, but be sensitive to your child's needs. Not all travels will be comfortable. Let her know what to expect whenever possible. Some of the best learning happens when children have to do something they resist.

**PREVENTIVE TIPS**

• Before you leave, give your school-age child a diary. Encourage her to keep up with it daily on your trip. A variation that both younger and older children enjoy is an album for collecting postcards, maps, napkins, and other souvenirs gathered along the way.
• Most children do better when you establish a destination and take side trips from there, rather than roaming from place to place. This saves packing and unpacking over and over.
• When your child meets other children and gets to know them, get their names and addresses. When you return home your child may want to start a pen-pal relationship. This is a great way to begin friendships around the world.
• Have a *family meeting* after the trip is over and evaluate what everyone liked best and would change the next time.
• *Trouble-Free Travel with Children* by Vicki Lansky (Deephaven, Minn.: Book Peddlers, 1991) is a helpful adult handbook.

# TUTORING

*"Does my child need a tutor?"*

**UNDERSTANDING THE SITUATION**

The question of whether a child needs a tutor is often considered by teachers and parents. Some may see it as a way to help a child who is struggling in school, while others may see it as an opportunity to advance their child into a special program or a special school in their community. For the most part, past negative connotations surrounding tutoring have diminished as adults have seen positive outcomes. Tutoring has changed dramatically in the last ten years, as have the reasons for it. The purpose of tutoring today should be positive: to help your child

become an independent learner and to become a more resourceful student by learning new strategies. This in turn aids in developing self-confidence. It is *not* meant to be a long-term arrangement, and it is *not* a tool to pressure your child to advance or to
increase performance. You might consider tutoring for your
child:

1. When your child is moved to a school that uses a different
   educational approach or assumes certain academic skills have
   already been acquired. For example, Dana moved from a
   school that used a self-discovery approach to a school that required her to have more academic skills. With six months of
   tutoring she learned the multiplication tables, the handwrit-
   ing, the spelling, and the reading that the other children in
   her new school had already mastered. Bruce moved from
   New Zealand to Seattle and found tutoring helped him understand the cultural differences. Both children's self-
   confidence grew.
2. When your child has learning difficulties or a learning style
   that places special demands on her. Beth is a very perceptive
   child who has trouble following directions in a class of thirty
   children. She learns best when involved in hands-on experiences as opposed to being talked to at length. Tutoring
   helped her improve her listening skills. She also learned the
   use of the computer as a helpful study aid.
3. When your child is dealing with critical family issues such as
   illness, death, divorce, job loss, moving, or other emotional
   issues at home, which may slow down learning. Many parents
   don't have the time or educational resources or experience to
   give the extra needed attention to schoolwork. When your
   child feels anxious about her learning or feels she needs help,
   it may affect her socially; she may act out or withdraw, and
   tutoring may be a helpful boost.

### WHAT TO SAY AND DO

Find the right person for your child. Tutors are usually experienced teachers, or professionals in a specific field, with the ability

to help your child. Some tutors belong to agencies that specialize in tutoring and some work privately out of their office, their home, or your home. Consider: Some tutors specialize in certain ages, some teach specific subjects only, some personality types will match your child's better than others. Seek referrals from a school counselor, teacher, or other professional, and interview before choosing.

Costs for tutoring will vary. This will be money well spent if your child grows more confident. Consider this preventive medicine.

Tutoring is most effective when the tutor and the classroom teacher meet and discuss a program designed for your child. The tutor ideally should be part of your child's teacher conference. Stay in close contact with both the teacher and the tutor.

Your child may feel that something is wrong with her if she is being tutored. Your enthusiasm and positive attitude are musts. *"Marnie, you have a soccer coach and a music teacher. Carol is a learning coach; she will help you with your language and math skills. Nothing is wrong with you. We are not trying to fix anything. You are a very bright girl. She will help learning be more fun!"*

Stay positive. Don't say, *"You won't have to do it long."* Say, *"Jana, you'll get to work with Carol up to winter break, and then we will decide how much longer."*

### PREVENTIVE TIPS

- Tutoring is merely enrichment. It is not a substitute for your much-needed interest and time spent reading with your child, playing different strategy games, and taking educational trips.
- Keep an open attitude. Your child is learning in a very different world from when you were in school. The schools cannot meet the needs of every child today. Take advantage of good enrichment when it is available.

# VIDEO GAMES

*"I'm competing with video games for my child's time and co-operation."*

## UNDERSTANDING THE SITUATION

Video games, like television, are a major source of conflict in family life today. You enjoy seeing your child's unending enthusiasm for Nintendo games. It has been suggested there may be benefits from some video games, such as developing hand-eye coordination, concentration, and logical thinking. Yet children do seem to become addicted to the games and tune out the world even more than they do with television. This is a very exasperating issue if you let it get out of hand. If you remind and coax and then begin yelling and threatening, the machine can quickly control your family life. If you allow these games in your home, apply proper management. Establish a routine, set firm limits with good communication, and be very consistent in following through.

## WHAT TO SAY AND DO

Do not nag, nag, nag. Establish a weekly chart with names and times the machine may be used—on the condition that chores and homework are done. One mother demanded equal time spent out of doors. If the rules are broken, unplug the machine and remove it if you must, but leave a hopeful note. *"Jason, we will try again next week."*

Use the video game as an incentive. *"As soon as you have dinner and do your homework, you may have thirty minutes on Sega."*

Keep a timer near the set. When the bell rings it is time for your child to stop. If you have to remind him more than once to stop, subtract time from his next game. Firmly and kindly say,

*"Joey, it seems you have chosen to not play the game at all tomorrow."* Do not yell, rant, or rave.

Be flexible, but mean what you say and do what you say you will do. If your child asks for special extended time, negotiate. That is healthy. *"Okay, Ryan. Convince me to let you have another half hour on the Nintendo."* When he hears *"I'm not convinced,"* he will negotiate with good thinking and use good reasoning rather than just whining, *"Please, oh please."*

## PREVENTIVE TIPS

- If you allow the game in your home, show interest in it. Take time to play games with your child.
- Comment on the skills he is learning from the machine. Comment on his efforts to follow the schedule.
- Take great effort to not let the video game take the place of reading, puzzles, or family outings. It is tempting, when children are happy and occupied before the screen, to put aside other activities.
- Use *family meetings* to negotiate the video schedule.

# WANDERING

*"My child will not stay with me in public places."*

## UNDERSTANDING THE SITUATION

The wandering child is a common problem. Many children feel adventurous and are oblivious to the dangers of becoming lost. Some children grow bored waiting for a parent who may be taking more time than the child's attention span will allow. Some children disappear for attention: It is truly exciting to see Mom all worked up and worried. Some children feel great control: It is a very powerful feeling to make Mom overreact with worry. Whatever the motive, wandering off is worrisome for you and very dangerous for your child. You need to *set clear limits* and be very consistent each time you go out. If you are sending your child on outings or field trips with friends or teachers, make sure a mature adult is aware that he may wander.

## WHAT TO SAY AND DO

Before going out, check your child's understanding of the limits. *"Jenny, we are going into the grocery store. Where will you be in the store? That's right. You may ride in the cart sitting down or walk right beside me."*

Do not go into morbid detail. *("Andrew, a strange man may take you, and you will never see Mommy again.")* This may create fear or be seen as a challenge to test the limits. Simply state, *"Andrew, stay with me."*

Take *time for teaching*. This may take months. Stay with your child. Have him hold your hand, a piece of your clothing, or one end of a rope; tether him with an expandable leash; or use a harness. *"Jeffrey, I do not want you to lose me, and I do not want to lose you."*

Give your child meaningful jobs to do to keep her occupied and feeling useful. In the store, send her on little errands while in your sight or have her add numbers on a calculator. On a walk, carry a list of things to look for and have her check them off as she sees them; read letters and numbers that mark your parking place in the parking lot. Engaging her interest may help prevent her from seeking excitement elsewhere.

Comment on good behavior and celebrate. *"You really helped me in the store. You stayed right with me and I finished with time to spare. We have time for an ice cream."*

### PREVENTIVE TIPS

- As mentioned above, wandering off is often a way of seeking attention. Tell your child the sequence of events for the morning and then for the afternoon. Tell her when she can expect *special time* with you so that she won't manipulate for attention.
- She may be wandering because she is bored. Be realistic about what you ask of her attention span. Do not expect her to stand still near your side while you talk to a friend for fifteen minutes. Children wander in the grocery store waiting for Mom to read all the ingredients on the packaging.
- Ask a children's librarian or knowledgeable bookstore clerk about children's books you might read together about wandering or showing responsibility.

*See also: Strangers*

# WATER SAFETY

*See: Safety*

# WHINING

*"My child is constantly whining."*

## UNDERSTANDING THE SITUATION

Whining for attention is one of the most irritating and tiring child behaviors. Common though it is, your child is not consciously thinking, *"I think I'll bug Mom with whining today."* She smay be whining and not even realize how she sounds. She may be tired, hungry, or feeling other stress. She may be bored. Coaxing, bribing, or scolding her will cause more discouragement and more whining, and you are likely to grow angry and fall into a power struggle. Stay calm and appear unimpressed by her whining. At any age, whining is just a symptom of how your child feels. Encourage her to get her needs met in a more direct way.

## WHAT TO SAY AND DO

Sometimes stopping what you are doing and holding her may work. Never label or call your child names. *"You whiner"* doesn't help. Instead, identify her feeling. *"Erin, I know you are hungry."* Calmly sit down with her and without words gently hold her, maybe rock her, and then say, *"I'll slice you an orange when you ask in a pleasant voice."*

Avoid embarrassing her in front of friends. Take *time out* together. With a *poker face* say, *"We will stay here until you feel you can join the rest of the children without whining."* If whining continues, ignore it; leave the room if you must.

Do not grant what she wants if she whines. When you make her lunch say, *"Suzy, I know you are feeling impatient and hungry. When you whine I may not hear you very well and I may not fix you what you want."*

Ask her to lower her voice. *"I cannot understand you. Lower your voice and try again."*

Comment on her big-girl voice and how good it makes you feel when she uses it. *"Thank you for using your pleasant voice. I know you are tired and frustrated, and I really appreciate your effort!"*

## PREVENTIVE TIPS

- Whining can be due to stress. Examine what may be the cause. Your child may need more rest or snacks during the day. She may be overstimulated or bored. She may need more *special time* with you.
- Five warm minutes with you first thing in the morning, after transitions such as naps, after day care, or after a big task like picking up toys may prevent an hour of whining for any age!
- Let your child know what to expect by sharing the schedule for the day. Discuss events of the day and plan *special time* together.
- At a good talking and listening time, talk about feelings. This is a good time to read a children's book together, such as *I Am Not a Crybaby* by Norma Simon (Morton Grove, Ill.: Whitman, 1989) or *Feelings* by Aliki Brandenberg (New York: Morrow, 1984).
- Whining into a tape recorder for fun is using your sense of humor, yet making her aware what it sounds like.

# WHY?

*"My child asks 'why?' all the time."*

### UNDERSTANDING THE SITUATION

A very common phenomenon in parenting is dealing with "why?" As soon as your very young child begins to talk it may seem that you hardly get a sentence out to answer a question before he flashes another "why?" your way. Sometimes the "whys" are a way to command attention. *("I belong when I keep Momma busy with 'why?' ")* If this is the dynamic with your child, you need to give plenty of positive attention at other times. For most children, however, the "why" is a sincere question, and, tiring as it may be, you need to spend time and answer questions to satisfy the young inquisitive mind. Curiosity is a wonderful gift to be cultivated. Your child's vocabulary is limited; your answers will help her learn more vocabulary and in time be able to ask more detailed questions.

### WHAT TO SAY AND DO

When your child asks "why?" ask him a question back. With sincerity, say, *"Andrew, why do you think the grass is green?"* Questions make children think; statements do not.

Describe all that is around you. Ask the questions before he asks you. *"Andrew, see the tractor up on the hill? The farmer is plowing. What is he plowing? What color is his tractor?"*

If you are tired of his "whys," let him know in a nice way. Firmly and kindly, say, *"Jimmy, I have answered about all I can right now. I want to listen to this song. No more questions until we get home, please."*

Encourage listening skills. *"Jamie, your questions are very good though I am tired of answering. Let's listen to this story on tape. The story lady will tell you all about frogs on this one. You have such good questions, listen for your answers."*

### PREVENTIVE TIPS

- Give *special time* regularly. The more time you spend listening to and talking with your child, the less likely his "whys" will be for getting attention.
- Read aloud together often. Reading promotes good listening and satisfies curiosity.
- Let your young child know what the day's schedule is. He will like to know what to expect, what is coming next, and when he will have time with you. Then he won't feel the need for the attention-getting behavior.

# WINNING AND LOSING

*"My child is a poor loser."*

### UNDERSTANDING THE SITUATION

It is frustrating and often embarrassing when your child is the one in the group who cannot enjoy playing a game without winning. This is a very common issue, especially when there is an older sibling or a competitive best friend who wants to remain the biggest, the fastest, and the best. In addition, competitive parents produce competitive children. You need to determine why your child is so invested in winning. Some children until the age of ten cannot handle competing against others. Most children up to age six do best with individual sports and classroom activity. From six to ten most children enjoy competing against themselves but fear losing to others. Competitive games that end with a winner and a loser are not good activities for children this age. Encourage cooperative games that concentrate on helping rather than defeating one another. With this and the use of Positive Parenting, poor-loser behavior can be eliminated. Healthy self-esteem and caring for others flourish in a cooperative environment.

## WHAT TO SAY AND DO

When possible, encourage cooperative games. All games can have their rules changed to encourage everyone to work together. Find ways for the total score to be the object or for all to have turns. Encourage helping one another reach the goal. Be creative.

When competition is a problem for your child, identify her feelings. *"Holly, you do not want to play because you are afraid Michael will be better than you."* Empathize. *"I understand that. I felt that way when I was your age and played with Maureen. Games are for fun whether you win or lose."* Give a *choice* and follow through. *"If the game is not fun for you, do not play. It is your choice."*

When children complain about your child in the middle of a game, talk to the whole group. Say, *"What do you all want to do about this? Do you want to stop playing?"* The group's decision will make it possible for your child to choose how to act. It is now her responsibility. If she loses control, stop the game and remove her for *time out*.

Never compare your child to another child. *("Jenna, if you were more like your sister and tried, you could win too.")* That supports the fear that others will be bigger, better, or faster than she is.

Use the language for winners. Look for what she does well. Play down her mistakes. Do not say, *"You'd better let me do that, it's too difficult for you."* Or *"Uh-oh, next time I'd better do that."* Instead, *encourage.* *"Nice try. This is not a race. You will get it."*

## PREVENTIVE TIPS

• Check your own attitude. Do you bring stories home from the office about getting ahead? Do you cheer on your winning football team and get angry when they lose? Is winning such a big part of your life that you cheer your child on to always win? He will mimic what you model.

• See a knowledgeable game-store or toy-store manager about games that build cooperation. "Friends Around the World" (Aristoplay, Box 7645, Ann Arbor, Mich., 48107) is a great game in which everyone works together against "the blob."
• Seek out outside activity with excellent leadership concentrating on learning the skills of the game and having fun.

*See also: Cheating*

# YELLING

*"My child startles and irritates with loud yells."*

## UNDERSTANDING THE SITUATION

Children yell or shriek for different reasons, some for the thrill of it, some for attention (*"Everyone looks at me when I yell"*), and some out of frustration (*"I yell to get my way"*). If you want the behavior to stop, do not yell back. Do not overreact. Kindly and with a firm *poker face*, tell your child that you are not going to answer him when he yells or shrieks. The cure may take some time, but it can be done. If you have established a bad reaction in the past, the yelling may get worse before it gets better. It will take your child time to understand that you will not react and that you will give your attention at more favorable times. Remember to express your unconditional love. *"I love you very much, although I do sometimes get frustrated with what you do."*

## WHAT TO SAY AND DO

Do not yell back. When you yell back at your child, you teach him to yell. He is a mimic, and you will get what you model. Talk softly, even try a whisper, when you want him to listen or talk softly.

Take *time to teach* your child to understand what causes her to yell. Help her understand strategy. *"Morgan, you yell when your brother comes near you. You think he is after your toy. He likes to hear you yell. Try walking away from him, and do not yell."*

Give her permission to yell to get her anger out. Indicate a place where she can go to yell. *"Sally, you yell when you are angry. If yelling makes you feel better, go into your room and close the door. Come out when you are done yelling."*

Tell her what to expect if there is yelling. *"Molly, we are going to be in the car for an hour. If there is any yelling, I will pull the car over."* Follow through with *action with few words*, and a *poker face*.

### PREVENTIVE TIPS

- Read children's stories about feelings together, such as *I Was So Mad* by Norma Simon (Morton Grove, Ill.: Whitman, 1974), *Feelings* by Aliki Brandenberg (New York: Morrow, 1984), and *Sometimes I Get Angry* by Jane Werner Watson, Robert E. Switzer, and J. Cotter Hirschberg (New York: Crown, 1986).
- Spend *special time* together on a regular basis. Be active with your child. Some parents love to wrestle with their children, plan bike outings, play ball, go on walks, and go to the park. When your child knows you will be joining her in play, she may yell for attention less often.
- Your child may yell when she is overtired or overstimulated. Watch her play and offer a change in activity before she falls apart and starts to yell.

# ZOO (AND OTHER OUTINGS)

*"My child ruins our trips to the zoo and other fun, planned outings."*

The zoo is one obvious and favorite choice for a busy parent who wants to spend some quality time with his or her child. However, a common complaint is *"I take a day off, pack a lunch, and plan a trip to the zoo intending that we will all have fun. When we arrive, she won't go in, she throws a tantrum, and ruins the day."* Your child is most likely feeling as frustrated as you. Both of you feel a lack of control over what is happening. The zoo and other outings can be more fun if you give up some control and offer more control to your child. This means mutual respect, taking into consideration what your child wants to do as well as what you want. This is worth working on, for better outings and better time together.

### WHAT TO SAY AND DO

Vary your *choices* of outings. The zoo is often the only place parents think of for an outing. It will be a more exciting adventure if it is not overused.

Give your child a feeling of control. *"Amanda, we have special time together Saturday morning. Here is a list of ideas. What would you like to do?"* Do not feel she always needs an elaborate outing. She may just want to stay home with you, especially if you work all week and she is in day care or school or with sitters.

If you want to go to the zoo (or any other specific place) and you know she won't choose it, do not make it your *special time* with her. *"Ronnie, the zoo is having a special showing of the baby elephants. We are going on Saturday morning. You may bring a friend."*

When you go on an excursion, limit the area you try to see according to what your child can handle. Call ahead to know what area is having a special event, such as washing the elephants, feeding time, or showing baby animals in the nursery at the zoo. The zoo is big and tiring for young children. If you all get overtired once at the zoo, your child may not want to go again.

End your outing commenting specifically on what you enjoyed. Your child needs to hear that you have as much fun with her as you do with a best friend. *"Elizabeth, I enjoyed climbing those steps with you. You are as much fun to be with as one of my buddies."*

### PREVENTIVE TIPS

- Prepare your child. Show her pictures of what she will see and do. Let her know what to expect.
- Be creative. Make a list of fun places to go and things to do in your city. This needs to change from year to year as your child grows and her interests change.
- Keep your expectations reasonable for your child's age and stage of development. Try to climb into your child's world and see the outing from his perspective.
- Plan for a successful day including meals and rest. Do not set out on an adventure right before lunch. Eat first or pack food. Outings get expensive when you buy food out and can leave you feeling broke and depressed—not the result you want!

# BIBLIOGRAPHY

Ames, Louise Bates, Sidney M. Baker, and Frances Ilg. *Child Behavior*. New York: Harper Perennial, 1992.

Clark, Jean Illsley. *Self-Esteem: A Family Affair*. New York: Harper and Row, 1980.

Clark, Jean Illsley, and Connie Dawson. *Growing Up Again, Parenting Ourselves, Parenting Our Children*. San Francisco: Harper-Hazelden, 1989.

Coloroso, Barbara. *Winning at Parenting. . . . without Beating Your Kids* (video and text). Littleton, Colo.: (kids are worth it!), 1989.

Dinkmeyer, Don, Sr., James S. Dinkmeyer, and Gary D. McKay. *Parenting Young Children*. New York: Random House, 1989.

Dreikurs, Rudolf, and Vicki Soltz. *Children: the Challenge*. New York: Penguin Books, 1964.

Faber, Adele, and Elaine Mazlish. *How to Be the Parent You Always Wanted to Be* (text and audio). New York: Hyperion, 1992.

———*How to Talk So Kids Will Listen and Listen So Kids Will Talk*. New York: Avon, 1982.

———*Siblings Without Rivalry: How to Help Your Children Live Together So You Can Live Too*. New York: Avon, 1987.

Ferber, Richard. *Solve Your Child's Sleep Problems*. New York: Simon and Schuster, 1986.

Garber, Marianne Daniels, Stephen W. Garber, and Robyn Freedman Spizman. *Good Behavior*. New York: Villard Books, 1987.

Glenn, Stephen H., and Jane Nelsen. *Raising Self-Reliant Children in a Self-Indulgent World*. Rocklin, Calif.: Prima Publishing, 1988.

Husmann, D. A., and Gordon A. McLorie. "Incontinence and Enuresis." *The Pediatric Clinics of North America 34* (October 1987): 1164–65.

Kurcinkaa, Mary Sheedy. *Raising Your Spirited Child*. New York: HarperCollins, 1991.

Meeks, Carolyn Ann. *Prescriptions for Parenting*. New York: Warner Books, 1990.

Nelsen, Jane. *Positive Discipline*. New York: Ballantine, 1987.

Satter, Ellyn. *How to Get Your Kid to Eat . . . But Not Too Much*. Palo Alto: Bull Publishing, 1987.

Schnebly, Lee. *Out of Apples*. Tucson: Manzanas Press, 1984.

# INDEX

and lack of friends, 184, 186, 188
and late developing speech, 347
lying and, 226
masturbation and, 227–28
meanness and, 233–35
moving and, 249, 251–52
naps and, 260
overactivity and, 277–78
peer pressure and, 280–81
pet care and, 284
Santa Claus and, 305
sexual play and, 319
sharing and, 327
showing off and, 332–33
stealing and, 350, 352
stubbornness and, 356
*see also specific feelings*
*Feelings* (Brandenberg), 65, 169, 199, 235,
    244, 270, 299, 332, 373, 398, 404
fighting, 169–75
    bullying and, 88
    with friends, 173–74, 180–84
    hitting and, 172–73, 197–200
    mealtime and, 232
    medications and, 236
    and misbehaving in cars, 90–91
    between parents, 169–71
    school buses and, 310
    between siblings, 6–7, 171–75
    television watching and, 368
    *see also* arguing
flatulence, 176–77
friends, 177–88
    athletic lessons and, 216
    choosing of, 177–79
    fantasies and, 162
    and fear of separating, 317
    fighting with, 173–74, 180–84
    grades and, 191
    holidays and, 201
    hospitals and, 207
    interrupting and, 210
    lack of, 184–88
    lying and, 226
    masturbation and, 228
    moving and, 248–49, 251

music lessons and, 219–20
overactivity and, 275
peer pressure and, 280
privacy and, 290–91
and refusing to go to school, 306, 309
restaurants and, 294–95
sadness and, 298
Santa Claus and, 304
sexual play and, 319–20
showing off and, 331–34
and sleeping away from home, 336–37
stealing and, 349–52
temper tantrums and, 371
thumb-sucking and, 376–78
and winning and losing, 400
"Friends Around the World," 101, 402
frustration, *see* anger and frustration

Gordon, Sol and Judith, 258, 321, 324
grades, 189–91
    peer pressure and, 281
    showing off and, 334
grandparents, 192–94
    and difficult to understand speech, 344
    nakedness and, 256
    overactivity and, 275
    stealing and, 349
*Grandpa's Face* (Greenfield), 36, 244, 299
Greenfield, Eloise, 36, 244, 289, 299

hairbrushing, 77–79
Hamilton, Leslie, 296–97
*Hating Book, The* (Zolotow), 86, 235
head banging, 195–96
healthful foods, eating of, 150–53
Henkes, Kevin, 74, 84, 126, 162, 175,
    184, 188, 263
Hest, Amy, 113–14, 116
Hirschberg, J. Cutter, 36, 169, 199, 270,
    373, 404
hitting:
    anger and, 30, 34, 197–99
    fighting and, 172–73, 197–200
    meanness and, 234
    new babies and, 260–63
    teasing and, 365

thumb-sucking and, 376–78
tooth fairy and, 381–83
television watching, 368–69
  anger and, 32–33
  bath time and, 46–48
  chores and, 108
  and cleaning up bedrooms, 53
  evening hassles and, 160
  fantasies and, 162
  fears and, 165
  and getting to bed, 57
  hitting and, 200
  homework hassles and, 204–6
  hospitals and, 207
  listening and, 221–22
  nightmares and, 267
  night wandering and, 264–65
  peer pressure and, 282
  possessions and, 285
  problem solving and, 26–27
  and questions about death, 132
  and questions about sexuality, 322
  setting limits on, 16–17
  stubbornness and, 356
  video games and, 393
Temper Tantrum Book, The (Preston and
    Bennett), 169, 199, 373
temper tantrums, 370–75
  head banging and, 195
  money and, 239
  shopping and, 328–30, 372
  and trips to zoo, 405
Tenth Good Thing about Barney, The
    (Viorst), 133, 284
There's Something in My Attic (Meyer),
    126, 268
thumb-sucking, 253, 376–78
time outs, 17–18
  belching and, 66
  biting and, 70–71
  bullying and, 85, 87
  climbing and, 111
  complaining and, 119
  dirty words and, 138–40
  feelings and, 168
  fighting and, 172–73, 181–82

flatulence and, 176
hitting and, 198
lying and, 225
mealtime and, 232
meanness and, 234
moodiness and, 243–44
overactivity and, 274–75, 278
pet care and, 283–84
roughhousing and, 296
showing off and, 333
talking back and, 361
temper tantrums and, 371, 374
whining and, 398
and winning and losing, 401
toilet training, 379–81
  dirty words and, 137–39
  encouragement and, 22, 379–80
  pregnancy and, 288
Tompert, Ann, 129, 317
Tools of the Trade, 8, 15–27
  see also specific Tools of the Trade
toothbrushing, 79–81
  dentists and, 80–81, 136
  encouragement and, 23
  listening and, 221–22
  and offering choices, 21, 79
tooth fairy, 381–83
toys, 285–87, 383–87
  bath time and, 46
  bed making and, 50
  birthdays and, 67, 69
  biting and, 70
  bossiness and, 73–74
  bullying and, 85–86
  car seats and, 96–97
  and choosing friends, 178
  chores and, 105
  and cleaning up bedrooms, 52–54
  complaining and, 119
  crying and, 121–22
  day care and, 129
  dentists and, 135–36
  fantasies and, 163
  and fear of dark, 125
  and fear of separating, 318
  feelings and, 167

## ABOUT THE AUTHOR

KAREN RENSHAW JOSLIN has over twenty years experience teaching parenting classes, and, just as importantly, raised three children herself. The techniques and ideas employed in this book are the product of her extensive professional experience as well as many hands-on ideas gleaned from twenty years of parents' suggestions in parenting classes.

Karen Renshaw Joslin's professional life has centered around a concern for the developing child. After teaching elementary school for over five years, and directing and teaching co-op preschools, Karen earned a Masters in Education from Seattle Pacific University, with emphasis in Creativity and Family Relations, in 1978. She is a Washington State certified public school teacher, and registered counselor. She has received certification from both Jean Clarke's *Self Esteem: A Family Affair*, and H. Stephen Glenn's *Developing Capable People* programs. She currently maintains a private counseling practice, designs positive self-help programs for parents, schools, hospitals, and corporations, and teaches her own Positive Parenting curriculum for Overlake Hospital in Bellevue, Washington.

Karen lives in Bellevue, Washington, with her husband, a pediatrician, and her youngest daughter.